WORLD POPULATION

A Reference Handbook

Other Titles in ABC-CLIO's
**CONTEMPORARY
WORLD ISSUES**
Series

Agricultural Crisis in America, Dana L. Hoag
American Homelessness, Third Edition, Mary Ellen Holmes
Biodiversity, Anne Becher
Endangered Species, Clifford J. Sherry
Environmental Justice, David E. Newton
Genetic Engineering, Harry LeVine III
Indoor Pollution, E. Willard Miller and Ruby M. Miller
Natural Disasters: Hurricanes, Patrick J. Fitzpatrick
The Ozone Dilemma, David E. Newton
Rainforests, Second Edition, Martin Gay
Recycling in America, Second Edition, Debra L. Strong
Work and Family in America, Leslie F. Stebbins

Books in the Contemporary World Issues series address vital issues in today's society such as terrorism, sexual harassment, homelessness, AIDS, gambling, animal rights, and air pollution. Written by professional writers, scholars, and nonacademic experts, these books are authoritative, clearly written, up-to-date, and objective. They provide a good starting point for research by high school and college students, scholars, and general readers, as well as by legislators, businesspeople, activists, and others.

Each book, carefully organized and easy to use, contains an overview of the subject; a detailed chronology; biographical sketches; facts and data and/or documents and other primary-source material; a directory of organizations and agencies; annotated lists of print and nonprint resources; a glossary; and an index.

Readers of books in the Contemporary World Issues series will find the information they need in order to better understand the social, political, environmental, and economic issues facing the world today.

WORLD POPULATION

A Reference Handbook

Geoffrey Gilbert

**CONTEMPORARY
WORLD ISSUES**

A B C 🦢 C L I O

Santa Barbara, California
Denver, Colorado
Oxford, England

Library of Congress Cataloging-in-Publication Data

Gilbert, Geoffrey, 1948–
    World population : a reference handbook / Geoffrey Gilbert.
        p. cm. — (Contemporary world issues)
Includes bibliographical references and index.
    ISBN 1-57607-229-0 (hard : alk. paper)
    1. Population—Handbooks, manuals, etc. 2. Population—Statistics.
3. Demography—Handbooks, manuals, etc. I. Title. II. Series.
    HB871.G47 2001
    304.6—dc21

This book is also available on the World Wide Web as an e-book. Visit www.abc-clio.com for details.

                                                                2001002707

07 06 05 04 03 02   10 9 8 7 6 5 4 3 2

ABC-CLIO, Inc.   ∞
130 Cremona Drive, P.O. Box 1911
Santa Barbara, California 93116-1911

This book is printed on acid-free paper   .
Manufactured in the United States of America

To the memories of
Carol Rae Gilbert and Tish Kurtz

Contents

Preface

People have expressed varying levels of concern about population over time, ranging all the way from complacency to near-panic. Likewise, the *reasons* given for concern have varied enormously. The size of a nation's population was once considered critical to its military readiness—more people meant more potential recruits for the army or navy. A big population was also thought to be a key to economic vitality, since with more consumers there would be more spending, more production, and more circulation of money and goods. Later, the economic argument began to run the other way: "excess" population would crowd the labor market, causing wages and living standards to fall. In recent decades, environmentalists have sounded alarms over the "carrying capacity" of our planet. Some believe we have already exceeded the Earth's capacity to support our species; others fear we are fast approaching that capacity limitation. Development economists have suggested that rapid population growth may hinder the prospects of economic advance in poorer nations. And political scientists have warned that the pressure of growing numbers on scarce resources can contribute—may *already* have contributed—to the breakdown of civil order in some societies.

Running directly counter to these concerns is a new one, or rather one not raised in a serious way since the 1930s: among the most economically advanced nations, fertility rates have dropped so sharply that population is now on a path toward stabilization and, very likely, actual decline in just a few years. No one knows what the full implications of this development will be, but clearly it introduces a new set of population worries into the realm of public discussion and debate. (Europe and Japan are at the leading edge of this demographic phenomenon; for the United States, depopulation appears to be ruled out by a high rate of immigration.)

It seems a safe bet that population concerns of the kind described above will be with us for years to come, with perhaps a shift of emphasis from time to time. The purpose of this book, then, is to serve as a convenient one-volume reference for those who want to know more about various global population problems and issues. The simplest questions about population can be answered with data, charts, and facts, all of which are included here. When issues are more complex, what is usually needed is a guide to reliable sources of information. This book will provide such guidance. It can be a starting point for research on a variety of population topics, whether they be historical, environmental, or policy-oriented. One of its primary aims is to give the reader an appreciation of the *controversial* aspects of population. From the publication of Malthus's classic 1798 population essay to the more recent battles between the "doomsters," led by Paul Ehrlich, and the "cornucopians," led by Julian Simon, population has been discussed in raised voices, if not shouts. That of course makes it a far more interesting subject to study than if it were entirely a matter of actuarial tables and scholarly monographs!

The best way to use this book is to start with the overview of world population offered in the first chapter. There a number of important terms are defined, demographic processes explained, and historical background issues outlined. The next chapter takes the reader on a tour of some highlights of the history of world population: first census counts, plagues, famines, key breakthroughs in disease control and birth control, major commissions and publications in the field of population, conferences, landmark judicial decisions, and billion-person milestones dating back to the first billion in 1804. Chapter 3 gives short biographies of a score of individuals—most still living—who have worked to advance our understanding of population, to expand the world's food supplies, or to shape population policy.

The statistical heart of the book is Chapter 4, where many tables of data on world population, broken down in a variety of ways, are given. Go there for facts, such as the current population of Brazil, the birth rate in Pakistan, the AIDS prevalence rate in sub-Saharan Africa, the ranking of the largest cities in the world, and the estimated world population in 2050. Chapter 5 presents ten key documents relating to world population (most in the form of excerpts). These include the first two chapters of Malthus's *Essay on Population*, plans of action from the world population conferences of 1974 and 1994, warnings about population trends from scientific organizations, and a fundamental document underpinning U.S. foreign policy regarding population.

Chapter 6 gives a directory of important organizations that gather and publish demographic data, advocate policy in this area, or simply study certain aspects of population. The educational and public services rendered by the Population Reference Bureau in Washington, D.C., cannot be overemphasized. It is probably the single best institutional resource for research projects on population issues. Chapter 7 offers a list of recently published or classic (and still in print) works on various aspects of population. These are mainly monographs, but several population handbooks are also listed. Be aware that the handbooks or yearbooks are periodically revised, sometimes annually. Chapter 8 provides reviews of over twenty videos dealing with population, all of them suitable for classroom use (though for different ages, as noted). Another key nonprint resource, and one that is clearly growing in importance all the time, is the Internet; therefore, an up-to-date listing of valuable websites for the study of population rounds out the chapter. The volume as a whole is completed by a glossary of technical terms and an index of subjects and names.

I am pleased to acknowledge the support and encouragement of my editor at ABC-CLIO, Alicia Merritt, who persuaded me to undertake this project in the first place. I am grateful, as well, to the reference, interlibrary loan, audio-visual, and computer-center staffs of Hobart and William Smith Colleges for cheerful compliance with all my requests. And thanks to two colleagues, Bill Atwell and Chi-Chiang Huang, who came through promptly with answers to my arcane questions. One could not ask for a more supportive scholarly environment than I have enjoyed at these colleges.

Geoffrey Gilbert

1

World Population: An Overview

In the waning months of the twentieth century the acronym "Y2K" was seen and heard everywhere. Shorthand for "year two thousand," Y2K referred to the major disruptions of commerce and communication thought likely to occur when computers proved unable to deal with the rollover from the year 1999 to the year 2000. But since 1999 happened to be the year in which the world's population reached 6 billion—or, with all the zeroes unfurled, 6,000,000,000—it was no surprise when a look-alike acronym, "Y6B," began showing up on bumper stickers, bulletin boards, and websites. On one level, Y6B merely recognized a new demographic milestone. (The Secretary-General of the United Nations visited the cribside of the symbolic 6 billionth person, a baby boy, at a Sarajevo hospital on October 12, 1999.) On a deeper level, however, Y6B signaled a sense of unease, even alarm, over the implications of 6 billion human beings now sharing the limited resources of one planet.

Demographers tell us it took most of human history for population to reach its first billion, around 1800. Subsequent additions of a billion people came much faster: 130 years, then 30 years, then 14, 13, and most recently, 12 years. The growth rate of world population has actually slowed in the past few decades, but total population continues to rise. We may see the arrival of Y7B by 2013, Y8B by 2028, and Y9B shortly after mid-century. It is entirely possible that the world's population will still be expanding at the end of the twenty-first century, even if some *national* populations begin to decline long before then. As we contemplate the prospect of another century of population growth, questions and concerns confront us on many sides: Will there be enough food to sustain a global population half again as large as the current one and living mainly in the poorer regions of the world? Can agricultural productivity keep advancing? Will scarcity-driven migrations destabilize the more prosperous regions? Will epidemics become more difficult to control? And what will be the impact of increasing population on global climate, wilderness areas, and biodiversity?

Some of these are questions we only learned to ask in the final decades of the twentieth century. The more basic ones, however, are almost as old as the written word. Excessive population is worried about in myths and philosophical writings of the ancient Babylonians, Chinese, Egyptians, and Greeks. In more recent times the inspiration for much of the pessimistic writing about world population has been the famed *Essay on the Principle of Population* (1798) by Thomas Robert Malthus. A mild-mannered English clergyman and professor, Malthus warned of the unequal powers of human increase and agricultural production, and of the terrible consequences that might follow from such inequality. The influence of the Malthusian perspective has been enormous, whatever its scientific merits. Perhaps the only modern thinker who can rival Malthus in the ability to provoke anxiety about the growth of population is Paul Ehrlich (b. 1932), author of *The Population Bomb* (1968) and many subsequent works on the theme of overpopulation and its impact on the environment. We shall return to both Malthus and Ehrlich later.

Although books on world population have often bordered on the apocalyptic—witness titles like *The Population Bomb* and *Famine, 1975!*—experts on population, known as demographers, do not as a rule go around wearing sackcloth and proclaiming the imminent demise of humankind by starvation. Nor are hunger and famine the only issues tackled at the conferences or in the journals devoted to population. A great many questions of public concern are related, directly or indirectly, to population, such as how to insure the well-being of a growing elderly population, how to improve access to family-planning, especially for women in poorer regions, how to balance the land-use needs of a growing population with the spiritual and recreational values to be found only in true wilderness, and how to manage the flows of migration in ways that serve the public interest. To get a handle on issues like these, some basic knowledge of demographic terms and principles is essential.

Population Growth Rates

Populations grow and decline; they rarely stand still. In a closed system—an isolated country, for example, or the world as a whole—population increases when births outnumber deaths, and shrinks when deaths outnumber births. A country of 100 million that had 3 million births and 1 million deaths during the year would record a 2 percent *increase* in population. With birth and death numbers reversed, the outcome would be a grim 2 percent *decline* in population. (Migration into or out of a country complicates things, of course. Immigrants, or those moving *into* a country on a permanent basis, add to its population; emigrants, or those moving *out* of a country, reduce it.) Continued over many years, even a low rate of growth can produce large changes in population. Demographers speak of the "doubling time" of a population, that is, the period of time in which the population, increasing at a constant rate, will double in size.

Consider the implications of various rates of growth. At a 2 percent growth rate, as in our example above, population would double in about 35 years. That is how fast population is currently growing in the countries of Colombia, Venezuela, Myanmar, and Zambia. (Unless otherwise noted, current demographic data presented in this chapter is taken from the highly useful *World Population Data Sheet: 2000 [WPDS]*, issued on an annual basis by the Population Reference Bureau.) At a growth rate of 3 percent a year, population would double even faster, in about 23 years. Niger, Angola, and Saudi Arabia are countries now experiencing 3 percent growth rates. When growth continues at a 4 percent pace, population doubles in about 18 years. It is virtually impossible to find a country in the world today experiencing a rate of natural increase that high. The Middle Eastern nation of Oman comes closest at 3.9 percent; continuing to grow at that rate, Oman's population would double in 18 years. (A demographic anomaly is the Gaza Strip, where in the late 1990s growth was 4.4 percent annually.)

In many parts of the world, the population growth rate has dropped below 2 percent, to 1 percent, 0.5 percent, even, in a few cases, to *negative* rates. If a population were growing 1 percent a year, as is currently the case in Thailand, Zimbabwe, and the tiny Pacific island state of Palau, it would take about 70 years to double in size. In countries that have fractional growth rates, the doubling time can rise above 100 years. Norway, for example, with a current annual growth rate of 0.3 percent, would need 217 years to double its population. And of course countries with negative growth rates can forget about doubling times; "halving times" are more relevant to them. Latvia, with a growth rate of *negative* 0.6 percent, could see its population cut in half in a little over a century. The same could happen to Bulgaria, Ukraine, and Russia, at current rates of depopulation. Obviously, these scenarios are strictly hypothetical since one thing we know with certainty is that no country will proceed for any considerable length of time at a constant annual rate of population increase or decrease.

Fertility

The population growth rates cited above were rates of "natural increase" (birth rate minus death rate), uncomplicated by migration. Most countries have little immigration or emigration anyway, the United States being a major exception, as will be discussed below. The birth and death rates that determine the rate of natural increase are usually given in numbers of births or deaths per thousand and are sometimes called "crude birth rate" and "crude death rate." The crude birth rate (CBR) for the United States has recently been 15—a relatively low number compared to other countries around the world. The CBR for the Philippines is 29, for Pakistan, 39, and for Nigeria, 42. The average CBR for sub-Saharan Africa is 41. For the world as a whole, it is 22. The only region of the world with a consistently lower CBR than the United States is Europe, where, for example, the CBR for Denmark, the United Kingdom, France, and the Netherlands is 12 or 13, and for Spain, Italy, Germany, Hungary, and Russia, it is 9.

What's "crude" about the CBR can best be shown by considering a very simple example of two countries, A and B, with populations of 1,000 each. In Country A there are 300 women of childbearing age, and 10 percent of them have babies in a given year. Thus the CBR in this country is 30. In Country B, there are only 150 women of childbearing age, yet 20 percent of them give birth in the same year. Since there are 30 births in Country B, just as in Country A, demographers will record exactly the same CBR in both countries. Yet the underlying fertility rates of the two countries are markedly different. The women of Country B have a much higher rate of childbearing, for which there may be various social, historical, religious, or other reasons, and if everything else about the two countries is the same, Country B will certainly end up more populous than Country A in the future.

It should be apparent that more refined measures of fertility than the crude birth rate are needed if we want to make meaningful comparisons between countries or regions of the world, or between different historical periods. One useful measure is the age-specific fertility rate (ASFR). Here we look at rates of childbearing by age group, for example, women aged 20–24 or women aged 25–29. The ASFR is generally given in numbers of live births per thousand women in the specified age range, usually a 5-year interval. For example, the ASFR in the United States for women in the age group 20–24 was 110 in the year 1995: for every 1,000 women in that age range, there were 110 live births in 1995. Some very interesting things can be learned from a table of ASFR data such as the one for the United States presented in Table 1.1 (Haupt and Kane 1997, 15). We see some noteworthy changes in the timing and rates of childbearing between 1955 and 1995. American women have dramatically reduced their overall fertility from the historically high levels of the "baby boom" era. This reduction is seen in each age group, most notably those in their early twenties. There has also been a clear shift to *later* childbearing. For example, in 1955 births to women in their early thirties were less than half as numerous as to women in their early twenties; by 1995 the proportion had climbed to three-quarters.

One other measure of fertility is very commonly cited by demographers and is, in fact, the most useful single number for projecting future levels of population. This is the total fertility rate (TFR), often shortened to simply "fertility rate." It is somewhat complicated to calculate and even to explain, but it is so important that we will take a moment to lay out the basic idea. No one can say, at the present time, how men and women in com-

TABLE 1.1
Live Births per 1,000 Women Ages 20–34
by Age Group, 1955–1995

Year	Ages 20–24	Ages 25–29	Ages 30–34
1955	241.6	190.2	116.0
1975	113.0	108.2	52.3
1995	109.8	112.2	82.5

ing decades will approach the vital question of family size. All we have to rely on are the data collected up to now. But if these data are complete enough to tell us, for a particular year, the age-specific fertility rates of women in a given country, we can compute its TFR. All we do is imagine—or "synthesize"—a "typical woman" who passes through her reproductive years bearing the same number of children in each sub-period of her life (usually 5-year spans) as the women *currently* in that age range are bearing. Thus, when we say that the TFR of Somalia in the year 2000 was 7.0, it means that as of that point in time the average Somali girl could be expected, as an adult, to give birth to seven children on the assumption that in each sub-period of her reproductive years she would bear children as frequently as Somali women in those age ranges *currently* were doing.

Needless to say, Somalia's TFR of 7.0 is extremely high—among the highest in the world. This should not, however, be taken as proof that Somali women possess a greater capacity for childbearing than women elsewhere in the world. The actual capacity to bear children is called fecundity by demographers. Fecundity and fertility are often confused with each other. Fertility refers to actual childbearing, fecundity, to the ability or potential to bear children. There is no evidence that the women of Zimbabwe, where the TFR is 4.0, are any less fecund than the women of Somalia, with their TFR of 7.0. Nor is there evidence that women in those nations of Europe and eastern Asia headed toward population decline have suffered any impairment of fecundity. Reduced fertility can be explained by many factors other than reduced fecundity, as will be discussed below.

The total fertility rate is a closely watched indicator of future population trends. In a society with low child mortality rates, a stable population requires a TFR of about 2.1. With the average woman producing two surviving children, the current generation would eventually be replaced by another generation of the same size (hence the term "replacement-level fertility"). A TFR above replacement level suggests future increases in population, a TFR below replacement level, just the opposite. On this basis, demographers are predicting the fastest future growth in the world will occur in Africa, since the TFRs for dozens of African nations are in the range of 5 to 7. At the other extreme, Europe's TFR at the turn of the twenty-first century was only 1.4 (Population Reference Bureau 2000). In the United States, it was 2.1.

Mortality

Everyone dies eventually. But in some countries and regions of the world, people on average die sooner than in others. One way to see this is through data on life expectancy at birth. As with the TFR, this is a hypothetical measure: it tells us how many years the average newborn could expect to live if he or she went through life facing the same mortality rates as people currently are experiencing in each age group. Life expectancies vary widely between continents, countries, and often among different areas of the same country. For example, the life expectancy at birth for all of Africa is 52, while for North America it is 77. (In northern Europe it is also 77, in western Europe, 78.) The highest life expectancy in the world is seen in Japan, where it is 81.

Differences in life expectancy correlate, statistically, with a number of factors, such as occupation, education, marital status (married folks live longer), race in those countries that are multiracial, and gender. Gender does matter when it comes to life expectancy: women live longer than men almost everywhere, and sometimes by a wide margin. In the former Soviet republic of Kazakhstan, for example, female life expectancy at birth is 70, male life expectancy, only 59. And in Russia itself, the figures are 73 and 61, respectively. In most countries the gender gap is less dramatic: in the United States, five years, in Japan, seven years, in China, four years. Truly anomalous are the countries where the gap is actually reversed, as in Afghanistan, Bangladesh, and Nepal (in each case, the life expectancy for males being one year *more* than for females).

Wherever life expectancies are short, one is sure to find high rates of mortality for infants and children. Consider two countries at opposite ends of the spectrum: Mali, in western Africa, and Israel, in the Middle East. The life expectancy in Mali is 53; the infant mortality rate (number of infant deaths annually per thousand live births) is 123. In Israel, by contrast, the life expectancy is 78, and the infant mortality rate is 6. It is tempting to go a step further and explain these differences in terms of per capita gross national product (GNP); that is, one might argue that the grim statistics for Mali as compared with Israel are fully accounted for by the fact that Israel has a per capita GNP about 65 times greater than that of Mali. But this would be simplistic. Economic development helps make healthier, longer lives possible, but, as Amartya Sen has shown, even some fairly "poor" nations or regions (China, Sri Lanka, the Indian state of Kerala) have achieved much more impressive life expectancies for their citizens than some "richer" nations (Brazil, Namibia, South Africa, Gabon). The more extensive public provision of health and education in the former group, Sen argues, makes a critical difference (Sen 1999, 46–49).

We saw in the previous section that rates of natural increase are calculated from crude birth and death rates. The crude death rate (CDR) is defined as the number of deaths per thousand people in a given year. In the United States the CDR is currently 9. It may at first appear surprising that the former Soviet republic of Tajikistan could have a much lower CDR of only 5 (Population Reference Bureau 2000). Since Tajikistan is a far less economically advanced nation than the United States, how can this difference in death rates be accounted for? The answer lies in the "crudeness" of the CDR, which takes no account of the age structure in a country. If a country has a large proportion of older citizens, then, other things equal, it will have a higher CDR than a country with a smaller proportion of older citizens. Tajikistan is a demographically "young" nation, with only 4 percent of its population over the age of 64, while the United States is much "older," with 13 percent past the age of 64. So, in spite of Tajikistan's lower death rate, the average Tajik has a shorter life expectancy than the average American (68 versus 77).

World Population — Past

Anthropologists believe that our species, *Homo sapiens*, made its first appearance perhaps two or three hundred thousand years ago in Africa. The population of these hunter-gatherers could never have been growing at a sustained, rapid rate, given their primitive mode of subsistence. In fact, it appears that up until the "agricultural revolution" began around 8,000 B.C., the worldwide population of humans never rose above a few million. Its annual growth rate for many millennia before 8,000 B.C. was probably under 0.01 percent, with a doubling time in the range of 8,000 to 9,000 years. With the beginnings of settled agriculture, however, this changed. There is no expert consensus on whether faster world population growth was the *cause* or the *effect* of the practice of agriculture, but a stepped-up rate of population growth evidently began around 10,000 years ago. From then until the time of Christ, the annual growth rate probably accelerated gradually from 0.01 to the much higher rate of 0.15 percent. Actual yearly additions to the global population also rose, from fewer than 400 per year in 5,000 B.C., to something over 300,000 per year in the era of 1 A.D. By the latter date, world population had reached a total of 200–300 million (Cohen 1995, 34–36; Livi-Bacci 1997, 30–32; Weeks 1998, 7–9).

Over the next 2,000 years, global population growth rates varied quite substantially from year to year, and even century to century, mainly due to swings in the death rate. Wars, plagues, famines—all made major dents in what might otherwise have been a steadier climb in population. Particularly notable was the bubonic plague (or "Black Death") of the fourteenth century, which reduced the populations of Europe and China by one-third. It has been estimated that Europe's population did not recover to its pre-plague levels of 1340 until the mid-1500s. Between 1650 and 1850, though, various forces combined to push world population to permanently higher levels and faster growth rates. Among these forces were the global dissemination of New World crops such as maize (Indian corn), potatoes, and manioc; the discovery and exploitation of fossil fuels; and the introduction of better hygiene and public sanitation. The combined effect of these developments was an improved level of nutrition for many of the world's people, along with reduced rates of disease. Mortality declined and life expectancy rose. By 1850, population was growing faster than 0.5 percent annually, for a net gain of 6 to 7 million people per year (Cohen 1995, 42–45; Livi-Bacci 1997, 47–55; Weeks 1998, 8).

The largest increase of world population in history, both in percentage terms and in absolute numbers, occurred during the twentieth century. Total population rose from 1.65 billion in 1900 to over 6 billion by 2000, with the peak annual rate of increase—around 2.2 percent—occurring in the early 1960s. The doubling time fell to as little as 32 years, probably the shortest we will ever know on a global basis. The century-long expansion (or, as some have called it, "explosion") of population was, once again, largely a matter of declining mortality. Science played an ever-increasing role in this, directly, through improvements in the prevention and treatment of disease, and indirectly, through the improved nutrition made possible by agricultural research (chemical fertilizers, pesticides, plant- and animal-breeding, etc.), research that in fact was well under way by the latter part of the nineteenth century. The mechanization of agriculture first seen in the United States and Europe also played a significant role in raising agricultural productivity and lowering the cost of food (Evans 1998, ch. 6–7; Weeks 1998, 8).

By the early twentieth century, most economically advanced nations had begun to lower their fertility rates, that is, couples in those nations had begun consciously to limit family size through the practice of contraception. This behavioral shift is fundamental to the "demographic transition" model featured in many population textbooks and discussions. According to this model, countries normally begin in a stage characterized by high levels of mortality and fertility. Population stays constant or fluctuates within narrow limits. In the second stage, death rates move downward (for reasons mentioned above), but since birth rates remain high, population increases rapidly. In the third stage, *birth* rates also decline as contraceptive practice becomes more widespread; population growth continues but less rapidly. In the final stage, birth rates descend to levels low enough to match death rates, bringing population growth to an end at a total population much larger than had been seen before the transition. At the risk of overgeneralizing, we can say that most developed nations entered the twentieth century already in the third stage of the model, with fertility declining, and finished the century in the final stage, at (or below) replacement levels of fertility. Poorer, less developed countries, mainly in Africa, Asia, and Latin America, started the century in the first stage, got to the second stage by mid-century, and by the last few decades were passing through the stage of declining fertility. It remains unclear how many of these nations will complete their demographic transition in the twenty-first century.

World Population—Present

At the opening of this new century, world population stands at just over 6 billion. One of the assertions sometimes made to dramatize the enormity of such a number is that there are more people alive today than have lived and died in all previous history. This is quite startling—and alas, quite untrue! One respected demographer has calculated that over the past 200,000 years, about 60 billion humans have been born. That would indicate that only 10 percent of all the humans who have ever lived are living today (Weeks 1998, 15). Nevertheless, 6 billion remains an almost incomprehensibly large number. To appreciate how large, an example may be useful. If we could get every man, woman, and child in the world to hold hands four feet apart from one another along a "skyway" extending from the Earth to the moon, the line would easily reach the moon. In fact, it would take *nineteen* such skyways to accommodate all of the Earth's present human inhabitants.

A nation's demographic characteristics are closely related to its overall economic status, as seen in Table 1.2 (based on the 2000 *WPDS*). The United Nations classifies all of Europe and North America, as well as Japan, Australia, and New Zealand, as "more developed" nations; all other countries are categorized as "less developed." A survey of the two groups in terms of per capita GNP would give us ample reason to call one group "rich" and the other "poor," at least relative to each other. As we see in the table, the total population of the rich countries today is only a quarter that of the poor ones. While the crude death rates of the two groups are similar, the birth rates are *not*. The poor nations, as noted earlier, have not brought down their fertility rates to the low levels reached by the rich. Indeed the total fertility rates of the two groups are poles apart: for the rich countries, TFR has dropped below replacement level; for the poor ones, it remains well above that level. As a result, the rate of natural increase for the less developed nations is much faster than for the more developed. On average, the rich populations are also older, with a larger proportion above age 64 and a smaller proportion under

TABLE 1.2
Demographic Differences between More Developed and Less Developed Nations

	More developed nations	Less developed nations
Population (millions)	1,200	4,900
Crude birth rate	11	25
Crude death rate	10	9
Natural increase	0.1%	1.7%
Total fertility rate	1.5	3.2
Life expectancy	75	64
Under age 15	19%	34%
Over age 64	14%	5%

age 15, than the poor populations. Life expectancy is over a decade longer for the more developed nations than for the less developed.

World Population—Future

How large will the world's population grow in the future? It's an easy question to ask, yet no one, expert or prophet, can answer it with any real confidence. In the near term, of course, we know that population will continue to grow. At the turn of the twenty-first century, the worldwide birth rate of 22 per thousand stood well above the death rate of 9 per thousand, yielding a 1.3 percent (or 13 per thousand) rate of natural increase. This continues the downward trend that began in the mid-1960s when the population growth rate had just peaked at about 2.2 percent annually. By 1980 it had fallen to 1.7 percent; by 1990, to around 1.5 percent. As long as the growth rate remains above *zero*, population will keep on growing. And as long as the total fertility rate stays as high as its current level of 2.9, the world will be on course not merely to replace its existing population but to *expand* it.

When demographers make projections of future population levels, they are careful to warn that such projections are only as good as the assumptions on which they are built. At the United Nations, projections are issued every two years by the Population Division. These are perhaps the most official estimates of future population available, and the most frequently cited by governments and the media. Critical assumptions must be made regarding fertility, which is believed likely to decline much more than mortality in the next several decades. As Table 1.3 shows, the UN offers three variants of its population projections, based on "high," "medium," and "low" future paths of fertility rates. It should be noted that all three paths track fertility *downward* from current levels; in other words, it is widely expected that the worldwide trend toward reduced fertility will continue. Note also that the lowest fertility assumption made by the UN produces a *negative* rate of population change by 2050. This possibility must be taken seriously, given the fact that demographers have been consistently caught off guard by the rapid decline of fertility rates in recent decades. Most attention, however, usually centers on the "medium-fertility" assumption, under which the annual growth rate slows to 0.34 percent by mid-century and

TABLE 1.3
UN Projections for 2050

	Growth rate (%)	World population (billions)
High-fertility variant	0.87	10.7
Medium-fertility variant	0.34	8.9
Low-fertility variant	−0.23	7.3

Source: United Nations Population Division. 1999. *World Population Prospects: The 1998 Revision.*

world population rises to 8.9 billion (United Nations Population Division 1999).

The five countries that are expected to contribute the most to population growth in the coming half-century are India, China, Pakistan, Indonesia, and Nigeria. (Sixth on the list is the United States.) Note that none of the five is presently considered a "more developed" nation. The "less developed" nations as a group are projected, on the medium-fertility path, to increase their share of world population from 80 percent to 87 percent by the year 2050. Indeed, by present projections, virtually *all* of the net increase in world population over the next five decades will occur in the poorer regions of the world. The richer nations, with their much smaller family sizes, will recede in demographic importance. For example, Europe and North America, which together represented 28.5 percent of world population in 1950, are projected to represent a mere 11.5 percent by mid-century (United Nations Population Division 1999).

How will AIDS affect world population in coming years? The largest impact will be felt in sub-Saharan Africa, which has by far the highest HIV prevalence rate of any region in the world. Of the roughly 30 million HIV/AIDS cases worldwide in the late 1990s, over 20 million were in sub-Saharan Africa. The worst-affected countries, with adult prevalence rates of 10 percent or more, were Botswana, Central African Republic, Cote d'Ivoire, Djibouti, Kenya, Malawi, Mozambique, Namibia, Rwanda, South Africa, Swaziland, Zambia, and Zimbabwe. In the central African nation of Uganda, it has been estimated that 40 percent of the armed forces are HIV-infected (Jeter 1999, 18). One of the grim demographic results of the disease has been lower life expectancies in some countries. By 2010–2015, life expectancies in many

African nations may be 15 or more years *lower* because of this terrible disease. In a number of AIDS-afflicted African countries, future populations will be smaller than they otherwise would have been, though because of continued high fertility, absolute declines in population are not yet predicted. For example, the population of Botswana will continue to grow, but by 2025 it is expected to be 23 percent less than it would have been without AIDS. Non-African nations that have had an above-average incidence of this disease are Brazil, Haiti, Cambodia, Thailand, and India (United Nations Population Division 1999).

Migration

So far, we have sidestepped the topic of migration. There is no direct impact on *total* world population from migratory flows since one country's loss is another's gain. If migration involves movement within a country, that country's total population is likewise unaffected. Migration does redistribute some people across national borders, however. And when it does, it affects population growth rates in the sending and receiving countries just as surely as fertility and mortality do. Demographers use a balancing equation to make all of this clear: for any individual country, births minus deaths, plus immigrants minus emigrants, or $(B - D) + (I - E)$, equals the yearly change in population. For the United States, the respective numbers in 1997 (in millions) were: $(3.9 - 2.3) + (1.1 - 0.3) = 2.4$. Thus population rose by 2.4 million for the year. Note that the "natural increase" of births minus deaths accounted for about two-thirds of the overall population gain. Net immigration, legal and illegal, provided the rest (McFalls 1998, 23).

Immigration into the United States during the 1990s reached levels not seen since the turn of the twentieth century. As had been true in that earlier time, it became a politically charged issue. Opponents claimed that immigrants took jobs from the native-born, lowered wage levels and working conditions for unskilled workers, placed a burden on public services such as education, and undermined national identity and unity. Some on the anti-immigration side made an issue of the "loss of border control," particularly with reference to the U.S. border with Mexico. Pro-immigration forces disputed most of these charges, arguing that immigration enriched the United States both culturally and economically. They also pointed to an indisputable fact: the United States has always been an immigrant nation.

Certain statistics are accepted by both sides: the immigrant flow of the 1990s, legal and illegal, was in the range of 1 million per year. This rate of immigration is expected to continue. The United States receives more immigrants annually than all other countries in the world combined. Current immigrants are less educated relative to the native-born U.S. population than their predecessors in recent decades. Most immigrants today are admitted on the basis of family ties to U.S. residents—a system that dates back to 1965. This policy has changed the regional origin of immigrants from mainly European to mainly Latin American and Asian. Indeed, because of the changing immigrant pattern, by 2050 Hispanics are projected to represent 24 percent of U.S. population and Asians 8 percent, compared with 11 and 4 percent, respectively, in 2000 (Martin and Midgley 1999, 23). A final demographic point: without immigration, the United States would much more closely resemble the other developed nations in terms of its TFR and population growth rate, with its population likely to stabilize much earlier.

Urbanization

As the world grows more populous, it also grows more urbanized. One of the underlying reasons is that as agriculture has become more intensive and productive, there has been less demand for labor in rural areas, and thus less of an economic rationale for people to remain there. At the same time, urban places exert a pull on rural populations due to the economic opportunities that cities are perceived to offer. Different countries define "urban" in different ways, but according to one common criterion, populations living in towns of at least 2,000 are considered to be urban. (In the United States, the cutoff line is 2,500.) There is considerable variation in the extent of urbanization from nation to nation. At one extreme is the 100 percent urbanization of the nations of Monaco, Singapore, and Kuwait. Italy, Libya, Chile, and Japan are four countries from as many continents that also would be considered highly urban (90, 86, 85, and 79 percent, respectively), with the United States close behind at 75 percent. By contrast, the two population giants, China and India, have relatively small urban components to their populations (31 and 28 percent). Asia as a whole is not very urbanized, and Africa even less so (35 and 33 percent). The African neighbors of Rwanda and Burundi are both extraordinarily *non*-urbanized, at 5 and 8 percent, respectively (Population Reference Bureau 2000).

Although cities have existed for many centuries, the "urban transition" that is redistributing so much of the world's population from rural to urban areas is relatively recent. In 1950, the world's three largest cities, New York, London, and Tokyo, had a combined population of about 28 million. By 1996, the three largest cities—now Tokyo, Mexico City, and Sao Paulo—numbered close to 61 million. In the late 1990s, about 45 percent of the world's people lived in urban places. This figure will surely climb; the world is likely to be half urban by 2005. Demographers at the UN anticipate that the developed countries will increase their level of urbanization from 76 to 84 percent between 2000 and 2030, while in the same period the less developed countries will increase their urbanization from 41 to 57 percent (Weeks 1998, 413; Gelbard, Haub, and Kent 1999, 17–18).

The effects of the continuing global trend toward urbanization have been both good and bad. On the positive side, urban residents achieve higher levels of health and education; they also have smaller families. (The so-called urban transition seems to be an integral part of the demographic transition referred to earlier.) The economic well-being of urban dwellers often exceeds that of the rural population. On the other hand, living conditions in many Third World cities are appalling, in part because the rapidity of urban growth has made it impossible for governments to provide an adequate infrastructure of streets, schools, housing, hospitals, and sanitation. A broader concern, and one that relates to both developed and developing nations, is that urban growth (or sprawl) is encroaching ever more deeply on lands needed for agriculture or valued for natural habitat.

Carrying Capacity

Is there a theoretical upper limit to the population the Earth can sustain? Joel Cohen presents an exhaustive analysis of this question in his 1995 book *How Many People Can the Earth Support?* Because there are so many possible constraints on population, whether ecological, biological, social, or technological; because "carrying capacity" can be defined in so many different ways;

and because of different views of what is an acceptable standard of living for human beings, the estimates of global carrying capacity have ranged from less than 1 billion to more than 1 trillion (or 1,000 billion). The earliest estimate cited by Cohen, that of the Dutch scientist Leeuwenhoek in 1679, was 13.4 billion people. The four most recent estimates, all from 1994, vary from 3 to 44 billion people. Before we despair of such wild diversity of opinion on carrying capacity, it is worth pointing out that the majority of the over 60 separate estimates gathered by Cohen cluster in a much narrower range, between 7.7 and 12 billion. This raises some concern for Cohen, who notes that the planet's current population has "entered the zone" believed by the majority of scholars to represent the sustainable upper limit. As he puts it, "the possibility must be considered seriously that the number of people on the Earth has reached, or will reach within half a century, the maximum number the Earth can support" at an acceptable living standard (Cohen 1995, 367). When one considers the ongoing trend toward urbanization and the view of one expert that "cities tend to grow on the best agricultural land" (Evans 1998, 201), the level of concern about carrying capacity is raised even higher. Still, there is at present nothing approaching consensus among scholars as to the true upper limit of the Earth's population.

Malthus and Overpopulation Fears

Those who are anxious about population size, at or below the global level, have always found inspiration in the writings of the English economist Thomas Malthus (1766–1834), in particular, his 1798 *Essay on the Principle of Population*. Yet Malthus is often misunderstood or misrepresented. His basic position was that population tends to increase at a "geometric" rate, such as 1, 2, 4, 8, 16, while food production, at best, can only increase at an "arithmetic rate," such as 1, 2, 3, 4, 5. This means the potential is ever-present for a gap to open up between the actual food supply and the food requirements of a growing population. Hasty readers might conclude from this that Malthus foresaw such a gap actually materializing in his own country or perhaps for the world as a whole. Indeed the commonest misconception about Malthus is that he *predicted* mass famine. He did not. Malthus identified a variety of "checks" on population, such as disease, hunger, war, infanticide, and even the simple postponement of marriage. He made clear that he approved of only one of them—the last. The point he stressed repeatedly was that population *must* be restrained by checks of some kind, and if the milder ones were insufficiently effective, then the harsher ones, like starvation and war, would be called into operation.

In a couple of ways, we now see the Malthusian analysis as distinctly premodern. First, the most obvious means of restraining population—artificial birth control—was absolutely rejected by Malthus on moral grounds. The only acceptable way to achieve smaller families and thus slower population growth, he said, was through the postponement of marriage. Malthus's position on this issue was not unusual for his time, or for a clergyman of the Church of England, which he was. But clearly he was on the wrong side of history in this regard. Second, environmental concerns were completely absent from the original Malthusian framework. For Malthus the consequences of overly rapid population growth took the form of depressed wages, urban crowding, infectious diseases, stunted growth among children, and other conventional miseries, never pollution or ecological degradation.

Modern Malthusians

In the century following Malthus's death, it seemed the Malthusian specter of overpopulation had been banished. Agricultural production grew at a remarkable rate and appeared fully capable of keeping pace with rising population. Famines were infrequent and localized. But in the 1950s and 1960s, as public health measures in the less developed nations sent mortality rates dramatically downward with no corresponding decrease in fertility rates, concerns about unsustainable population growth were voiced once again. The loudest Malthusian echo, though hardly the first of the postwar era, was Paul Ehrlich's *The Population Bomb*, published in 1968. "The battle to feed all of humanity is over," warned the Stanford biologist. "In the 1970s the world will undergo famines—hundreds of millions of people are going to starve to death" (Ehrlich 1968, xi). The same grim message had been delivered the previous year in William and Paul Paddock's starkly titled *Famine, 1975!* At the same time, Malthusian fears about the possible destabilizing effects of rapid population growth in Third World countries were having an impact on U.S. foreign policy—hence the support for family-planning efforts in the U.S. foreign aid program (Ross 1998, ch. 4; see also "National Security Study Memorandum 200" in Chapter 5, this volume).

For Ehrlich, unlike Malthus, the concern about population has been environmental, global, and immediate. His *Population Bomb* gave a powerful added boost to the environmental movement launched by Rachel Carson's *Silent Spring* (1962). The first Earth Day, in 1970, was inspired largely by the messages in these two books. Since then, Ehrlich has raised many concerns about the depletion of renewable and nonrenewable resources, the degradation of the environment, and the international tensions that can be attributed, often directly, to population growth. He warns that current population trends will lead not just to poverty and misery, as depicted by Malthus, but to ecological disaster. Given the Earth's finite carrying capacity, human population can grow only so large. At the limit there can be only two possible solutions (short of migration to other planets): lower birth rates or higher death rates. Although Ehrlich sees the second solution as more likely, he takes every opportunity to advocate those personal and public actions that could lower birth rates. He was an enthusiastic cofounder of the advocacy group Zero Population Growth (ZPG) in 1968.

Hard on the heels of *The Population Bomb* came the sensational *Limits to Growth* (1972), a report by a team of MIT scholars who used computer modeling to simulate the future direction of the global economy, environment, and population. The scholars began, reasonably enough, by assuming that population growth, agricultural production, resource depletion, industrial production, and pollution were interdependent processes, each affecting the others through "feedback loops." The computer model, capable of sorting out the complex connections among the variables and of projecting current trends into the future, signaled a crisis ahead. Global population was already so large and fast-growing, nonrenewable resources were being exploited so rapidly, and pollution rates were likely to increase so substantially in coming decades that by the year 2100 economic growth would have halted. Worse yet, population would have gone into worldwide decline due to food crises and rising death rates. The future depicted in *Limits to Growth* was alarming indeed.

Population Optimists

Gloomy views of population growth have undoubtedly been influential in recent times, but they have not gone unchallenged. Two of the strongest *anti*-Malthusian voices have been those of Ester Boserup (1910–1999), a Danish economist, and Julian Simon (1932–1998), a U.S. economist. Boserup, in her classic study, *The Conditions of Agricultural Growth* (1965), noted that Malthus and his followers saw population change as dependent on agricultural conditions. Population would grow if land was abundant or crop yields generous but not otherwise. Her own research, however, convinced Boserup that frequently the direction of causation ran the other way: population change could lead to changes in agricultural practices. In particular, rapid population growth, by putting pressure on resources, could *induce* changes in agricultural techniques, such as shifts from slash-and-burn methods to settled cultivation, or innovations in plant varieties, more systematic crop rotations, or improvements in farm tools (Boserup 1965). In short, population pressure could be a force for dynamic, positive change.

Julian Simon offers a broader and even more optimistic view of population growth than Boserup. A growing population, he argues, tends to raise, not lower, the standard of living. Why? Because the most critical resources for improving human welfare are, quite simply, human ingenuity and imagination. And the way to have more of these is to expand population. (That is the message behind the title of Simon's controversial 1981 book, *The Ultimate Resource*.) Simon disputes many of the pessimistic claims made by the neo-Malthusians regarding the impact of population. He asserts, for example, that contrary to the warnings of environmentalists like Ehrlich, natural resources and energy are *not* becoming scarcer, or more expensive in constant-dollar terms, as population continues to grow. Advances in technology have brought down the extraction costs, in labor hours per unit, for most resources and thereby actually increased the known and available reserves of those resources. Likewise, pollution in the United States has abated in recent decades, despite a growing population. Meanwhile, the world's per capita food production has been on the rise for many years, and famines have become less frequent. Hence population growth ought to be seen, according to Simon, more as a means for solving problems than as a problem in itself.

The Changing Age Structure

When fertility rates fall as low as they have in most developed nations, there are important impacts on the age structure of the population. The proportion of children and adolescents in the population shrinks, while the proportion of elderly expands. With mortality rates also declining, life expectancy rises. You get an older, "grayer" population. These trends, while affecting some of the world's poorer nations, are most clearly seen at present in the rich ones. The developed nations often have 15 percent of their populations over the age of 64, while in the less developed nations a more common figure is 5 percent or less. Among the rich countries, there are usually fewer than 25 percent under the age of fifteen, while that figure can rise to between 40 and 50 percent in some poorer countries today (Haupt and Kane 1997, 5). In Italy, which has been Europe's leader in recording low fertility rates, the population over 60 now outnumbers the population under 20 years of age.

An obvious concern with graying populations is how to support the growing number of citizens who are no longer active in the labor force. Many national pension systems, including Social Security in the United States, were established long ago, when life expectancies were much shorter than they are today. Pay-as-you-go systems, under which the taxes paid by current workers are used to fund current benefits to retirees, function well when there are many workers per retired person but less well when the worker to retiree ratio falls. If that ratio falls far enough—it is now below two to one in Austria and Belgium, and headed toward one to one by 2030—the system may collapse.

Aging populations also raise difficult issues of fairness in the allocation of a society's resources. As the elderly population continues to expand and requires increasing amounts of social services, there will inevitably be strains on private and public sources of funding to provide those services. Some believe that a shift of social resources away from the young and toward the older generations has been under way for years. Intergenerational conflicts of interest may prove hard to avoid. The political process will be tested. It has been clear for some time in the Western democracies that senior citizens, by virtue of their high participation rates in the electoral process, wield considerable influence over legislation that affects their well-being. Such political clout can only increase in the coming decades as the so-called gray lobby increases in size.

The developed countries face dramatic challenges in regard to their aging populations, but they are not alone. Indeed the largest increases in elderly populations over the coming half-century will be found among the *developing* countries. By mid-century, three-quarters of the world's elderly will live in these countries. Yet these are precisely the countries least able to bear the financial burden of a growing senior citizenry. Old-age pensions are virtually unknown in the poorer countries; the elderly traditionally rely on their adult children for support. As modernization proceeds, such traditional practices are weakening. Unless new social-support arrangements can be found, the outlook for the elderly in the developing nations will be worrisome at best.

Population Policies: Pronatalist

Throughout history, governments have attempted to modify the direction of population change, both upward and downward. Pronatalist polices, aimed at more births and faster population growth, have been pursued in times and places where national well-being has been equated with population size. It is sometimes the fear of *de*population, with consequent loss of national power and influence, that drives pronatalist efforts. (This has been true of France, according to many observers.) On the other hand, *anti*-natalist policies, aimed at *slower* population growth, have been thought more likely to serve the economic and social interests of the people in a number of countries, generally poorer, high-fertility countries in Africa and in south and western Asia.

In light of the "birth dearth" and graying population problems noted in the previous section, governments in some of the 60-odd countries now experiencing below-replacement fertility rates have made efforts to raise the birth rate. In Europe and Japan, especially, where attitudes toward immigration have historically been more hostile than in the United States, higher birth rates offer the only means to halt an eventual decline in population. Sweden has pursued a pronatalist policy, at least implicitly, since the 1970s. Family benefits were made quite generous, in the form of cash payments, tax incentives, and extended maternity leaves. The effort seemed to pay off during the 1980s, as the Swedish fertility rate (TFR) rose from 1.7 to 2.1, but during the

1990s fertility slumped to its lowest rate ever (1.5), perhaps due to adverse economic conditions. Japan has tried similar pronatalist policies—with a similar lack of sustained success. Hungary, a formerly socialist nation, provides child allowances and maternity leave benefits, in addition to an extensive child-care network for working mothers. Experts believe the effect on fertility has been positive, but only in the sense of preventing Hungary's TFR from falling any *lower* than its current 1.3 (Kent 1999, 4–5).

Although in recent years the United States has seen its fertility rate drop to approximately replacement level, and even briefly below that level, there is no prospect of U.S. depopulation—and thus no push for a pronatalist policy—as the new century opens. In fact, the Census Bureau projects a more than doubling of the U.S. population, to 571 million, by the end of the twenty-first century (see Chapter 5). What differentiates the United States from nearly all other developed nations is a heavy rate of net *immigration*. Without it, the demographic future of the United States would much more closely resemble that of the other industrialized countries. With it, the nation will see population expand significantly, owing to the number of immigrants themselves, their relative youthfulness, and their high rates of fertility. If immigration policy can be thought of as a form of population policy, then the United States has accepted (if only implicitly) a policy strongly favoring a larger national population.

Population Policies: Antinatalist

For over half a century, policies aimed at slowing population growth in developing countries have been discussed, debated, and, with wide variations, implemented. An influential rationale for antinatalist policies was provided in a 1958 study by Ansley Coale and Edgar Hoover, who argued that high rates of population growth jeopardized long-term economic development by diverting resources from growth-enhancing investments to the mere maintenance of population. Reduced fertility, on the other hand, could speed economic development by freeing more resources for investment in productivity-enhancing activities (Coale and Hoover 1958). On the basis of this kind of thinking, the industrialized nations began funding population programs in the less developed countries (LDCs) in the 1960s and 1970s, with the United States playing a leading role.

By 1997, 68 nations were on record as desiring to limit their population growth; the majority were in Africa. Over twice that many countries had governments that provided subsidies for family-planning activities. Poorer nations, less able to raise the needed public funds, have received considerable financial and technical support for family planning from the UN Population Fund (UNFPA), the United States Agency for International Development (USAID), nongovernmental agencies like International Planned Parenthood, and private foundations, such as the Ford and Rockefeller Foundations. What seems to be agreed on all sides is that no single family-planning model fits every country. Each country's efforts must be tailored to its own traditions, culture, and perceptions of what needs to be done (Jain 1998, ch. 1).

In addition to providing information about contraceptive choices and actually delivering contraceptive services to clients, some family-planning programs offer more general health services to women and children, and some engage in propaganda to change attitudes about family size. (Soap operas delivering messages about the benefits of smaller families seem to have been quite effective in changing attitudes and behavior in some countries.) In recent years, the trend has been away from placing a narrow emphasis on birth control per se. Policymakers have come to understand that fertility is inextricably linked to women's status in society, and that higher levels of education and opportunity for women tend to result in later childbearing and smaller completed families. A 1995 study by the Alan Guttmacher Institute found that, in countries as diverse as Peru, Egypt, and Indonesia, teenage childbearing was *far* more prevalent among women who had less than seven years of schooling than among those who had more than seven years. Maternal education has also been shown to be correlated with lower mortality rates for children in most societies—another benefit of expanding educational opportunity for girls (Gelbard, Haub, and Kent 1999, 21–24).

Population Policies: China and India

What population policies have been followed by the world's two population giants, China and India? China, with approximately 1.3 billion people in 1999 and a TFR now below replacement level at 1.8, has pursued a forceful national program of slower population growth for more than two decades. India, with around 1 billion people and a TFR of 3.3, has followed a more decentralized system of family planning in the years since India became the first developing nation to offer family-planning services in 1951 (Population Reference Bureau 2000; Jain 1998, 53). A comparison of the two cases will be instructive.

China's fertility rate began falling first in its cities during the 1960s. There was no explicit national policy aiming for smaller families until 1971, when the *wan xi shao* campaign began. The translation is *later* (marriage), *longer* (intervals between births), *fewer* (children). This program evolved into the "one-child policy" of 1979 that has been the focus of so much international attention. Under the one-child policy, couples are given incentives and disincentives to limit themselves to a single child. Urban couples with one child who pledge not to have any more children receive monthly child-support allowances until the child reaches the age of 14, promises of higher pensions in their own retirement, and more spacious housing. The child receives preferential treatment in applying to schools and for jobs. In rural areas, a modified policy offers added monthly payments in cash and kind to couples who pledge to stop at one child. One-child families also get the same grain ration and the same size plots for private cultivation as larger families, thus reaping an indirect advantage. The Chinese provinces may implement additional policies on an individual basis, and some of these have included higher taxes on families who have more than two children, and even imposition on the parents of full maternity costs and medical and educational costs for such children (Weeks 1998, 32, 538).

Whether the one-child policy has been a success is debatable. China once set a goal of capping national population at 1.2 billion by the year 2000. That limit has already been breached, and while the TFR has fallen below replacement level, China's current population is so youthful, with so many young adults entering their childbearing years, that the total population is bound to increase for a few more decades at least. Some also question how much of the fall in fertility has been due to the one-child policy. Much of the extraordinary drop from a TFR of 7.5 in 1963 to 2.5 in 1983 occurred *before* the new policy was announced in 1979. And much of China's fertility decline might have occurred even in the absence of a strict antinatalist policy. But criticism of the one-child policy has been directed less at its efficacy than at its coercive features. When incentives and disincentives become strong enough, the policy looks like compulsory birth control. One of the policy's worst side effects, in a culture that values male children above female, can be seen in the neglect of infant girls and sex-selective abortion of female fetuses (Weeks 1998, 32–33; Sen 1999, 220–221).

India has been seeking slower population growth ever since its first five-year plan (for 1951–1956) called for the creation of family-planning centers throughout the country. At that time, the Indian TFR stood at 6.0. Early efforts focused on information, education, and research into contraceptive methods. Results were disappointing, with fertility declines seen mainly in a few states, in the upper classes, and in cities. Determined to do better, Indira Gandhi's government in 1976 revamped the program, increased the monetary incentives to participants, and suggested that state legislatures consider passing laws that ordered compulsory sterilization after the birth of a couple's third child. (One state actually did so.) Controversy and violence ensued, and Gandhi's party was defeated in elections a year later. Her return to office in 1980 brought a renewed commitment to the national family-planning effort, as did her son's rise to power in 1984. Rajiv Gandhi promised a broader, higher-quality national program, with more generous rewards to women who limited their family sizes. But demographic results at the national level were, and have continued to be, less than impressive. According to some observers, the program has been overly bureaucratic, inconsistent, and inflexible. Too much reliance has been placed on sterilization (first male, later female) rather than on offering couples an array of contraceptive choices (Livi-Bacci 1997, 191–94; Weeks 1998, 532–534; Jain 1998, ch. 3).

Fertility *has* declined in India, but not nearly as quickly as policymakers once projected. Although they hoped at one time to see replacement-level fertility achieved by the end of the twentieth century, the revised goal is to reach that mark by the period 2011–2016. As with China, this will entail continued population growth for decades to come, due to the demographic momentum of large numbers of Indians about to enter or already in their reproductive years. How much of India's fertility decline is due to its population policy and how much to general modernization trends is unclear. The rates of fertility reduction vary widely across the states of India. It has been noted that where fertility is highest, for example, in the northern states of Uttar Pradesh,

Bihar, and Rajasthan, educational levels, especially for females, are low. In Kerala and Tamil Nadu, by contrast, fertility is low (TFRs of 1.7 and 2.2, respectively) while educational levels and literacy rates are high. Women are accorded more economic rights and opportunities here than in other Indian states, and family-planning programs are less heavy-handed than they are in states with much higher fertility rates (Sen 1999, 221–224; Jain 1998, 73).

Global Population Policy

There is no super-government with the authority to impose population policies on sovereign states around the world. Nor, aside from the most alarmed neo-Malthusians, is there any real support for sweeping measures to limit population. But the views of the international community on population matters can have an impact on the deliberations of national policymakers and on the academic, media, and political elites who shape the policies. Over the years, the most important forum for debating population policy has been a series of decennial, UN-sponsored world population conferences, which now go by the official title of International Conference on Population and Development (ICPD). These conclaves, to which most governments send delegations, have been held in Bucharest (1974), Mexico City (1984), and Cairo (1994), with rather different messages conveyed to the world on each occasion.

At Bucharest, ideology dominated the proceedings. The financial support of rich countries for family-planning programs in the poorer ones was attacked by some delegates as self-serving, if not imperialistic. A number of national delegations made clear their opposition to policies aimed at lowering population growth rates. "Economic development is the best contraceptive," in the words of one slogan voiced at the conference. Acrimony aside, the Bucharest meetings did put the nations assembled there on record as approving, for the first time, an international population "plan of action." The plan included a numerical target for reduced birth rates in the developing countries, a statement of the "basic human right" of all couples to make their own decisions about family size, and support for full gender equality in education, politics, and economic life (Weeks 1998, 545; Livi-Bacci 1997, 183–184).

In Mexico City, ten years later, delegates were startled by the announcement of a new U.S. position that population was a "neutral phenomenon," neither helpful nor harmful to economic advancement. Many developing nations had come to the conclusion since 1974 that rapid population growth could indeed pose a threat to their chances for social and economic progress. The new, less activist U.S. position could be traced to antiabortion politics in the United States and to the intellectual influence of Julian Simon (see above) in the Reagan administration. Population experts saw the main significance of the conference in the unanimous acceptance of the idea that population growth was a matter of concern apart from economic development (Weeks 1998, 545–547).

The most recent UN population conference, held in Cairo in 1994, drew delegates from 183 nations. The "program of action" that emerged was lengthier than previous "plans of action," ambitious, and wide-ranging. Topics addressed include the empowerment of women, internal and international migration, the environment, technology, nongovernmental organizations (NGOs), education, and more. No numerical goals were set for fertility or population growth rates, although goals *were* set for life expectancies and (reduced) child mortality rates. One expert has concluded that Cairo produced three major accomplishments: it firmly removed the taboo against public discussion of family-planning and birth control; it elevated the concerns and rights of women in the control of fertility; and it saw the return of the United States to a position of shared leadership on issues of world population (Cohen 1995, 71–72). As of now, no plans have been announced for another decennial conference in 2004.

References

Boserup, Ester. 1993 (1965). *The Conditions of Agricultural Growth: The Economics of Agrarian Change under Population Pressure.* London: Earthscan Publications.

Coale, Ansley J., and Edgar M. Hoover. 1958. *Population Growth and Economic Development in Low-Income Countries: A Case Study of India's Prospects.* Princeton: Princeton University Press.

Cohen, Joel E. 1995. *How Many People Can the Earth Support?* New York: W. W. Norton.

Ehrlich, Paul. 1968. *The Population Bomb*. New York: Ballantine.

Evans, L. T. 1998. *Feeding the Ten Billion: Plants and Population Growth*. Cambridge: Cambridge University Press.

Gelbard, Alene, Carl Haub, and Mary M. Kent. 1999. "World Population beyond Six Billion." *Population Bulletin*, 54, no. 1: 1–44.

Haupt, Arthur, and Thomas T. Kane. 1997. *The Population Handbook*, 4th ed. Washington, DC: Population Reference Bureau.

Jain, Anrudh (ed.). 1998. *Do Population Policies Matter? Fertility and Politics in Egypt, India, Kenya, and Mexico*. New York: Population Council.

Jeter, Jon. 1999. "A Continent Ravaged by AIDS." *Washington Post National Weekly Edition*, Dec. 20–27, p. 18.

Kent, Mary Mederios. 1999. "Shrinking Societies Favor Procreation." *Population Today*, 27, no. 12: 4–5.

Livi-Bacci, Massimo. 1997. *A Concise History of World Population*, 2nd ed. Malden, MA: Blackwell Publishers.

McFalls, Joseph A., Jr. 1998. *Population: A Lively Introduction*, 3rd ed. Washington, DC: Population Reference Bureau.

Malthus, Thomas Robert 1993 (1798). *An Essay on the Principle of Population*. Edited by Geoffrey Gilbert for Oxford World's Classics. New York: Oxford University Press.

Martin, Philip, and Elizabeth Midgley. 1999. "Immigration to the United States." *Population Bulletin*, 54, no. 2: 1–44.

Meadows, Donella H., Dennis L. Meadows, Jorgen Randers, and William W. Behrens III. 1972. *The Limits to Growth: A Report for the Club of Rome's Project on the Predicament of Mankind*. 2nd ed., 1974. New York: Universe Books.

Paddock, William, and Paul Paddock. 1967. *Famine, 1975! America's Decision: Who Will Survive?* Boston: Little, Brown.

Population Reference Bureau. 2000. *2000 World Population Data Sheet (WPDS)*. Washington, DC: Population Reference Bureau.

———. 1999. *World Population: More than Just Numbers*. Washington, DC: Population Reference Bureau.

Ross, Eric B. 1998. *The Malthus Factor: Poverty, Politics and Population in Capitalist Development*. New York: Zed Books.

Sen, Amartya. 1999. *Development as Freedom*. New York: Alfred A. Knopf.

Simon, Julian. 1981. *The Ultimate Resource*. Princeton: Princeton University Press.

———. 1996. *The Ultimate Resource 2*. Princeton: Princeton University Press.

Specter, Michael. July 10, 1998. "The Baby Bust: A Special Report; Population Implosion Worries a Graying Europe." *New York Times*.

United Nations Population Division of the Department of Economic and Social Affairs of the United Nations Secretariat. 1999. *World Population Prospects: The 1998 Revision*, vol. 1, *Comprehensive Tables*. New York: United Nations.

Weeks, John R. 1998. *Population: An Introduction to Concepts and Issues*, 7th ed. Belmont, CA: Wadsworth.

2

Chronology

This chapter places on a time line some of the key events in the history of world population: the first censuses in a number of countries, the founding of major population organizations, the publication of important scholarly works, the occurrence of extraordinary epidemics and famines, and the convening of international population conferences. The years in which world population achieved whole billions are also noted (most recently 6 billion in 1999). Sources for this chronology are given at the end of the chapter. Obviously there is no single place to find a full history of world population. Three books, however, by Cohen (1995), Livi-Bacci (1997), and Weeks (1998), have proven to be especially informative not only on the history of population but many other aspects of the subject.

8000 B.C. The "agricultural revolution" begins, with about 4 million human beings on Earth. Hunter-gatherers shift to more settled patterns of living, which include livestock-herding and the cultivation of grains; population begins growing more rapidly.

1000 B.C. Egyptians are using a primitive form of birth control (condoms).

5 B.C. Caesar Augustus orders a census of the entire Roman empire.

1 A.D. World population stands at about 210 million.

2 A.D.   Under the Han dynasty, China counts the number of households, i.e., conducts a primitive census.

100 A.D.   The city of Rome's population of 650,000 is unrivaled by any other city in the world.

1086   William the Conqueror orders a survey of English lands and landholdings, from which modern historians have derived a population estimate for England of around 1.5 million.

1347   The bubonic plague, or "Black Death," returns to Europe after an absence of six or seven centuries, appearing first in Sicily and spreading rapidly in the following years. Its cause is the bacillus *Yersinia pestis*, spread by rodent-borne fleas. By 1400 the plague's toll is nearly one-third of Europe's population.

1492   Christopher Columbus's arrival in the West Indies marks the opening stage of a long-term population catastrophe for the indigenous American peoples as a result of their vulnerability to the pathogens carried by Europeans. The population of Aztecs in central Mexico, for example, falls from about 6.3 million in 1548 to 1.9 million in 1580.

1500   The population of Europe, battered by periodic returns of the plague, still has not recovered to the level it had reached in 1300.

1679   Dutch scientist A. van Leeuwenhoek offers an early quantitative estimate of Earth's maximum population, or carrying capacity: 13.4 billion.

1721   Japan conducts a nationwide count of population; scholars believe population surveys were undertaken in Japan as early as the ninth century A.D.

           The practice of inoculating people against smallpox is introduced in rural England: a small extract from a smallpox pustule is transferred from an infected individual to one who has not previously been infected. A mild case of the disease results, but thereafter the inoculee enjoys a natural immunity to smallpox.

1749   Sweden is among the first nations in Europe to establish a population register and census, conducted locally by clergymen.

1771   An outbreak of bubonic plague in Moscow takes 57,000 lives in one season.

1774   With the death of Louis XV from smallpox, popular opposition to smallpox inoculation in France crumbles.

1776   George Washington orders smallpox inoculation for all his troops.

1787   The kingdom of Spain, in its first census, counts 10.4 million people.

1790   The first U.S. census, mandated by the Constitution, finds a total national population of 3.9 million.

1797   Edward Jenner, an English country doctor, notices that milkmaids rarely contract smallpox. He assumes that by getting cowpox milkmaids acquire immunity to the more deadly smallpox. Jenner develops a vaccine for humans based on cowpox that proves to be fully protective against smallpox. Thus, vaccination replaces inoculation in the prevention of smallpox.

1798   The publication of Thomas Robert Malthus's *Essay on the Principle of Population* marks a milestone in the study of human population and the social, economic, and moral implications of population size. Malthus warns that population tends to increase more rapidly than the means of subsistence, and that in the absence of other checks, famine and disease will act as the ultimate checks.

1800   Only one city in the world has 1 million people—London; two centuries later there will be 325 additional cities of that size or larger.

1801   England conducts its first census.

1804   There are 1 billion people on Earth.

1817   An outbreak of cholera in Calcutta spreads beyond its usual bounds; British colonial troops pass the disease to Nepalese and Afghan foes. Within a few years, ships' crews carry it even further, to Ceylon, Indonesia, China, and Japan, as well as into the Middle East and down the eastern African coast.

1831   An outbreak of cholera at Mecca during the annual Muslim pilgrimage leads to a widespread epidemic throughout the Islamic world. In many subsequent years, cholera outbreaks accompany the annual pilgrimage—for a final time in 1912.

1843   Vulcanization of rubber opens the way to mass production of inexpensive condoms.

1846   Failure of the potato crop initiates a great famine in Ireland; within a few years, over a million Irish die and over a million emigrate from the island.

1854   English physician John Snow discovers, during a cholera outbreak in London, that the disease is caused *not* by "miasma," or "bad air," but rather by the presence of fecal waste in drinking water. Snow publishes his finding in 1855; not until 1883 is the actual bacterium, *Vibrio cholerae*, observed under the microscope by Robert Koch.

               The Dutch establish plantations of quinchona trees in Java; an extract from the trees' bark, quinine, is effective in treating malaria.

1882   Robert Koch announces his discovery of the bacillus responsible for tuberculosis.

1891   E. G. Ravenstein, a well-known British scholar, pub-
        lishes a carefully calculated estimate of the world's
        current population as well as its future supportable
        population; his first estimate is later judged to have
        been remarkably accurate, but not his figure for the
        Earth's maximum population, 5.99 billion (surpassed
        in 1999).

1909   The International Office of Public Hygiene is estab-
        lished in Paris to monitor worldwide outbreaks of
        such diseases as cholera, typhus, yellow fever, and
        smallpox.

1915   The newly established Rockefeller Foundation under-
        takes to study and bring under control deadly mos-
        quito-borne yellow fever, sending teams of scientists
        to Latin America and Africa. By 1935 an effective vac-
        cine for prevention of the disease has been developed
        in the Rockefeller Foundation laboratories; in 1950
        Max Theiler is awarded the Nobel Prize in medicine
        for this work.

1916   Margaret Sanger opens the first U.S. birth-control clin-
        ic in Brooklyn.

1918–   Global influenza pandemic takes an estimated 25–40
1919   million lives; U.S. servicemen returning home from
        war in Europe bring the virus with them, leading to
        550,000 U.S. deaths.

1921   The first family-planning clinic in the United King-
        dom is opened by Marie Stopes, English feminist,
        birth-control activist, and author of the pioneering sex
        manual *Married Love* (1919).

        The first vaccine effective against tuberculosis is pro-
        duced.

1927   World population reaches 2 billion.

        The discovery of penicillin opens the way to control
        many infectious diseases.

1929   Population Reference Bureau is founded in Washington, D.C.

1930   At a conference in Lambeth (London), the Anglican communion resolves that contraception, under appropriate circumstances, is morally acceptable.

              In reaction to the Anglican decision earlier in the year Pope Pius XI issues the encyclical *Casti Connubii*, reasserting the Roman Catholic position that contraception is contrary to the purpose of the conjugal act and therefore immoral.

1931   Population Association of America is founded by Alfred Lotka and others; it becomes the leading professional society of demographers in the United States.

1943   The Great Bengal (India) Famine claims roughly 3 million lives, mostly due to lowered resistance to disease.

1944   Norman Borlaug arrives at the Mexican research center later known as Centro Internacional para Mejoramiento del Mais y Trigo (CIMMYT), or International Maize and Wheat Improvement Center. Borlaug leads efforts to develop high-yield wheat and maize, with major funding from the Rockefeller Foundation.

1945   Demographer Frank Notestein formulates the theory of "demographic transition"; it soon becomes an influential framework for analyzing national trends in mortality, fertility, and population growth.

1946   The U.S. baby boom (also experienced in several other countries heavily involved in World War II) begins; the peak year of the boom in the United States is 1957.

              United Nations Population Division is established with Frank Notestein, an architect of the modern science of demography, its first director.

1948   The publication of *Our Plundered Planet*, by Fairfield Osborn, raises the issue of a correlation between rapid population increase and environmental degradation; William Vogt's *Road to Survival* warns of the impact of a population explosion among the "backward billion."

The passage of the Eugenics Protection Act in postwar Japan legalizes abortion; an already declining Japanese birth rate falls even faster.

The World Health Organization is established.

1951   The draft outline of India's first Five-Year Plan calls for a national population policy that includes family planning, and specifically the provision of facilities for sterilization. The final draft of the plan, released in 1952, states that a reduction in the country's birth rate would benefit the economy as well as the health of mothers and children.

1952   Population Council is founded in New York at the instigation and under the sponsorship of John D. Rockefeller III.

International Planned Parenthood Federation is established, with headquarters in London and birth-control pioneer Margaret Sanger as its first president. Its original members are from India, the United States, the United Kingdom, Netherlands, Sweden, West Germany, Singapore, and Hong Kong; by 1990 the IPPF has 107 member organizations representing 150 nations.

1955   A vaccine against polio, developed by Jonas Salk of the University of Pittsburgh Medical School, is proved effective in human trials.

1958   Coale and Hoover's book *Population Growth and Economic Development in Low-Income Countries* argues that population growth hinders poor countries' prospects for economic growth; the view becomes highly influential in government and academic circles.

1958–
1961   Mao Zedong's crash industrialization program in China, known as the "Great Leap Forward," leads to

1958–
1961
cont.

famine deaths in the range of 30 million. The estimate of 30 million is based on the difference between *expected* Chinese mortality in those years and *actual* mortality; experts consider this the worst famine in history.

1960

There are 3 billion people on Earth.

International Rice Research Institute (IRRI) is established by the Rockefeller and Ford Foundations in the Philippines to develop high-yield varieties of rice.

U.S. Food and Drug Administration (FDA) approves oral contraceptives, or "the pill"; from 1965 on, it is the most common form of birth control in the United States.

1961

Agency for International Development (AID) is established within the U.S. State Department; within a few years it becomes the main conduit for U.S. financial assistance to global family-planning efforts.

1962

The release of dwarf, high-yield wheat inaugurates the so-called Green Revolution, raising hopes that rapid increases in world food supplies will match the high rate of population increase, especially in the developing nations.

Serious research begins on oral rehydration therapy (ORT) to combat the devastating mortality effects of diarrhea, especially for children in the poorer countries; clinical trials are conducted by the International Centre for Diarrhoeal Diseases Research in Bangladesh from 1964 to 1968. Successful results are announced in a *Lancet* journal article in 1968. ORT now offers a safe, effective, and inexpensive treatment for cholera.

1963

The growth rate of world population reaches its all-time high of about 2.2 percent annually; by 2000 it will fall to about 1.3 percent.

1964

This year marks the closing of the U.S. baby boom.

1965   The Supreme Court, in *Griswold v. Connecticut*, gives married couples the right to practice birth control; a later decision (1972) extends the right to unmarried couples.

President Johnson declares, in his State of the Union address: "I will seek new ways to use our knowledge to help deal with the explosion in world population and the growing scarcity in world resources." Senate hearings are commenced, and the Agency for International Development prepares to get involved in family-planning efforts abroad. U.S. funding of such efforts rises during LBJ's term from $2 million to $35 million annually.

1966   IRRI releases its first high-yield rice.

1967   The United Nations Population Fund (UNFPA) is authorized.

The best-selling book *Famine, 1975!* by William and Paul Paddock advocates a harsh policy of "triage" in dealing with expected famines: provide aid only to those countries that have a reasonable chance of bringing their population growth under control.

1968   The publication by the Sierra Club of Paul Ehrlich's *The Population Bomb* builds public awareness of the effects of rapid population increase.

Zero Population Growth (ZPG) is founded by Ehrlich and others.

Pope Paul VI issues the encyclical *Humanae Vitae*, restating traditional Catholic opposition to all forms of birth control except the "rhythm method."

UN conference on human rights held in Iran results in the Teheran Proclamation; article 16 identifies the control of one's own fertility, and access to the means of achieving this, as a basic human right.

1969   UNFPA begins operations as the major international source of family-planning assistance.

A United Nations General Assembly resolution calls on governments to provide their citizens with the knowledge and means necessary to control their fertility.

President Nixon declares in a message to Congress: "The experience of this decade has . . . shown that lower rates of population growth can be critical for speeding up economic development and social progress."

1970   Nobel Peace Prize is awarded to Norman Borlaug for his work in advancing the Green Revolution, by which food crop yields have been greatly increased in many developing countries.

Global population growth is a major concern voiced on the first Earth Day, on April 22.

1972   Publication of *The Limits to Growth*, sponsored by the Club of Rome, renews worries about an unsustainable growth of world population.

The Nixon-appointed Commission on Population Growth and the American Future, chaired by John D. Rockefeller III, recommends stabilized domestic population, an end to illegal immigration, liberalized state laws on abortion, and other measures; Nixon declines to endorse the report.

1973   *Roe v. Wade* decision by the Supreme Court legalizes abortion in the United States.

1973–
1974   Famine in Ethiopia claims more than 100,000 lives, recalling the great Ethiopian famine of 1888–1892, in which one-third of the country's population died.

1974   Famine in Bangladesh claims 26,000 lives, according to the government, but unofficial estimates place the toll at 100,000 or more.

There are 4 billion people on Earth.

The first international conference on population to be attended by official government representatives is held in Bucharest. The conference is highly contentious and politicized, but a world population plan of action is adopted (see Chapter 5). "Economic development is the best contraceptive" becomes the most quoted phrase from the conference.

President Echeverria of Mexico reverses his previous opposition to family-planning. The country's General Law of Population is altered to permit the sale and purchase of contraceptives. The Catholic church refrains from actively opposing the change of policy.

Worldwatch Institute is founded in Washington, D.C.

A National Security Council memorandum, ordered by President Nixon, details the possible adverse effects on U.S. national interests from rapidly rising world population; contents are classified (declassified in 1989).

1975   At the World Conference of the International Women's Year, a "world plan of action" points to ways that improved education, status, and employment for women would affect age at marriage, as well as the spacing and number of children.

1976   India's national government, under prime minister Indira Gandhi, authorizes state legislatures to enact policies of compulsory sterilization to limit birth rates; the ensuing period of "national emergency" culminates in Gandhi being voted out of office.

1979   China implements its one-child policy; its previous family-planning programs of the 1960s and 1970s had already brought down fertility rates substantially. In 2000, Chinese women average more than one child each, but their total fertility rate (TFR) of 1.8 is still below replacement level.

1980   Upon concluding its global smallpox eradication and vaccination project, the World Health Organization declares smallpox *eradicated*, the first such total elimination of an infectious disease in human history. During the twentieth century, smallpox took an estimated 300 million to 500 million lives.

A government interagency report, solicited by President Carter in 1977 and issued as *The Global 2000 Report to the President: Entering the Twenty-first Century*, warns that "if present trends continue, the world in 2000 will be more crowded, more polluted, less stable ecologically, and more vulnerable to disruption than the world we live in now"; population trends are identified as a worrisome variable. In response to *Global 2000*, President Carter requests that Congress double its funding of international population assistance; it declines to do so.

1981   The first diagnosis of AIDS is made in the United States.

The Office of Management and Budget proposes eliminating U.S. funding for population assistance from the first Reagan budget, a move defeated by Secretary of State Alexander Haig and Vice-President George Bush.

1984   The second UN-sponsored world population conference is held in Mexico City; it reaffirms the plan of action adopted at Bucharest (1974). The U.S. delegation asserts the Reagan administration position that population growth is not a significant obstacle to economic development. It also announces that henceforth no U.S. funds will go to NGOs that offer clients abortion information or services, even if they do so at their own expense. Observers see a clear departure from previous U.S. leadership on population policy.

The International Planned Parenthood Federation, after 17 years of U.S. financial support, loses that funding after it refuses to accept new U.S. conditions on abortion provision and counseling (the so-called Mexico City policy).

The European Parliament passes a resolution calling on member nations to follow pronatalist policies to head off a crisis of low birth rates.

1986   The Reagan and Bush administrations withhold U.S. funds from UNFPA through 1992, on grounds that some UNFPA monies help fund coercive population practices in China (denied by UNFPA). Some of the funds are reallocated to other family-planning programs abroad.

The National Research Council publishes *Population Growth and Economic Development: Policy Questions*, in which it is argued that population growth in less developed countries can be advantageous if it triggers certain kinds of "market reactions," such as more clearly defined property rights; the study finds "little support for either the most alarmist or the most complacent views concerning the economic effects of population growth" (p. vii).

1987   World population reaches 5 billion; "Day of Five Billion" observed on July 11.

Nafis Sadik, a Pakistani obstetrician, is appointed executive director of the UNFPA; she is the first woman to be appointed the head of a UN agency.

1988   Mifepristone, or RU 486, is approved for use in France (in Great Britain, 1991; in Sweden, 1992).

The United Nations General Assembly endorses a decision by the World Health Organization that December 1 be declared World AIDS Day; the occasion is marked every year afterward, on December 1, in hopes of raising awareness about the disease.

1989   President Bush vetoes a foreign aid bill that includes $15 million for the UNFPA but later signs a revised bill

1989
cont.

that increases the population aid budget by $20 million (with no money for UNFPA).

The Governing Council of the UN Development Fund recommends, and the UN officially declares, July 11 as a permanent World Population Day, with themes to be chosen annually to highlight important issues (for example, in 1996, reproductive health and HIV/AIDS; and in 2000, saving women's lives).

1990

The FDA approves Norplant, a contraceptive implant for women.

1992

The FDA approves the use of an injectable contraceptive for women, Depo-Provera (previously used in 80 other countries).

In an unprecedented step, the Royal Society of London and the U.S. National Academy of Sciences issue a joint statement urging a "more rapid stabilization of world population" as a partial remedy for environmental degradation that threatens to become irreversible (see Chapter 5).

Another statement by scientists, this one signed by over 1,500, including half the living Nobel laureates in science, calls for stabilization of world population. This "Warning to Humanity" stresses the damage suffered by the environment from overconsumption by the developed nations and rapidly expanding populations among the developing nations (see Chapter 5).

At Rio de Janeiro, the United Nations Conference on Environment and Development, also known as the Earth Summit, approves a report that includes this statement: "The growth of world population and production, combined with unsustainable consumption patterns, places increasingly severe stress on the life-supporting capacities of our planet."

1993

President Clinton issues an executive order, two days after his inauguration, rescinding the Mexico City policy of 1984 and indicating an intention to restore U.S. financial support for UNFPA.

A UN-sponsored Conference on Human Rights convenes in Vienna and issues, at its conclusion, the "Vienna Declaration and Programme of Action"; part II, para. 41, states: "The World Conference on Human Rights reaffirms, on the basis of equality between women and men, a woman's right to accessible and adequate health care and the widest range of family planning services, as well as equal access to education at all levels."

At an international science summit on world population held in New Delhi, representatives from 58 scientific academies endorse a statement that reads in part: "In our judgment, humanity's ability to deal successfully with its social, economic, and environmental problems will require the achievement of zero population growth within the lifetime of our children."

The World Health Organization declares tuberculosis (TB) to be a global emergency; at century's end, the disease is claiming 2 million lives each year, with 1 billion new TB infections expected between 2000 and 2020, resulting in 35 million deaths.

Genocidal tribal conflict in Burundi takes 100,000 lives.

1994   The third UN-sponsored world population conference, now titled International Conference on Population and Development (ICPD), is held in Cairo; it adopts a Program of Action to be followed by all participating nations.

Genocidal tribal conflict in Rwanda takes an estimated 1 million lives.

The Zapatista uprising in Chiapas, Mexico, is attributed by some observers (in part) to population pressures on the available land; land scarcity in Chiapas is exacerbated by concentrated landholding patterns.

1995   According to a report issued by the UN's Intergovernmental Panel on Climate Change, "the balance of evidence suggests that there is a discernible human influence on global climate."

1995–   Famine in North Korea, caused by natural disasters
1999   and economic mismanagement, takes the lives of 2 million (by U.S. estimate).

1996   At the UN World Food Summit, held in Rome, delegates from 173 nations sign a Plan of Action calling for progress toward world population stabilization, as well as wiser management of natural resources and less excessive consumption. More concretely, the conference calls for a reduction by half in the number of malnourished people in the world by 2015.

1997   Media mogul Ted Turner donates $1 billion to the United Nations in support of its efforts in the areas of population, health, and environment.

    A U.S. Department of State Strategic Plan asserts that "stabilizing population growth is vital to U.S. interests. . . Not only will early stabilization of the world's population promote environmentally sustainable economic development in other countries, but it will benefit the U.S. by improving trade opportunities and mitigating future global crises."

1998   The bicentennial of Malthus's *Essay on the Principle of Population* (1798) is widely noted, with commentators debating the merits, realism, and relevance of the Malthusian theory in the contemporary world.

    The United Nations issues new, lower projections of world population for the year 2050; its medium (most likely) estimate is 8.9 billion.

1999   India becomes the second nation, after China, to reach a population of 1 billion.

The ICPD + 5 forum held at the Hague (Feb. 8–12) reviews progress toward the goals set at the 1994 UN population conference in Cairo, in an atmosphere of general disappointment; many goals have not been met.

Officially on October 12, Earth has 6 billion people.

2000   U.S. Congress restores funding for UNFPA at a reduced level.

The U.S. Census Bureau issues its first-ever projection of U.S. population to the end of the twenty-first century, putting the number in the year 2100 at 571 million, or about double its current level.

The UN predicts in a report issued June 27 that in those African nations with the worst AIDS infection rates, between one-half and two-thirds of all current 15-year-olds will eventually die of the disease.

According to the Census Bureau, whites have become a racial-ethnic minority in California, their numbers having declined during the 1990s, whereas the numbers of Asians, Hispanics, and blacks all increased.

The FDA grants approval to the abortion drug RU-486, or mifepristone, to be marketed under the name "Mifeprex"; 620,000 European women have already used the drug.

Nafis Sadik, executive director of the UNFPA, retires after 14 years, to be replaced on January 1, 2001, by Thoraya Obaid of Saudi Arabia. Obaid had been in charge of the UNFPA division for Europe and the Arab States; she holds a Ph.D. in literature from Wayne State University in Detroit and has much experience in international civil service.

2001   Immediately upon taking office, President George W. Bush reinstates the "Mexico City policy" banning U.S. funds to international family-planning agencies that

2001   counsel or provide abortions. Some observers expect
cont.   an ironic result: reduced funding to these agencies
        will mean less ability to provide contraceptives and
        thus more abortions.

        In a much firmer statement than the one issued in
        1995, the Intergovernmental Panel on Climate Change
        (IPCC) now concludes that man-made gases have
        "contributed substantially to the observed warming
        over the last 50 years," and warns that by the year
        2100 temperatures may be as much as 11 degrees
        Fahrenheit above their 1990 levels, *far* higher than pre-
        viously estimated. The report is unanimously
        approved by 150 scientists at a meeting of the IPCC in
        Shanghai.

2013   World population is set to pass the 7 billion mark
        according to UN projections.

2028   World population is set to pass 8 billion.

2050   World population is expected to reach 9.3 billion
        according to the UN's "middle variant" projection
        (2001).

References

Booth, William. 2000. "California, the Majority Minority State." *Washington Post National Weekly Edition,* Sept. 4.

Brown, Lester et al. 1999. *Beyond Malthus: Nineteen Dimensions of the Population Challenge.* New York: W. W. Norton.

Coale, A., and E. Hoover. 1958. *Population Growth and Economic Development in Low-Income Countries.* Princeton: Princeton University Press.

Cohen, Joel. 1995. *How Many People Can the Earth Support?* New York: W. W. Norton.

Evans, L. T. 1998. *Feeding the Ten Billion: Plants and Population Growth.* Cambridge: Cambridge University Press.

Green, Marshall. 1993. "The Evolution of US International Population Policy, 1965–92: A Chronological Account." *Population and Development Review* 19, no. 2: 303–321.

Himes, N. E. 1976. *Medical History of Contraception*. New York: Shocken Books.

Hinde, T. 1995. *The Domesday Book: England's Heritage, Then & Now.* London: Tiger Books International.

Holloway, Marguerite. 2001. "Aborted Thinking: Reenacting the Global Gag Rule Threatens Public Health." *Scientific American* 284, no. 4 (April): 19-21.

Livi-Bacci, Massimo. 1997. *A Concise History of World Population*, 2nd ed. Malden, MA: Blackwell.

Malthus, Thomas Robert. 1798. *An Essay on the Principle of Population.* Edited by Geoffrey Gilbert. New York: Oxford University Press.

McNeill, William H. 1976. *Plagues and Peoples.* New York: Anchor Press.

Meadows, Donella H. et al. 1972. *The Limits to Growth: A Report for the Club of Rome's Project on the Predicament of Mankind.* New York: Universe Books.

Noonan, John T. 1986. *Contraception: A History of Its Treatment by the Catholic Theologians and Canonists.* Cambridge, MA: Harvard University Press.

Paddock, William, and Paul Paddock. 1967. *Famine, 1975! America's Decision: Who Will Survive?* Boston: Little, Brown.

Population Division of the Department of Economic and Social Affairs of the United Nations Secretariat. 2001. *World Population Prospects: The 2000 Revision.* New York: United Nations.

Sen, Amartya K. 1981. *Poverty and Famines: An Essay on Entitlement and Deprivation.* Oxford: Oxford University Press.

Struck, Doug. 2000. "For North Korea, the Worst Is Over." *Washington Post National Weekly Edition,* Sept. 11.

Weeks, John R. 1998. *Population: An Introduction to Concepts and Issues.* 7th ed. Belmont, CA: Wadsworth.

Working Group on Population Growth and Economic Development. 1986. *Population Growth and Economic Development: Policy Questions.* Washington, DC: National Academy Press.

3

Biographical Sketches

Many people have contributed to the debate over world population. Some, like Thomas Malthus, Paul Ehrlich, and Julian Simon, have forged the basic theoretical and policy frameworks within which population issues are addressed. Others, like John Bongaarts and Paul Demeny, have refined our understanding of key demographic processes. More practical-minded individuals, like Margaret Sanger and Nafis Sadik, have helped shape new population policies at the national and international levels. And scientists like Norman Borlaug, M. S. Swaminathan, and Walter Plowright, have led the research efforts that are making it possible to continue balancing the world's growing population with its food supply. No claim is made that the individuals featured below are the "right" people. Indeed it is quite clear that the chapter could be much longer. For example, Margaret Sanger and Maria Stopes, birth-control pioneers in the United States and Britain, had courageous counterparts in many other countries. Malthus was preceded as a population theorist by the sixteenth-century Italian thinker Botero, and ultimately by ancient Greek and Chinese philosophers. Advances in agricultural science have come from a succession of innovators in many countries. Those singled out in this chapter have, as the saying goes, "stood on the shoulders of giants."

John Bongaarts (1945–)

Nothing will play a larger role in determining the future size of the world's population than trends in the fertility rate. Demographer John Bongaarts has presented an influential model of fertility, according to which there are four basic determinants of a society's fertility rate: the proportion of women married, the proportion who are physically unable to bear children (infecund), the rate of abortion, and the proportion of women using contraception. These four variables account for almost all observed differences in fertility among nations. At the global level, therefore, we will have to see further change in one or more of the variables before fertility, which has been declining for years, settles at (or below) replacement level. The variable most likely to change: the proportion of women using contraception.

Dutch by birth and citizenship, Bongaarts wrote his doctoral thesis on the "demographic transition" (University of Illinois, 1972). He has long been associated with the Population Council in New York City, where he is currently vice-president in the policy research division. He has served on many panels, committees, and boards, and has briefed the U.S. vice-president and the secretary of state on population matters.

Norman Borlaug (1914–)

His admirers see in Norman Borlaug's lifework a decisive refutation of Malthus. The famed eighteenth-century English parson had worried about the danger of human numbers outpacing any possible increase in food production, with famine the ultimate control. As the populations of the developing nations shot upward in the second half of the twentieth century, a "Malthusian" crisis appeared imminent in Asia and Africa. The occurrence of widespread famines was taken almost for granted in the West. But the so-called Green Revolution of the 1960s, for which Borlaug was principally responsible, helped keep food supplies growing as fast as, and in many cases *faster* than, the population. Some observers credit the agricultural innovations of Borlaug and his colleagues with saving millions of lives, especially in the developing world.

An Iowa native, Borlaug earned his bachelor's degree in forest management and his Ph.D. in plant pathology (University of Minnesota, 1942). In 1944 he accepted the invitation of the Rockefeller Foundation to lead a research effort in Mexico aimed at improving that country's wheat production. Over many years of patient experimentation, he and his team developed the dwarf, high-yielding wheat varieties that, in combination with chemical fertilizers and irrigation, allowed Mexico to greatly increase its grain output and reduce its dependency on food imports. The Mexican research center that evolved out of the original research program—known by its acronym CIMMYT—soon achieved worldwide renown. Borlaug was invited to develop similar crop varieties in India and Pakistan; his remarkable success in doing so helped move the subcontinent from famines in the 1960s to much greater food security in subsequent decades. His plant-breeding practices were also emulated at the International Rice Research Institute (IRRI) in the Philippines, and today most Asian rice bowls are filled with hybridized rice.

In 1970, Borlaug was awarded the Nobel Peace Prize for his efforts to reduce world hunger through agricultural science. He has not rested on his laurels, however. First at Cornell University, then at Texas A & M, he has held distinguished professorships. He continues to mentor young scientists at CIMMYT in Mexico. And in recent years he has turned his attention to the food situation in sub-Saharan Africa. Working with Japanese philanthropist Ryoichi Sasakawa and former president Jimmy Carter, Borlaug, under the auspices of the Sasakawa-Global 2000 foundation, initiated field trials of new varieties of wheat, sorghum, cassava, and cow peas in several African countries. As with his earlier efforts, these projects have produced startling increases in crop yields. Borlaug is the first to admit, however, that long-term success in Africa will be a challenge, given the lack of physical infrastructure, the extraordinary levels of poverty, the lack of social cohesion, and the high rates of population increase. He continues to worry about global population, in spite of all he has done to banish the Malthusian specter.

Ester Boserup (1910–1999)

One of the most notable demographic thinkers of the twentieth century was the Danish economist Ester Boserup. In her classic study *The Conditions of Agricultural Growth* (1965), she turned Malthusian theory on its head and in the process gave valuable ammunition to the "cornucopian" side of the population debate. Under simple Malthusian theory, population levels were thought to depend on food supplies. Thus an improvement in agricultural techniques could pave the way to a rapid increase in population. But what if the relationship worked in a reverse direction, with faster population growth the *cause*, rather than the *effect*, of improved methods of agricultural production? That, in essence, was Boserup's contention in her 1965 book. Her empirical research convinced her that agricultural advances were spurred by population pressure and not the other way around. In particular, the pressure of more people on the land (that is, rising population *density*) had led to such historic innovations as the plow, crop rotation, irrigation, the use of fertilizers, and so on. These notions clearly ran counter to the neo-Malthusian orthodoxy of the 1950s, 1960s, and 1970s, which regarded population growth as likely to jeopardize economic development.

Boserup was educated at the University of Copenhagen, where she studied economic theory, sociology, and agriculture. She began her career as an economic planner in the Danish government during World War II. Later she spent a decade—much of it in the study of European agriculture—at the United Nations Economic Commission for Europe in Geneva, Switzerland. In 1957 she moved to India to assist Gunnar Myrdal (later a Nobel laureate in economics) in his research on Asian economic development. Her extensive travel as part of this project and a subsequent period of research in Africa in 1964–1965 gave Boserup a firsthand grasp of development issues and an impatience with purely theoretical approaches to development. Her interest in the way modernization affected the status of women led her to write *Woman's Role in Economic Development* (1970).

Population optimists like Julian Simon were delighted to welcome Boserup to their ranks. As they saw it, her work demonstrated that population growth need not have any negative impact on human well-being; in fact, it could be highly beneficial. Although the environmentalist camp remained skeptical, they respected the empirical and multidisciplinary qualities of Boserup's scholarship.

Lester R. Brown (1934–)

Few public-interest organizations have been as closely identified with their founder as the Worldwatch Institute has been with Lester Brown. Since 1974 Brown has built Worldwatch into one of most recognized names in the environmental movement. Its annual *State of the World* report, always coauthored by Brown, has assumed the status of a semiofficial document; it is now translated into all of the world's major languages and used in hundreds of college and university courses in the United States and abroad. Brown has demonstrated a flair for "getting out the word" in a variety of formats: *Vital Signs* and *State of the World* annuals, monographs (the Environmental Alert series), the bimonthly magazine *World Watch*, interviews, and speeches.

Consistently throughout his career, Brown has expressed concern about world population, most recently in the 1994 book *Full House: Reassessing the Earth's Population Carrying Capacity* (with H. Kane) and the 1999 book *Beyond Malthus: Nineteen Dimensions of the Population Challenge* (with G. Gardner and B. Halweil).

Educational credentials in agriculture and public administration—along with firsthand experience both in farming (tomato-growing in New Jersey) and in the federal government—may help explain Lester Brown's willingness to view environmental issues broadly. He sees the problems of the environment as complex and interrelated. Solutions will not come from specialists working only within their narrow fields of expertise. Hence the useful role of an organization like Worldwatch that can supply government officials, the media, and the public with analysis that is readable and broad-gauged rather than narrowly technical.

In early 2000, Worldwatch announced that Lester Brown would be leaving the presidency of the institute to assume the position of chairman of the board. He will continue as a Worldwatch senior researcher. Brown has received numerous honorary degrees, prizes, and fellowships, among them, the MacArthur Fellow award (1986), the United Nations Environment Prize (1987), and the Blue Planet Prize (1994). His board memberships include the Council on Foreign Relations and Zero Population Growth.

Joel E. Cohen (1944–)

Curious people through the centuries have asked the simple question, how high can our planet's population go? Their answers, and a fascinating review of the entire subject, may be found in Joel Cohen's 1995 book *How Many People Can the Earth Support?* With doctoral training in applied mathematics, population sciences, and tropical public health at Harvard, and as head of the Laboratory of Populations at Rockefeller University and Columbia University, Cohen is well qualified to tackle the issue. He carefully notes a host of difficulties and complications that must be overcome before one can estimate the Earth's carrying capacity. Surprisingly, the middle value (or median) of past maximum-population estimates turns out to be quite close to actual UN projections of world population by the middle of the twenty-first century. Indeed Cohen's survey of previous estimates of maximum global population—back to 1679—strongly suggests that the world is approaching what many demographic thinkers have deemed to be the upper limits of sustainable population.

Formerly a member of Harvard's Society of Fellows, Cohen has been elected to the American Academy of Arts and Sciences, the American Philosophical Society, and the National Academy of Sciences. He has won the Tyler Prize for Environmental Achievement (1999) and a MacArthur Fellowship. His writings have ranged across demography, ecology, epidemiology, and mathematics.

Paul Demeny (1932–)

No one will insist—with the possible exception of economists—that our most personal decisions are based on economics. Still, the demographer Paul Demeny, a distinguished scholar at the Population Council in New York, believes that the timing of a country's "fertility transition"—the all-important move to smaller families—is mainly determined by four economic factors. They are (1) the direct cost to parents of rearing and educating their children, (2) the indirect costs in lost earnings when a parent, usually the mother, is kept out of the job market by child-rearing activities, (3) the earnings that children can bring home to their families, and (4) the contribution children can make to their parents' old-age security relative to other systems of economic support, such as state pensions. All of this suggests that government policies to speed the transition to lower fertility should be simple enough to devise, though perhaps not as easy to carry out. For example, policies discouraging child labor and requiring children to remain in school, encouraging women to enter or reenter the labor force, or providing for old-age assistance, will all tend to raise the costs and lower the benefits of childbearing.

A widely respected figure in the demographic profession, Paul Demeny immigrated to the United States from Hungary in 1956, earned his Ph.D. in economics from Princeton University in 1961, and founded the journal *Population and Development Review* in 1974. He continues as the journal's editor to this day, and *Population and Development Review* remains a refreshingly readable source of population information and perspective.

Nicholas Eberstadt (1955–)

At the various councils, foundations, and government agencies concerned with population matters, there has long been a dominant view about the world's population: it is growing too fast, damaging the environment, and dampening the economic prospects of poorer nations. But for years there has also been a vigorous dissent from the "neo-Malthusian" orthodoxy. Julian Simon, Peter Bauer, Ester Boserup, and two resident scholars at the American Enterprise Institute, Ben Wattenberg and Nicholas Eberstadt, have challenged the mainstream view. In a widely noted article in *The Public Interest* (Fall 1997), Eberstadt explores the possibility that a population "implosion" is now under way around the world. Fertility rates are declining virtually everywhere, and in Europe and parts of east Asia the drop is so severe that populations may well *shrink* in the foreseeable future. The social and economic implications are immense. On its current path, Italy, for example, will become, within two generations, a place where most children have no siblings, aunts, uncles, or cousins. (China is moving in the same direction.) The concept of family will be fundamentally altered. Europe will face massive immigration pressures. Some Asian societies will have to cope with a "bride shortage" due to abortion practices that favor male offspring. In many countries a growing elderly population will need to be supported on a dwindling base of younger workers.

Because he does not share the view that population growth needs to be curbed, Eberstadt is not favorably impressed by the financial support that U.S. charitable foundations have given to international family-planning—or "population control," as he prefers to call it. He has written about the crucial role of the Rockefeller and Ford Foundations in the 1950s and 1960s in launching these efforts, and the renewed interest shown in such activities by a more recent generation of U.S. philanthropists, such as Ted Turner, Bill Gates, and Warren Buffett. It is Eberstadt's view that "ordinary American taxpayers" have become less supportive of aid to international population programs and that wealthy philanthropists are stepping in to cover the difference out of their own pockets.

Eberstadt presents his provocative ideas on television and radio programs, in the pages of leading public-affairs journals and newspapers, and before congressional committees. He has been a consultant to the Departments of State and Defense, the World Bank, and the Census Bureau. Holding three degrees from Harvard and one from the London School of Economics, he has been for many years a visiting fellow at Harvard's Center for Population and Development Studies. His most recent book is *Prosperous Paupers and Other Population Problems* (2000).

Paul R. Ehrlich (1932–)

In recent decades, the individual most responsible for sounding the alarm over the impact of human population on the natural environment has been Paul Ehrlich. His 1968 book *The Population Bomb* was an international best-seller. It has been credited, along with Rachel Carson's *Silent Spring*, with helping to launch the environmental movement. The urgent tone (and premature pessimism) of this work is evident in its much-quoted opening lines: "The battle to feed all of humanity is over. In the 1970s and 1980s hundred of millions of people will starve to death in spite of any crash programs embarked upon now." Ehrlich's powerful and persuasive prose echoes the original population warning of Malthus in 1798. But while Malthus analyzed population mainly in economic terms, Ehrlich stresses the *ecological* costs of overpopulation. He points to things like pollution, species extinction, and depletion of the ozone layer as potential costs of too rapid population growth. His simple equation, $I = P \times A \times T$, makes the impact (I) on the environment depend directly on population (P), the average level of consumption or affluence (A), and the level of technology (T). Obviously a rising population has harmful effects on the environment unless offset by lower consumption rates or more beneficent kinds of technology.

The clear role of population (P) in the formula above helps account for Ehrlich's persistent emphasis, in books, articles, and television appearances, on limiting human numbers. He believes families should aim for two children at most, preferably one. Not surprisingly, he was a cofounder of the organization Zero Population Growth (ZPG). But his environmental concerns have broadened more recently—as may be seen in his 1997 book *The Stork and the Plow* (coauthored with Anne Ehrlich and Gretchen Daily)—to include the advocacy of less wasteful lifestyles in the developed world, a reduction of the income gap between rich and poor nations, and better education and improved status for women, one benefit of which would be reduced family size. Ehrlich has not hesitated to support strong government measures to achieve the limits on population he thinks are so imperative. This is one of several areas in which he differs sharply with the population optimists, led by Julian Simon (until his death in 1998).

Ehrlich earned his Ph.D. in biology from the University of Kansas and has been for many years on the faculty at Stanford University, where he is Bing Professor of Population Studies. His special research interest has been in the genetics, ecology, and population dynamics of checkerspot butterflies. His many honors include prizes from the Royal Swedish Academy of Sciences, the United Nations, the World Wildlife Fund, and the MacArthur Foundation. His writings include hundreds of articles, *The Population Explosion* (1990, with A. H. Ehrlich), *Betrayal of Science and Reason: How Anti-Environmental Rhetoric Threatens Our Future* (1996, with A. H. Ehrlich), and the books cited above.

Werner Fornos (1933–)

For the past quarter-century, Werner Fornos has been the Paul Revere of the population-awareness community, sounding the alarm about overpopulation to every kind of audience, attending population conferences all over the world, and serving as president of the Population Institute. As with most neo-Malthusians, Fornos stresses the environmental degradation caused by excessive population growth. But what is distinctive in his approach to overpopulation is a clear focus on the downward trend in the *quality of life* as human numbers continue to climb. He worries about the squalor and misery experienced by millions around the world as they crowd into super-large cities. He points to the poverty, illiteracy, and disease rates found in those parts of the world where 95 to 99 percent of future population growth is expected to take place. When he looks at his adopted country— Fornos was granted U.S. citizenship in 1953 after arriving in this country *four* times as a stowaway—he sees a need for greater action on two fronts. First, the United States needs to support international family-planning programs more generously. Second, it needs to establish its own population policy. The United States has faster population growth than any other industrialized nation, with serious consequences for global warming and other environmental problems.

A graduate of the University of Maryland, Fornos served for four years as a Maryland state legislator before joining the Population Institute. In February 2000, he had the honor of receiving the Order of Merit, the highest award granted by the German government to a noncitizen.

Garrett Hardin (1915–)

Few writers on population have been more outspoken—or controversial—than Garrett Hardin. Like his fellow ecologist Paul Ehrlich, Hardin has expressed deep alarm over global population trends. But Hardin's focus is less on the scientific than the ethical and societal aspects of overpopulation. His highly influential 1968 essay "The Tragedy of the Commons" argues that common resources—village grazing lands and ocean fish stocks, for example—tend to be systematically overexploited by individuals acting on the basis of expected benefits to themselves, without due regard to the *social* cost of what they do. Even population decisions may be viewed in this light. When people choose to have additional children, they do not take fully into account the costs that an additional human life will impose on society or the environment. The result is overpopulation.

Hardin took on a related taboo subject in his 1974 article "Lifeboat Ethics: The Case against Helping the Poor." There he argued that if a lifeboat is loaded to capacity and can transport to safety only its current occupants, they must refuse to pull on board any others who may be struggling in the water nearby. Otherwise *all* will perish. By analogy, Hardin continued, if the Earth's resources can support only a limited population, then the self-sufficient or economically developed nations must either refuse assistance to those unable to feed their citizens or condition such assistance on strict population-control measures. Coercion by the state, Hardin has said, may be required to achieve the stabilization of population. So, too, may the tightening of border controls in high-wage countries (like the United States) subject to mass immigration from low-wage countries. He favors zero net immigration to the United States.

Hardin's undergraduate degree is from the University of Chicago (1936); his doctoral degree in biology is from Stanford (1941). He was for many years professor of human ecology at the University of California, Santa Barbara. His books include *Living within Limits: Ecology, Economics and Population Taboos* (1993), *The Immigration Dilemma: Avoiding the Tragedy of the Commons* (1995), and *The Ostrich Factor: Our Population Myopia* (1999).

He Kang (1923–)

He Kang, the Chinese minister of agriculture from 1983 to 1990 and a key agricultural planner from as early as 1979, seems never to have been daunted by the challenge of keeping food supplies growing fast enough to feed the world's most populous nation. Superficially it might not seem a difficult task, since China several years ago reached below-replacement fertility (fewer than two children per woman) as a result of its "one-child policy." But the relative youthfulness of China's population gives it what demographers call "momentum." With millions of Chinese entering their childbearing years, population—and the demand for food—will continue to increase for many years to come.

He Kang's rise to a position of high influence in the agricultural bureaucracy coincided with the similar rise to paramount political influence in China by Deng Xiaoping, a pragmatist determined to lead the country away from the deadening effects of government controls and central planning. Deng wanted peasant farmers to have more decisionmaking authority and a chance to make profits by their hard work. Implementation of the new approach, under He Kang's inspired guidance, led to quick results: grain output rose from 305 million tons in 1978 to a record 407 million tons in 1984. Other types of agricultural production—meat, sugar, fish catches, cotton—also showed impressive gains. By 1986 He Kang could boast that China had achieved basic self-sufficiency in food and clothing, a welcome refutation of the gloomier predictions of some Western writers in the 1960s.

Thomas Homer-Dixon (1956–)

Thomas Homer-Dixon, director of the Peace and Conflict Studies Program at the University of Toronto, has for some years now been contributing to a complex way of understanding what may lie ahead for poor but populous regions of the world. He argues that rapid population growth, in many places, is depleting and degrading the available supplies of renewable resources such as cropland, forests, and fresh water. The supplies that remain are often under the control of powerful, privileged interests who exploit them without regard for the long-term effects on the majority of the population. Growing environmental scarcities can contribute, in Homer-Dixon's view, to outbreaks of "ecoviolence." Indeed he believes we have already seen ecoviolence occur in Chiapas (Mexico), the Gaza Strip, South Africa, and Pakistan and are likely to see more of it in the future.

A native and citizen of Canada, Homer-Dixon earned his Ph.D. in political science at MIT (1989). He has presented his research at the World Economic Forum in Davos, Switzerland, and has twice briefed the vice-president of the United States. His most recent book is *Environment, Scarcity, and Violence* (1999).

Thomas Robert Malthus (1766–1834)

The most commonly cited name in the history of population studies (and controversies) is Malthus. The adjective "Malthusian" has entered the English language as a term suggestive of the frightening possibilities of overpopulation. Thomas Robert Malthus came from a middle-class family in the south of England. Shortly after graduation from Cambridge University in 1788, he was ordained a clergyman in the Church of England. In 1805 he was appointed professor of history and political economy at the East India College, where he taught for the rest of his life. His *Essay on the Principle of Population* was published anonymously in 1798, with significant revisions incorporated into later editions. Malthus was an economist who shared many of the free-market views of his great classical predecessor Adam Smith.

In his population theory, Malthus argued that human numbers tend to increase more rapidly than the food supply needed for subsistence. He pointed to the explosive rates of population growth observed under favorable conditions, for example, in the American colonies, and to the finite amount of land available for the production of food. Although it is commonly asserted that Malthus *predicted famine* for the human race, this is quite untrue. Malthus merely stated that population must be restrained by some combination of "checks," and that if all other checks failed to limit population, famine would do the grim job. He believed that some checks were more benign in their operation than others, and he particularly favored what he called "moral restraint"—the postponement of marriage, with chastity in the interim.

Malthus became one of the most controversial public figures of his time, and even today the evaluations of his ideas range from highly critical to warmly appreciative. Environmentalists applaud his attention to the impact of rapid population growth, and believe his concerns are even more pertinent in our world of 6 billion people than in his world of 1 billion. Critics, on the other hand, argue that Malthus underestimated the potential of technological progress in agriculture; that he wrongly blamed the poor for their own misery; and that by rejecting birth control (on moral grounds), he failed to grasp the most effective and humane means of avoiding overpopulation. His *Essay* remains available in many editions, continuing to invite new generations of readers to confront difficult issues.

Donella H. Meadows (1941–2001)

If there was one book that marked the climax of the "population panic" that took hold of much of the world from the mid-1960s to the mid-1970s, it was *The Limits to Growth* (1972), by Donella Meadows, Dennis Meadows, J. Randers, and W. W. Behrens. Other books, such as Paul Ehrlich's *The Population Bomb* (1968) and the Paddock brothers' *Famine, 1975!* (1967), had sounded the alarm, but *Limits to Growth* created an immediate sensation, partly because it seemed to rest on solid scientific foundations and partly because it predicted disaster. *Limits to Growth*, sometimes known as the "Club of Rome report" after the organization that sponsored it, was based on a computer model (World3) pioneered by Jay Forrester at MIT. Statistical information on current trends in resource use, energy use, pollution, and population growth was fed into the computer to see whether those trends were sustainable on a long-term basis. The computer's answer: absolutely not. Within a century at most, all the key variables *including population* would turn downward. The world system could not achieve an equilibrium in time to avoid collapse.

Much controversy ensued. Academic conferences were convened, more models were developed, World3 itself was refined, and more recent data was fed into it. In 1992 three of the four original authors of *Limits to Growth*, including Donella Meadows, who taught environmental studies at Dartmouth College, issued a new study. Its title, *Beyond the Limits: Confronting Global Collapse, Envisioning a Sustainable Future*, gave a fair indication of its basic message. Current trends were still pushing the world toward disaster; indeed on some important variables the world system had already *overshot* its limits. But the worst possibilities might still be avoided through a combination of voluntary cutbacks in consumption, slower (eventually zero) population growth, and greater efficiency in the use of energy and materials.

Donella (Dana) Meadows received her B.A. at Carleton College in 1963 and a Ph.D. in biophysics at Harvard in 1968. She was the author or coauthor of nine books. In addition to her adjunct teaching duties at Dartmouth, she was an organic farmer, a journalist, and a systems analyst on the local as well as global level. Her weekly newspaper column, "The Global Citizen," was nominated for a Pulitzer Prize in 1991. A selection of the columns was published as *The Global Citizen* in 1991. That same year she was chosen as a Pew Scholar in Conservation and the Environment, and in 1994 she was awarded a five-year MacArthur Fellowship.

Walter Plowright (1923–)

The awarding of the 1999 World Food Prize to Walter Plowright put the spotlight on a resourceful scientist and a costly disease, neither well known to the public. The disease, rinderpest, has plagued humankind since the era of the Roman empire. It is a highly infectious viral disease that is nearly always fatal to cattle and other hoofed animals, and thus devastating in its impact on those who depend on livestock herds. In the eighteenth century, outbreaks of rinderpest killed 200 million cattle in western Europe, wreaking such havoc that one result was the founding of the world's first veterinary school in Lyon, France, where veterinary science was born. An outbreak during the 1890s wiped out between 80 and 90 percent of the cattle in sub-Saharan Africa, causing untold human suffering. As recently as the 1980s an outbreak of rinderpest in Nigeria brought losses estimated in the billions of dollars.

Walter Plowright, an English-born and -trained veterinary scientist, devoted much of his career to developing an effective vaccine against rinderpest. He did most of the research at the Mugaga Laboratory of the East African Veterinary Research Organization in Kenya from 1956 to 1971. Ultimately he was able to produce a vaccine known as TCRV (tissue culture rinderpest vaccine) that proved to be safe, effective, cheap to produce, and stable even in tropical climates. The resulting gains in food security and, indirectly, economic security for millions of people in Africa and Asia have been enormous. One estimate puts the value of the Plowright vaccine to the economy of India during the period 1965–1998 at close to $300 billion. So effective is the vaccine that there are now just a few pockets of rinderpest still in existence, in Somalia, Sudan, and Pakistan. The Food and Agriculture Organization (FAO) of the United Nations hopes to eradicate the disease from the entire world by the year 2010, a scientific accomplishment on par with the eradication of smallpox.

Nafis Sadik (1929–)

As executive director of the United Nations Population Fund (UNFPA) from 1987 to 2000, Nafis Sadik directed the world's largest multilateral provider of financial and technical assistance to family-planning programs. Her rank as Under-Secretary-General of the United Nations and her long service as head of the UNFPA suggest leadership qualities beyond the ordinary. Born in India, she is now a citizen of Pakistan. She received her medical training in that country and at Johns Hopkins University. She was an administrator of women's and children's hospital wards in Pakistan between 1954 and 1963, and she held leadership positions in Pakistan's early family-planning programs before joining the UNFPA in 1971. Her position as head of the UNFPA made her one of the highest-ranking women in the United Nations.

Sadik has opposed "top-down" population policies that focus on quantitative targets and quotas. That, she believes, can be a counterproductive and at times coercive approach. She prefers, as do a growing number of population officials around the world, to build family-planning programs around the health and educational needs of girls and women, giving them a stronger voice in decisions that directly affect their lives. The International Conference on Population and Development (ICPD), at its 1994 Cairo meeting, essentially adopted the Sadik approach. Access to reproductive health services was recognized as an issue of human rights. In practical terms, this means access to information and to contraceptives. Sadik has often observed that there are still tens of millions of women in the developing world who would use contraceptives if they were available. She has urged the developed nations, particularly the United States, to provide more funding to global efforts to enhance women's health and reproductive choices.

Sadik has written many articles on population and economic development and edited several books, including *Making a Difference: Twenty-five Years of UNFPA Experience* (1994). She has received many international awards and honors.

Margaret Sanger (1879–1966)

The career of Margaret Sanger, U.S. birth control pioneer, demands a full-length biography to be told properly. Born in Corning, New York, the sixth of eleven children, Sanger saw her mother die at the age of 50, worn out by eighteen pregnancies. (It happens that Francis Place, the greatest nineteenth-century advocate of birth control, also was born into a very large family.) As a young woman, Sanger trained to be a nurse. Following marriage and an early association with New York intellectuals and anarchists, as well as participation in several hard-fought labor disputes on the eve of World War I, she began working with women in some of New York's poorest neighborhoods. The plight of these women, lacking the most basic health services and sexual information, angered the young midwife. When she tried to publish an article on venereal disease in 1912, the censors suppressed it. Two years later, her advocacy of contraception in her feminist magazine, *The Woman Rebel*, earned her an indictment for breaking the postal obscenity laws. Sanger fled to Europe but returned the following year; charges against her were dropped.

In 1916 Sanger opened the first U.S. birth control clinic in a Brooklyn tenement. It was modeled on a Dutch facility she had visited while in Europe. Nine days after the clinic's opening, Sanger and her colleagues were arrested for distributing contraceptive information. She served thirty days in jail but won a partial victory on appeal: the court ruled that contraception could be prescribed, for "medical reasons," by a doctor (not a nurse, as Sanger wanted). This cleared the way for Sanger to open a doctor-operated clinic in 1923. With all the publicity she had received, and a wealthy second husband willing to bankroll her cause, Sanger assumed leadership of the international birth control movement. An overseas lecture tour took her as far away as Japan and India, where she helped found organizations that still exist today. She sponsored the first world population conference in Geneva, Switzerland, in 1927, an event that led to the establishment, the following year, of the International Union for the Scientific Study of Population.

Sanger was instrumental in the founding of Planned Parenthood in the United States and later the International Planned Parenthood Federation, of which she was the first president from 1952 to 1959. She had a lifelong interest in seeing more effective, less costly forms of birth control developed. In the early 1950s she persuaded a wealthy friend to fund the biological research that led to the development of oral contraceptives. Today, population agencies around the world, including UNFPA, have shifted away from an emphasis on population quotas and targets, and back toward Sanger's original vision of family-planning as a means of giving women, through improved health care, more control over their own lives.

Amartya K. Sen (1933–)

According to economist Amartya K. Sen, the "Malthusian" explanation of famine is not very compelling in modern times. The

Malthusian point of view blames famine on insufficient food supplies relative to population; the cause can be drought, devastating cyclones, or ravaging floods. But Sen asserts that people can experience famine even when adequate stocks of food are within reach, for the simple reason that they lack the financial means (or "entitlements") to purchase that food. A shortage of purchasing power, in other words, can be as lethal as an actual shortage of food. In his 1981 book, *Poverty and Famines: An Essay on Entitlement and Deprivation*, Sen developed this line of thought not only theoretically but empirically. A careful examination of several twentieth-century famines led him to the conclusion that starvation had occurred in Bengal (1943), Ethiopia (1972-1974), and Bangladesh (1974) not because of a sharp drop in the supply of food available in those countries but because large numbers of people, for reasons such as inflation and unemployment, lacked sufficient means to purchase food. A shortage of entitlements also contributed to famine in the Sahel of Africa in the early 1970s.

Sen's analysis points to a view of famine that makes it more the product of human institutions relating to markets and property rights than of any natural forces. If famine is to be averted, exchange entitlements in countries prone to food insecurity must be more equally distributed than they have often been in the past. In an exchange economy, nothing else can insure that *food*, too, will be more equally distributed.

Born in West Bengal, India, Amartya Sen was educated at Presidency College, Calcutta, and at Trinity College, Cambridge (Ph.D., 1959). He has taught at universities in India, the United States, and Britain. In 1998, the year he won the Nobel Prize in Economics, he resigned a professorship at Harvard to return to Trinity College, Cambridge, as its master. Sen is a leading authority in the technical field of welfare economics, but he is better known to the public for his studies of poverty, hunger, and inequality. These include the 1981 book cited above and two works coauthored with Jean Dreze: *Hunger and Public Action* (1989) and *The Political Economy of Hunger* (1990–1991).

Julian L. Simon (1932–1998)

Discussions of world population are often tinged with apprehension, gloom, and pessimism, for which the writings of Thomas R. Malthus are partly to blame. The strongest antidote to neo-Malthusian gloom may be found in the writings of Julian Simon, who proved to be the foremost *anti*-Malthusian of the twentieth century. In scores of articles, several books, and many television interviews and newspaper columns, Simon tried to take the curse off population growth, arguing that increased human numbers should be viewed in a *positive* light, not just as a liability but as a long-term asset. The liability came in the form of increased short-run demands on existing stocks of resources. The asset took the form of human inventiveness: more human beings meant more minds capable of innovative thinking and technological advances that could *stretch* the stocks of resources. For Simon, the evidence that population growth had in fact been benign in its impact was to be seen in falling resource prices, rising life expectancies, and a host of other indicators of environmental and material well-being. For good reason he was labeled a "cornucopian."

Simon's optimism on population posed a vigorous challenge to the more sober views of environmentalists. His main opponent in the arena of demographic controversy was biologist Paul Ehrlich, author of the 1968 bestseller *The Population Bomb*. In that book and in many other forums, Ehrlich had warned of impending famines, natural resource shortages, and dangerous rates of pollution—all attributable, more or less, to excessive population growth. Simon countered with reams of data pointing to trend lines that were positive, not negative. History demonstrated that whenever a particular resource became scarce and costly, human ingenuity found ways to conserve it or substitute around it. Always Simon emphasized creativity and adaptability, which he believed the "doomsayers" either ignored or underestimated. His position on immigration was fully consistent with his population optimism: he advocated an open immigration policy for the United States.

For a demographic thinker, Simon had a rather unconventional academic career. His graduate degrees were in business economics (University of Chicago), as were his early research interests. His final academic position was professor of business administration at the University of Maryland. He was also a senior fellow at the Cato Institute—an indication of the free-market orientation of much of his writing. His main books include *The Economics of Population Growth* (1977), *The Ultimate Resource* (1981; revised in 1996 as *The Ultimate Resource 2*), and *The Economic Consequences of Immigration* (1989).

Marie Stopes (1880–1958)

Much like her contemporary Margaret Sanger on the other side of the Atlantic, Marie Stopes fought for the reproductive rights of women in Britain in the early decades of the twentieth century. In 1921 she opened the first birth control clinic in the United Kingdom. Located in north London, the "Mothers' Clinic" employed only female nurses and doctors and had a clientele of mainly poor women. In the face of much opposition, Stopes opened other clinics around Britain, including a horse-drawn caravan. Like Sanger, Stopes took an interest in the varieties of contraceptive techniques and even designed a cervical cap that was dispensed at her clinics. She wanted family-planning clinics to be opened in every country in the world. (The international organization which today bears her name, Marie Stopes International, operates in more than 30 countries.)

Born in Edinburgh, Stopes graduated with honors from University College London and then earned her doctorate at the University of Munich. Her first marriage was a personal fiasco that prompted her to write *Married Love* (1918), a sex manual that became a best-seller. Stopes received thousands of letters from grateful readers of the book; her other book, *Wise Parenthood* (1918), dealt with the specifics of birth control. Stopes's second marriage, to Humphrey Roe, was much more successful than her first. Roe shared her commitment to the cause of birth control and helped finance the publication of her books and the operation of her clinics. The couple had one child, Harry, born in 1924.

M. S. Swaminathan (1925–)

In the 1950s and 1960s, India was perceived by many as a demographic train wreck waiting to happen. Its population was growing far more rapidly than its agricultural output. In some years the only thing standing between the Indian masses and famine was the flotilla of U.S. grain ships arriving at the nation's ports. Yet the worst did not happen, and much of the credit for averting Malthusian disaster in India goes to M. S. Swaminathan. Born in the southern Indian state of Tamil Nadu and educated first in India and then at Cambridge University (Ph.D. in genetics, 1952), Swaminathan went on to the University of Wisconsin for postgraduate study. He was offered a professorship there but declined it: "I asked myself, why did I study genetics? It was to produce enough food in India. So I came back." At the Indian Agricultural Research Institute in New Delhi, of which he was the director by 1966, Swaminathan became the architect of India's Green Revolution, leading the efforts to adapt high-yield wheat varieties from Mexico to conditions in India. This involved the cross-breeding of Mexican semi-dwarf plants developed by Norman Borlaug with Japanese and local strains to create a superior wheat for Indian agriculture. But it also involved big administrative challenges, like persuading the Indian government to import sufficient quantities of wheat seeds, and getting farmers to adopt new seed varieties, chemical fertilizers, and pesticides. The success of Swaminathan's efforts is evident in a simple statistic: from a wheat output of 12 million tons in the early 1960s, India has now reached 70 million tons and is virtually self-sufficient in basic foodstuffs.

For the achievements outlined above, and for his leadership both nationally and internationally in trying to develop more ecofriendly and sustainable agricultural practices, Swaminathan has received numerous honors. These include the World Food Prize (1987), the Tyler Environment Award (1991), the Honda Award (1991), the United Nations Environment Program's Sasakawa Prize (1994), and the Volvo Environment Prize (1999). The money that came with these awards helped their recipient establish and sustain the M. S. Swaminathan Research Foundation and, under its aegis, the Centre for Research on Sustainable Agricultural Development, in Chennai, Madras. The purpose of the center, which has a staff of 150, is to advance the cause of environmentally sound and socially equitable agriculture. Swaminathan was named the UNESCO-Cousteau Professor in Ecotechnology for Asia in 1996.

4

Statistics and Graphs

When the topic is population, there are clearly a great many questions that can be answered only by *numbers*. Although not every population question is quantitative, many are: How many people are there on the planet? How has the population grown over the centuries and millennia, and how rapidly is it likely to grow in the coming 50 or 100 years? How many people are born and die every minute, every day, and every year, at current rates? What are the world's most populous cities and countries, and how might the rankings change in the next few decades? These questions are but a small sampling of the many that can best be answered with graphs and tables of data. We will start with a table that gives the number of births and deaths for various time spans, from years down to seconds. (See Table 4.1.)

TABLE 4.1
World Vital Events per Time Unit, 2000

	Births	Deaths	Natural increase
Year	131,389,622	54,409,824	76,979,798
Month	10,949,135	4,534,152	6,414,983
Day	358,988	148,661	210,327
Hour	14,958	6,194	8,764
Minute	249	103	146
Second	4.2	1.7	2.4

Table 4.2 gives the U.S. Census Bureau's estimates of world population, year by year, back to 1950 and forward to the middle

of this century. It also provides information on the annual percentage rates of population growth and the actual numbers of people added each year. Note the steady decline in population growth rates assumed to be in effect from 1986 through the next five decades.

TABLE 4.2
Total Midyear Population for the World, 1950–2050

	Population	Average annual growth rate (%)	Average annual population change
1950	2,555,078,074	1.47	37,783,610
1951	2,592,861,684	1.61	42,057,724
1952	2,634,919,408	1.71	45,334,288
1953	2,680,253,696	1.77	47,968,370
1954	2,728,222,066	1.87	51,447,715
1955	2,779,669,781	1.89	52,953,889
1956	2,832,623,670	1.95	55,820,377
1957	2,888,444,047	1.94	56,498,740
1958	2,944,942,787	1.76	52,326,211
1959	2,997,268,998	1.39	42,063,403
1960	3,039,332,401	1.33	40,781,960
1961	3,080,114,361	1.80	56,083,390
1962	3,136,197,751	2.19	69,508,948
1963	3,205,706,699	2.19	71,110,065
1964	3,276,816,764	2.08	69,021,089
1965	3,345,837,853	2.08	70,227,393
1966	3,416,065,246	2.02	69,742,104
1967	3,485,807,350	2.04	71,868,340
1968	3,557,675,690	2.08	74,665,661
1969	3,632,341,351	2.05	75,268,761
1970	3,707,610,112	2.07	77,580,647
1971	3,785,190,759	2.01	77,006,527
1972	3,862,197,286	1.96	76,511,302
1973	3,938,708,588	1.91	75,889,828
1974	4,014,598,416	1.82	73,625,631
1975	4,088,224,047	1.75	72,167,756
1976	4,160,391,803	1.73	72,536,792
1977	4,232,928,595	1.70	72,474,692
1978	4,305,403,287	1.74	75,373,540
1979	4,380,776,827	1.72	75,928,390
1980	4,456,705,217	1.70	76,259,715
1981	4,532,964,932	1.76	80,436,954
1982	4,613,401,886	1.73	80,530,264
1983	4,693,932,150	1.68	79,634,655
1984	4,773,566,805	1.68	81,036,085

(continues)

TABLE 4.2, continued

	Population	Average annual growth rate (%)	Average annual population change
1985	4,854,602,890	1.70	83,004,818
1986	4,937,607,708	1.73	85,962,468
1987	5,023,570,176	1.71	86,583,085
1988	5,110,153,261	1.67	86,179,948
1989	5,196,333,209	1.67	87,422,136
1990	5,283,755,345	1.56	83,182,744
1991	5,366,938,089	1.53	82,725,730
1992	5,449,663,819	1.48	81,337,993
1993	5,531,001,812	1.44	79,976,536
1994	5,610,978,348	1.41	79,887,428
1995	5,690,865,776	1.36	77,746,508
1996	5,768,612,284	1.35	78,192,518
1997	5,846,804,802	1.32	77,770,099
1998	5,924,574,901	1.31	77,934,526
1999	6,002,509,427	1.29	77,632,256
2000	6,080,141,683	1.26	77,258,877
2001	6,157,400,560	1.24	76,849,827
2002	6,234,250,387	1.22	76,299,210
2003	6,310,549,597	1.19	75,477,418
2004	6,386,027,015	1.16	74,526,549
2005	6,460,553,564	1.14	73,759,794
2006	6,534,313,358	1.12	73,307,780
2007	6,607,621,138	1.10	72,774,552
2008	6,680,395,690	1.07	72,012,218
2009	6,752,407,908	1.05	71,226,645
2010	6,823,634,553	1.03	70,770,206
2011	6,894,404,759	1.02	70,638,751
2012	6,965,043,510	1.01	70,466,862
2013	7,035,510,372	0.99	70,232,623
2014	7,105,742,995	0.98	69,932,071
2015	7,175,675,066	0.97	69,613,925
2016	7,245,288,991	0.95	69,172,133
2017	7,314,461,124	0.93	68,537,288
2018	7,382,998,412	0.92	67,877,546
2019	7,450,875,958	0.90	67,134,642
2020	7,518,010,600	0.88	66,371,114
2021	7,584,381,714	0.86	65,530,746
2022	7,649,912,460	0.84	64,563,881
2023	7,714,476,341	0.82	63,596,837
2024	7,778,073,178	0.80	62,587,177
2025	7,840,660,355	0.78	61,682,010
2026	7,902,342,365	0.77	60,869,928
2027	7,963,212,293	0.75	59,981,878

(continues)

TABLE 4.2, continued

	Population	Average annual growth rate (%)	Average annual population change
2028	8,023,194,171	0.73	59,060,143
2029	8,082,254,314	0.72	58,089,926
2030	8,140,344,240	0.70	57,189,977
2031	8,197,534,217	0.68	56,329,702
2032	8,253,863,919	0.67	55,336,454
2033	8,309,200,373	0.65	54,292,787
2034	8,363,493,160	0.63	53,249,118
2035	8,416,742,278	0.62	52,278,271
2036	8,469,020,549	0.60	51,366,513
2037	8,520,387,062	0.59	50,352,314
2038	8,570,739,376	0.57	49,313,531
2039	8,620,052,907	0.56	48,338,547
2040	8,668,391,454	0.55	47,462,555
2041	8,715,854,009	0.53	46,648,317
2042	8,762,502,326	0.52	45,741,361
2043	8,808,243,687	0.51	44,825,944
2044	8,853,069,631	0.50	44,003,864
2045	8,897,073,495	0.48	43,234,092
2046	8,940,307,587	0.47	42,454,580
2047	8,982,762,167	0.46	41,502,870
2048	9,024,265,037	0.45	40,456,148
2049	9,064,721,185	0.43	39,484,645
2050	9,104,205,830		

Note: Data updated May 10, 2000.

Source: U.S. Bureau of the Census, *International Data Base.*

Table 4.3 presents the 1998 long-range population projections of the United Nations. The "instant replacement" column makes an arbitrary assumption that the world shifts immediately to a total fertility rate of 2.1; that will not happen, of course, but it offers a hypothetical point of reference. The "constant" column assumes that total fertility rates around the world remain unchanged from 1995 onward—another unrealistic assumption, and one that leads to an astonishing estimate of global population by the year 2150: 256 billion. That would be more than 40 times the current population! The "medium" projection reflects the UN demographers' sense of what is *most likely* to happen in the future, based on past and current trends, but they hedge their bets by bracketing the "medium" estimates with "low" and "high" alternative estimates.

TABLE 4.3
UN Long-Range World Population Projections:
Various Growth Rate Scenarios, 1995–2150 (in millions)

Year or period	Instant replacement	Low	Low-medium	Medium	High-medium	High	Constant
			Population				
1995	5,666	5,666	5,666	5,666	5,666	5,666	5,666
2000	5,962	6,028	6,028	6,055	6,082	6,082	6,113
2025	7,424	7,275	7,275	7,824	8,379	8,379	9,069
2050	8,310	7,343	7,547	8,909	10,409	10,674	14,421
2075	8,663	6,402	7,024	9,319	12,026	13,149	26,048
2100	8,924	5,153	6,324	9,459	13,430	16,178	52,508
2125	9,142	4,074	5,779	9,573	14,735	19,986	113,302
2150	9,349	3,236	5,329	9,746	16,218	24,834	255,846
			Growth Rates (per year)				
2000	1.02	1.24	1.24	1.33	1.42	1.42	1.52
2025	0.71	0.50	0.50	0.84	1.17	1.17	1.65
2050	0.29	−0.23	−0.07	0.34	0.69	0.87	2.02
2075	0.13	−0.73	−0.39	0.11	0.51	0.83	2.57
2100	0.11	−0.92	−0.40	0.04	0.40	0.83	2.93
2125	0.09	−0.93	−0.34	0.06	0.37	0.86	3.16
2150	0.09	−0.92	−0.32	0.08	0.39	0.87	3.32

Note: Each "growth rate" is for the five-year period preceding the given year, e.g., 1995–2000.

Sources: Population Division of the Department of Economic and Social Affairs of the United Nations Secretariat. 1999. *World Population Prospects: The 1998 Revision*, vol. 1, *Comprehensive Tables.* New York: United Nations; Population Division of the Department of Economic and Social Affairs of the United Nations Secretariat. 2000. *Long-range Population Projections: Based on the 1998 Revision.* New York: United Nations.

Table 4.4 is a companion to Table 4.3, giving a more detailed breakdown of the UN's long-range population projections by major area. It is based on the medium or maximum-likelihood scenario for population growth (see Table 4.3). An interesting feature of Table 4.4 is the possibility that Africa's share of world population will grow from 12 percent in 1995 to 24 percent in 2150, while Europe's share will shrink from 13 percent to 5 percent. North America's share could decline to a mere 4 percent.

Tables 4.5 and 4.6 give the rankings of the top twenty nations by population for 1950, 2000, and then—with the inevitable uncertainty that goes with demographic *projections* into the future—for 2025 and 2050. It is interesting to note that China and India will continue to outdistance all other countries in the world, as they have in the past, although their own rank-order will be reversed some time between 2025 and 2050.

TABLE 4.4
UN Long-Range World Population Projections by Major Area, 1995–2150

Year	Total	Africa	Europe	Latin America and the Caribbean	North America	Oceania	Asia excluding China and India	China	India
				Population (millions)					
1995	5,666	697	728	480	297	28	1,282	1,221	934
2000	6,055	784	729	519	310	30	1,391	1,278	1,014
2025	7,824	1,298	702	697	364	40	1,912	1,480	1,330
2050	8,909	1,766	628	809	392	46	2,262	1,478	1,529
2075	9,319	2,077	549	857	390	48	2,423	1,386	1,589
2100	9,459	2,215	515	877	388	49	2,476	1,340	1,600
2125	9,573	2,264	508	894	390	50	2,512	1,338	1,617
2150	9,746	2,308	517	912	398	51	2,558	1,361	1,642
				Percentage					
1995	100	12	13	8	5	1	23	22	16
2000	100	12	13	8	5	1	23	22	16
2025	100	13	12	9	5	1	23	21	17
2050	100	17	9	9	5	1	24	19	17
2075	100	20	7	9	4	1	25	17	17
2100	100	22	6	9	4	1	26	15	17
2125	100	23	5	9	4	1	26	14	17
2150	100	24	5	9	4	1	26	14	17

Source: Population Division of the Department of Economic and Social Affairs of the United Nations Secretariat. 2000. *Long-range Population Projections: Based on the 1998 Revision.* New York: United Nations.

TABLE 4.5
Top Twenty Countries Ranked by Population, 1950 and 2000

	1950			2000	
1	China	562,579,779	1	China	1,261,832,482
2	India	369,880,000	2	India	1,014,003,817
3	United States	152,271,000	3	United States	275,562,673
4	Russia	101,936,816	4	Indonesia	224,784,210
5	Japan	83,805,000	5	Brazil	172,860,370
6	Indonesia	83,413,921	6	Russia	146,001,176
7	Germany	68,374,572	7	Pakistan	141,553,775
8	Brazil	53,443,075	8	Bangladesh	129,194,224
9	United Kingdom	50,127,000	9	Japan	126,549,976
10	Italy	47,105,000	10	Nigeria	123,337,822
11	Bangladesh	45,645,964	11	Mexico	100,349,766
12	France	41,828,673	12	Germany	82,797,408
13	Pakistan	39,448,232	13	Philippines	81,159,644

(continues)

TABLE 4.5, continued

	1950				2000	
14	Ukraine	36,774,854		14	Vietnam	78,773,873
15	Nigeria	31,796,939		15	Egypt	68,359,979
16	Mexico	28,485,180		16	Turkey	65,666,677
17	Spain	28,062,963		17	Iran	65,619,636
18	Vietnam	25,348,144		18	Ethiopia	64,117,452
19	Poland	24,824,000		19	Thailand	61,230,874
20	Egypt	21,197,691		20	United Kingdom	59,508,382

Source: U.S. Census Bureau, *International Data Base;* updated in May 2000.

TABLE 4.6
Top Twenty Countries Ranked by Projected Population, 2025 and 2050

	2025				2050	
1	China	1,464,028,860		1	India	1,619,582,271
2	India	1,377,264,176		2	China	1,470,468,924
3	United States	338,070,951		3	United States	403,943,147
4	Indonesia	301,461,556		4	Indonesia	337,807,011
5	Pakistan	213,338,252		5	Nigeria	303,586,770
6	Nigeria	204,453,333		6	Pakistan	267,813,495
7	Brazil	200,606,553		7	Brazil	206,751,477
8	Bangladesh	177,499,122		8	Bangladesh	205,093,861
9	Russia	135,951,626		9	Ethiopia	187,892,174
10	Mexico	133,834,712		10	Congo (Kinshasa)	181,922,656
11	Philippines	121,981,773		11	Philippines	153,913,427
12	Japan	120,235,271		12	Mexico	153,162,145
13	Ethiopia	115,042,931		13	Vietnam	119,003,660
14	Vietnam	105,763,268		14	Russia	118,233,243
15	Congo (Kinshasa)	105,300,502		15	Egypt	113,002,084
16	Egypt	95,164,237		16	Japan	101,228,471
17	Iran	88,409,309		17	Iran	100,198,725
18	Germany	85,414,825		18	Saudi Arabia	91,112,265
19	Turkey	82,204,623		19	Tanzania	88,280,060
20	Thailand	70,549,199		20	Turkey	86,473,786

Source: U.S. Census Bureau, *International Data Base;* updated in May 2000.

Table 4.7 presents some of the key demographic data for every country in the world, as reported in the Population Reference Bureau's *2000 World Population Data Sheet (WPDS).* Those who want to make a serious study of world population are well advised to get a current copy of the *WPDS,* available in both wall chart and booklet form, since it provides for each country not only the data given in Table 4.7 but much more: the population doubling time, projections of population to 2025 and 2050, the percent of population under the age of 15 and over 64 (usually known as "dependent"), life expectancies for males and females, percent of population urbanized, percent with HIV/AIDS, contraceptive prevalence for married women, and per capita gross national product (GNP). This information may also be obtained online from the Population Reference Bureau, but the electronic format is not as flexible and useful as the booklet.

TABLE 4.7
Demographic Data and Estimates for the Countries and Regions of the World, 2000

	Population mid-2000 (millions)	Births per 1,000 pop.	Deaths per 1,000 pop.	Natural increase (annual %)	Infant mortality rate	Total fertility rate
World	6,067	22	9	1.4	57	2.9
More developed	1,184	11	10	0.1	8	1.5
Less developed	4,883	25	9	1.7	63	3.2
Less developed (excluding China)	3,619	29	9	1.9	69	3.7
AFRICA	800	38	14	2.4	88	5.3
Sub-Saharan Africa	657	41	16	2.5	94	5.8
Northern Africa	*173*	*27*	*7*	*2.0*	*51*	*3.6*
Algeria	31.5	29	6	2.4	44	3.8
Egypt	68.3	26	6	2.0	52	3.3
Libya	5.1	28	3	2.5	33	4.1
Morocco	28.8	23	6	1.7	37	3.1
Sudan	29.5	33	12	2.2	70	4.6
Tunisia	9.6	22	7	1.6	35	2.8
Western Sahara	0.3	46	18	2.9	150	6.8
Western Africa	*234*	*42*	*14*	*2.8*	*89*	*5.9*
Benin	6.4	45	17	2.8	94	6.3
Burkina Faso	11.9	47	18	2.9	105	6.8
Cape Verde	0.4	37	9	2.8	77	5.3
Cote d'Ivoire	16.0	38	16	2.2	112	5.2
Gambia	1.3	43	19	2.4	130	5.6
Ghana	19.5	34	10	2.4	56	4.5
Guinea	7.5	42	18	2.4	98	5.5
Guinea-Bissau	1.2	42	20	2.2	130	5.8
Liberia	3.2	50	17	3.2	139	6.2
Mali	11.2	47	16	3.1	123	6.7

(continues)

TABLE 4.7, continued

	Population mid-2000 (millions)	Births per 1,000 pop.	Deaths per 1,000 pop.	Natural increase (annual %)	Infant mortality rate	Total fertility rate
Mauritania	2.7	41	13	2.7	92	5.5
Niger	10.1	54	24	3.0	123	7.5
Nigeria	123.3	42	13	2.8	77	6.0
Senegal	9.5	41	13	2.8	68	5.7
Sierra Leone	5.2	47	21	2.6	157	6.3
Togo	5.0	42	11	3.1	80	6.1
Eastern Africa	*246*	*42*	*18*	*2.4*	*102*	*6.0*
Burundi	6.1	42	17	2.5	75	6.5
Comoros	0.6	38	10	2.8	77	5.1
Djibouti	0.6	39	16	2.3	115	5.8
Eritrea	4.1	43	13	3.0	82	6.1
Ethiopia	64.1	45	21	2.4	116	6.7
Kenya	30.3	35	14	2.1	74	4.7
Madagascar	14.9	44	14	2.9	96	6.0
Malawi	10.4	41	22	1.9	127	5.9
Mauritius	1.2	17	7	1.1	19	2.0
Mozambique	19.1	41	19	2.2	134	5.6
Reunion	0.7	20	5	1.4	9	2.2
Rwanda	7.2	43	20	2.3	121	6.5
Seychelles	0.1	18	7	1.1	9	2.0
Somalia	7.3	47	18	2.9	126	7.0
Tanzania	35.3	42	13	2.9	99	5.6
Uganda	23.3	48	20	2.9	81	6.9
Zambia	9.6	42	23	2.0	109	6.1
Zimbabwe	11.3	30	20	1.0	80	4.0
Middle Africa	*96*	*46*	*16*	*3.0*	*106*	*6.6*
Angola	12.9	48	19	3.0	125	6.8
Cameroon	15.4	37	12	2.6	77	5.2
Central African Republic	3.5	38	18	2.0	97	5.1
Chad	8.0	50	17	3.3	110	6.6
Congo	2.8	40	16	2.4	109	5.3
Congo, Democratic Republic of (former Zaire)	52.0	48	16	3.2	109	7.2
Equatorial Africa	0.5	41	16	2.5	108	5.6
Gabon	1.2	38	16	2.2	87	5.4
Sao Tome and Principe	0.2	43	9	3.4	51	6.2
Southern Africa	*50*	*26*	*13*	*1.3*	*51*	*3.1*
Botswana	1.6	32	17	1.6	57	4.1
Lesotho	2.1	33	13	2.1	85	4.4
Namibia	1.8	36	20	1.7	68	5.1
South Africa	43.4	25	12	1.3	45	2.9
Swaziland	1.0	41	22	1.9	108	5.9

(continues)

TABLE 4.7, continued

	Population mid-2000 (millions)	Births per 1,000 pop.	Deaths per 1,000 pop.	Natural increase (annual %)	Infant mortality rate	Total fertility rate
NORTH AMERICA	306	14	9	0.6	7	2.0
Canada	30.8	11	7	0.4	5.5	1.5
United States	275.6	15	9	0.6	7.0	2.1
LATIN AMERICA AND THE CARIBBEAN	518	24	6	1.8	35	2.8
Central America	*136*	*26*	*5*	*2.1*	*34*	*3.1*
Belize	0.3	32	5	2.7	34	3.9
Costa Rica	3.6	22	4	1.8	13	3.2
El Salvador	6.3	30	7	2.4	35	3.6
Guatemala	12.7	37	7	2.9	45	5.0
Honduras	6.1	33	6	2.8	42	4.4
Mexico	99.6	24	4	2.0	32	2.7
Nicaragua	5.1	36	6	3.0	40	4.4
Panama	2.9	22	5	1.7	21	2.6
Caribbean	*36*	*22*	*8*	*1.3*	*47*	*2.6*
Antigua and Barbuda	0.1	22	6	1.6	17	2.2
Bahamas	0.3	21	5	1.5	18.4	2.2
Barbados	0.3	14	9	0.5	14.2	1.8
Cuba	11.1	14	7	0.7	7	1.6
Dominica	0.1	16	8	0.8	14.6	1.9
Dominican Republic	8.4	28	6	2.2	47	3.1
Grenada	0.1	29	6	2.3	14	3.8
Guadeloupe	0.4	17	6	1.1	10.0	2.0
Haiti	6.4	33	16	1.7	103	4.7
Jamaica	2.6	22	7	1.6	24	2.6
Martinique	0.4	15	6	0.9	9	1.8
Netherlands Antilles	0.2	17	6	1.1	14	2.2
Puerto Rico	3.9	17	8	0.9	11.3	2.1
St. Kitts-Nevis	0.04	20	11	0.9	24	2.2
St. Lucia	0.2	19	6	1.2	16.8	2.5
St. Vincent and the Grenadines	0.1	19	7	1.2	20.4	2.0
Trinidad and Tobago	1.3	14	7	0.7	16.2	1.7
South America	*345*	*23*	*6*	*1.7*	*34*	*2.7*
Argentina	37.0	19	8	1.1	19.1	2.6
Bolivia	8.3	30	10	2.0	67	4.2
Brazil	170.1	21	6	1.5	38	2.4
Chile	15.2	18	5	1.3	10.5	2.4
Colombia	40.0	26	6	2.0	28	3.0
Ecuador	12.6	27	6	2.1	40	3.3
French Guiana	0.2	27	3	2.4	18	3.4
Guyana	0.7	24	7	1.7	63	2.7

(continues)

TABLE 4.7, continued

	Population mid-2000 (millions)	Births per 1,000 pop.	Deaths per 1,000 pop.	Natural increase (annual %)	Infant mortality rate	Total fertility rate
Paraguay	5.5	32	6	2.7	27	4.3
Peru	27.1	27	6	2.1	43	3.4
Suriname	0.4	26	7	1.9	29	2.4
Uruguay	3.3	16	10	0.7	14.5	2.3
Venezuela	24.2	25	5	2.0	21.0	2.9
OCEANIA	31	18	7	1.1	29	2.4
Australia	19.2	13	7	0.6	5.3	1.7
Federal States of Micronesia	0.1	33	7	2.6	46	4.7
Fiji	0.8	22	7	1.5	13	3.3
French Polynesia	0.2	21	5	1.6	10	2.6
Guam	0.2	28	4	2.4	9.1	3.5
Kiribati	0.1	33	8	2.5	62	4.5
Marshall Islands	0.1	26	4	2.2	31	6.6
Nauru	0.01	19	5	1.4	25	3.7
New Caledonia	0.2	21	5	1.7	7	2.7
New Zealand	3.8	15	7	0.8	5.5	2.0
Palau	0.02	18	8	1.0	19	2.5
Papua-New Guinea	4.8	34	10	2.4	77	4.8
Solomon Islands	0.4	37	6	3.1	25	5.4
Tonga	0.1	27	6	2.1	19	4.2
Vanuatu	0.2	35	7	2.8	39	4.7
Western Samoa	0.2	31	6	2.5	25	4.2
ASIA	3,684	22	8	1.4	56	2.8
Asia (excluding China)	2,420	26	8	1.7	64	3.3
Western Asia	189	28	7	2.1	55	4.0
Armenia	3.8	10	6	0.4	15	1.3
Azerbaijan	7.7	15	6	0.9	17	1.9
Bahrain	0.7	22	3	1.9	8	2.8
Cyprus	0.9	14	8	0.6	8	1.9
Georgia	5.5	9	8	0.2	15	1.2
Iraq	23.1	38	10	2.8	127	5.7
Israel	6.2	22	6	1.5	6.0	2.9
Jordan	5.1	33	5	2.9	34	4.4
Kuwait	2.2	24	2	2.2	13	3.2
Lebanon	4.2	23	7	1.6	35	2.4
Oman	2.4	43	5	3.9	25	7.1
Palestinian Territory	3.1	41	5	3.7	27	6.0
Qatar	0.6	20	2	1.8	20	4.2
Saudi Arabia	21.6	35	5	3.0	46	6.4
Syria	16.5	33	6	2.8	35	4.7
Turkey	65.3	22	7	1.5	38	2.5

(continues)

	Population mid-2000 (millions)	Births per 1,000 pop.	Deaths per 1,000 pop.	Natural increase (annual %)	Infant mortality rate	Total fertility rate
United Arab Emirates	2.8	24	2	2.2	16	4.9
Yemen	17.0	39	11	2.8	75	6.5
South Central Asia	*1,475*	*28*	*9*	*1.9*	*75*	*3.6*
Afghanistan	26.7	43	18	2.5	150	6.1
Bangladesh	128.1	27	8	1.8	82	3.3
Bhutan	0.9	40	9	3.1	71	5.6
India	1,002.1	27	9	1.8	72	3.3
Iran	67.4	21	6	1.4	31	2.9
Kazakhstan	14.9	14	10	0.4	21	1.7
Kyrgyzstan	4.9	22	7	1.5	26	2.8
Maldives	0.3	35	5	3.0	27	5.4
Nepal	23.9	36	11	2.5	79	4.6
Pakistan	150.6	39	11	2.8	91	5.6
Sri Lanka	19.2	18	6	1.2	17	2.1
Tajikistan	6.4	21	5	1.6	28	2.7
Turkmenistan	5.2	21	6	1.5	33	2.5
Uzbekistan	24.8	23	6	1.7	22	2.8
Southeast Asia	*528*	*24*	*7*	*1.7*	*46*	*3.0*
Brunei	0.3	25	3	2.2	24	3.4
Cambodia	12.1	38	12	2.6	80	5.3
East Timor	0.8	34	16	1.8	143	4.6
Indonesia	212.2	24	8	1.6	46	2.8
Laos	5.2	41	15	2.6	104	5.6
Malaysia	23.3	25	5	2.1	8	3.2
Myanmar	48.9	30	10	2.0	83	3.8
Philippines	80.3	29	7	2.3	35	3.7
Singapore	4.0	13	5	0.8	3.2	1.5
Thailand	62.0	16	7	1.0	22	1.9
Vietnam	78.7	20	6	1.4	37	2.5
East Asia	*1,493*	*15*	*7*	*0.8*	*29*	*1.8*
China	1,264.5	15	6	0.9	31	1.8
China, Hong Kong SAR	7.0	7	5	0.3	3.2	1.0
China, Macao SAR	0.4	10	3	0.7	6	1.2
Japan	126.9	9	8	0.2	3.5	1.3
Korea, North	21.7	21	7	1.5	26	2.3
Korea, South	47.3	14	5	0.9	11	1.5
Mongolia	2.5	20	7	1.4	34	2.7
Taiwan	22.3	13	6	0.7	6.6	1.5
EUROPE	728	10	11	−0.1	9	1.4
Northern Europe	*96*	*12*	*11*	*0.1*	*6*	*1.7*
Denmark	5.3	12	11	0.1	4.7	1.7
Estonia	1.4	8	13	−0.5	9	1.2
Finland	5.2	11	10	0.2	4.2	1.7
Iceland	0.3	15	7	0.9	2.6	2.0

(continues)

TABLE 4.7, continued

	Population mid-2000 (millions)	Births per 1,000 pop.	Deaths per 1,000 pop.	Natural increase (annual %)	Infant mortality rate	Total fertility rate
Ireland	3.8	15	9	0.6	6.2	1.9
Latvia	2.4	8	14	−0.6	11	1.2
Lithuania	3.2	10	11	−0.1	9	1.3
Norway	4.5	13	10	0.3	4.0	1.8
Sweden	8.9	10	11	−0.1	3.5	1.5
United Kingdom	59.8	12	11	0.1	5.7	1.7
Western Europe	*183*	*11*	*10*	*0.1*	*5*	*1.5*
Austria	8.1	10	10	0.0	4.9	1.3
Belgium	10.2	11	10	0.1	5.6	1.6
France	59.4	13	9	0.3	4.8	1.8
Germany	82.1	9	10	−0.1	4.7	1.3
Liechtenstein	0.03	14	7	0.7	18.4	1.6
Luxembourg	0.4	13	9	0.4	5.0	1.7
Monaco	0.03	20	17	0.3	–	–
Netherlands	15.9	13	9	0.4	5.0	1.6
Switzerland	7.1	11	9	0.2	4.8	1.5
Eastern Europe	*304*	*9*	*13*	*−0.5*	*14*	*1.2*
Belarus	10.0	9	14	−0.5	11	1.3
Bulgaria	8.2	8	14	−0.6	14.4	1.1
Czech Republic	10.3	9	11	−0.2	4.6	1.1
Hungary	10.0	9	14	−0.5	8.9	1.3
Moldova	4.3	11	11	0.0	18	1.5
Poland	38.6	10	10	0.0	9	1.4
Romania	22.4	11	12	−0.2	20.5	1.3
Russia	145.2	8	15	−0.6	17	1.2
Slovakia	5.4	11	10	0.1	8.8	1.4
Ukraine	49.5	8	14	−0.6	13	1.3
Southern Europe	*145*	*10*	*10*	*0.0*	*7*	*1.3*
Albania	3.4	18	5	1.3	22	2.2
Andorra	0.1	11	3	0.8	6	1.2
Bosnia-Herzegovina	3.8	13	8	0.5	12	1.6
Croatia	4.6	11	12	−0.1	8.2	1.5
Greece	10.6	10	10	0.0	6.7	1.3
Italy	57.8	9	10	−0.1	5.5	1.2
Macedonia	2.0	15	8	0.6	16.3	1.9
Malta	0.4	12	8	0.4	5.3	1.8
Portugal	10.0	11	11	0.1	5.4	1.5
San Marino	0.03	11	7	0.4	9	1.2
Slovenia	2.0	9	10	−0.1	5.2	1.2
Spain	39.5	9	9	0.0	5.7	1.2
Yugoslavia	10.7	11	11	0.1	10	1.6

Source: Population Reference Bureau. *2000 World Population Data Sheet (WPDS).* Washington, DC: Population Reference Bureau.

Tables 4.8 and 4.9 provide a backward and forward view of the world's largest *urban* populations. Table 4.8 reveals that only five cities had populations over 10 million in 1975, but a quarter-century later the number of such cities had almost quadrupled. Perhaps more astonishing is the fact that by 2015, the world's second-, third-, and fourth-most-populous cities, with over 20 million residents each, will be names that did not make the top-five list in 1975: Bombay, Lagos, and Dhaka.

TABLE 4.8
Cities with over 10 Million Inhabitants, 1975, 2000, 2015 (in millions)

	1975			2000			2015	
1	Tokyo	19.8	1	Tokyo	26.4	1	Tokyo	26.4
2	New York	15.9	2	Mexico City	18.1	2	Bombay	26.1
3	Shanghai	11.4	3	Bombay	18.1	3	Lagos	23.2
4	Mexico City	11.2	4	Sao Paulo	17.8	4	Dhaka	21.1
5	Sao Paulo	10.0	5	New York	16.6	5	Sao Paulo	20.4
			6	Lagos	13.4	6	Karachi	19.2
			7	Los Angeles	13.1	7	Mexico City	19.2
			8	Calcutta	12.9	8	New York	17.4
			9	Shanghai	12.9	9	Jakarta	17.3
			10	Buenos Aires	12.6	10	Calcutta	17.3
			11	Dhaka	12.3	11	Delhi	16.8
			12	Karachi	11.8	12	Manila	14.8
			13	Delhi	11.7	13	Shanghai	14.6
			14	Jakarta	11.0	14	Los Angeles	14.1
			15	Osaka	11.0	15	Buenos Aires	14.1
			16	Manila	10.9	16	Cairo	13.8
			17	Beijing	10.8	17	Istanbul	12.5
			18	Rio de Janeiro	10.6	18	Beijing	12.3
			19	Cairo	10.6	19	Rio de Janeiro	11.9
						20	Osaka	11.0
						21	Tianjin	10.7
						22	Hyderabad	10.5
						23	Bangkok	10.1

Source: Population Division of the Department of Economic and Social Affairs of the United Nations Secretariat. 2000. "World Urbanization Prospects: The 1999 Revision, Data Tables, and Highlights." Working Paper no. ESA/P/WP.161. New York: United Nations.

A fuller picture of what has been, and will be, happening to the most heavily populated of the world's cities is provided in Table 4.9. Here we see some remarkable contrasts: Tokyo and

Osaka, Japan's biggest cities, are not expected to grow at all between 2000 and 2015, but Lagos, Nigeria, and Dhaka, Bangladesh, both of which expanded at more than a 5 percent annual rate from 1975 to 2000, will continue to grow quite rapidly, at 3.7 and 3.6 percent, respectively, from now until 2015. The only city that is expected to grow at an appreciably *faster* rate in the next 15 years than it did in the past 25 is Shanghai, China. A final pattern worth noting: four urban giants of the Asian subcontinent, Bombay, Delhi, Dhaka, and Karachi, have seen and will continue to see burgeoning growth of a kind that is sure to strain the capacities of urban authorities to provide adequate services to their residents.

TABLE 4.9
The World's Top 19 Cities by Population and
Their Growth Rates, 1975–2015

Urban	Population (in millions)			Growth rate (percent)	
agglomeration	1975	2000	2015	1975–2000	2000–2015
1 Tokyo	19.8	26.4	26.4	1.2	0.0
2 Mexico City	11.2	18.1	19.2	1.9	0.4
3 Bombay	6.9	18.1	26.1	3.9	2.4
4 Sao Paulo	10.0	17.8	20.4	2.3	0.9
5 New York	15.9	16.6	17.4	0.2	0.3
6 Lagos	3.3	13.4	23.2	5.6	3.7
7 Los Angeles	8.9	13.1	14.1	1.5	0.5
8 Shanghai	11.4	12.9	14.6	0.5	0.8
9 Calcutta	7.9	12.9	17.3	2.0	1.9
10 Buenos Aires	9.1	12.6	14.1	1.3	0.7
11 Dhaka	2.2	12.3	21.1	6.9	3.6
12 Karachi	4.0	11.8	19.2	4.3	3.2
13 Delhi	4.4	11.7	16.8	3.9	2.4
14 Osaka	9.8	11.0	11.0	0.4	0.0
15 Jakarta	4.8	11.0	17.3	3.3	3.0
16 Beijing	8.5	10.8	12.3	0.9	0.9
17 Metro Manila	5.0	10.9	14.8	3.1	2.1
18 Rio de Janeiro	7.9	10.6	11.9	1.2	0.8
19 Cairo	6.1	10.6	13.8	2.2	1.7

Source: Population Division of the Department of Economic and Social Affairs of the United Nations Secretariat. 2000. "World Urbanization Prospects: The 1999 Revision, Data Tables, and Highlights." Working Paper no. ESA/P/WP.161. New York: United Nations.

Table 4.10 documents the current extent and death toll of the late twentieth-century plague, HIV/AIDS, with data from the World Health Organization's annual report on this disease. As noted elsewhere in this book, AIDS has been most devastating in sub-Saharan Africa, where the prevalence rate is almost 15 times greater than in North America and 37 times greater than in Western Europe. AIDS deaths in Africa numbered over 2 million in 1999, causing the number of AIDS orphans to continue rising past 12 million.

TABLE 4.10
The Worldwide HIV/AIDS Epidemic (2000)

Region	People living with HIV/AIDS, 1999	Adult prevalence (%)	AIDS orphans (cumulative)	AIDS deaths, 1999
Sub-Saharan Africa	24,500,000	8.57	12,100,000	2,200,000
North Africa, Middle East	220,000	.12	15,000	13,000
South and South-east Asia	5,600,000	.54	850,000	460,000
East Asia, Pacific	530,000	.06	5,600	18,000
Latin America	1,300,000	.49	110,000	48,000
Caribbean	360,000	2.11	85,000	30,000
Eastern Europe and Central Asia	420,000	.21	500	8,500
Western Europe	520,000	.23	9,000	6,800
North America	900,000	.58	70,000	20,000
Australia and New Zealand	15,000	.13	<500	120
Global	34,300,000	1.07	3,200,000	2,800,000

Source: World Health Organization, "Report on the Global HIV/AIDS Epidemic—June 2000."

Not only tables but *graphs* can be useful in presenting some important features of the global population picture, as it stands today and as it has developed over the centuries and millennia. Figure 4.1 depicts world population over the past 7,000 years. On the scale used, world population would not be seen to rise above the horizontal axis at any time in the past 200,000 years—until about 3000 B.C. At that time it began a slow ascent, so slow that in 1500 it remained under one-half billion. Since 1500, however, there has been an astonishing rise in world population. By 2000 it had crossed the 6 billion line, and it is now expected to

FIGURE 4.1
Estimated Human Population from 5000 B.C. to the Present

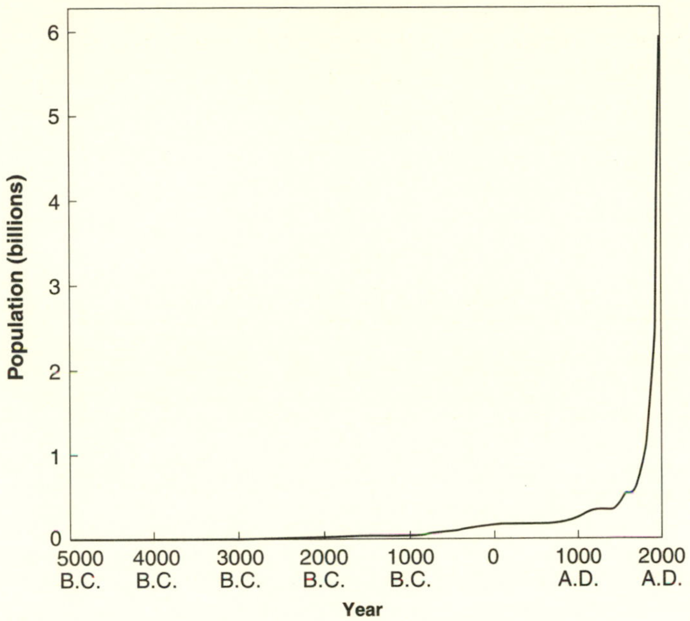

Source: Based on data given in Colin McEvedy and Richard Jones. 1978. *Atlas of World Population History.* New York: Viking Penguin.

reach 9 billion by mid-century. The growth of our species has been truly explosive in recent times.

Figure 4.2 shows not only the rising curve of total world population (projected to 2050) but also the actual increments of population, beginning in 1750. These increments are given on a per-decade basis. They allow us to see that the gains in population were relatively small in the eighteenth century, visibly larger in the nineteenth, and simply enormous during the twentieth century—and into the twenty-first. For those who feel some anxiety about the size of global population, the only reassuring aspect of Figure 4.2 is the lessening of growth per decade after the 1980s. Each subsequent decade adds, or will add, less to world population than the previous decade; the 2040s are expect-

FIGURE 4.2
Long-Term World Population Growth, 1750–2050

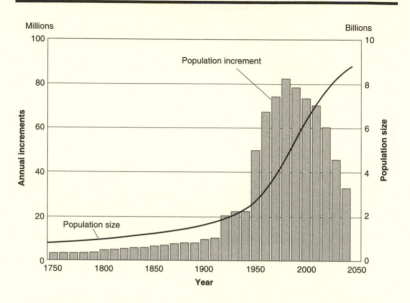

Source: Population Division of the Department of Economic and Social Affairs of the United Nations Secretariat. 1999. "The World at Six Billion." Working Paper no. ESA/P/WP.154. New York: United Nations. Reprinted by permission.

ed to give the smallest numerical boost to global population since the 1940s.

The actual and projected year-by-year growth rate of world population during the period 1950–2050 may be seen in Figure 4.3. Several things are clear from this graph: the fastest population growth in history was recorded in the early 1960s, at around 2.2 percent annually; growth has been decelerating ever since then; and the downward trend will continue steadily to the middle of this century, according to demographers. By 2050, the growth rate is expected to have slowed quite dramatically—to less than half of one percent annually. That will be the lowest growth rate in well over a century. (And of course the *absolute* populations of several countries, mainly in Europe, will be shrinking long before 2050, barring unforeseen developments.)

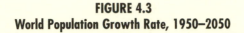

FIGURE 4.3
World Population Growth Rate, 1950–2050

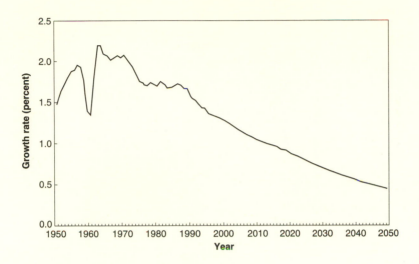

Source: U.S. Census Bureau, *International Data Base* (May 10, 2000).

Figures 4.4 and 4.5 illustrate the theory and reality of demographic transition, as outlined in Chapter 1. In Figure 4.4, we see high birth and death rates before the transition begins (Stage I). Then the death rate begins to decline (Stage II). The birth rate may remain high for a period of time, but eventually it, too, starts to decline (Stage III). Finally, both rates stabilize at new lower levels (Stage IV). Actual population growth is slow or zero in Stage I, rapid in Stages II and III, and again slow or zero in Stage IV.

The demographic reality corresponding to the theory depicted in Figure 4.4 can be seen in Figure 4.5, which tracks crude birth and death rates for a group of thirteen European countries from 1850 to 1990 and for a group of 106 less developed countries from 1950 to 1990. (Data for less developed regions is generally not as complete as for the developed European countries.) A couple of things are immediately evident in the graph: first, the downward trends in birth and death rates in Europe have not been smooth, but they *have* been long-lasting and have clearly brought the continent to the final stage of the demographic transition; and second, the less developed countries

FIGURE 4.4
Demographic Transition Model

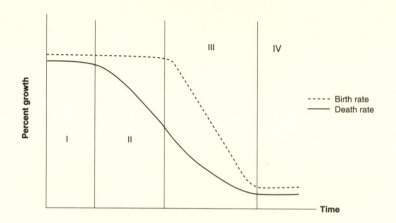

FIGURE 4.5
Crude Birth and Death Rates in Developed and Developing Countries

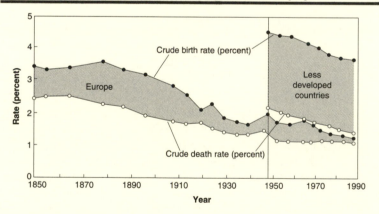

Source: Allen C. Kelley. 1988. "Economic Consequences of Population Change in the Third World." *Journal of Economic Literature,* 26, no. 4, 1688. Reprinted with permission.

began their own mortality and fertility transitions at significantly higher death and birth rates, at mid-twentieth century, than
were seen in Europe a century earlier. Although both rates have
declined, birth rates remain far above death rates—more so than

FIGURE 4.6
Population Pyramid for Nigeria, 2000

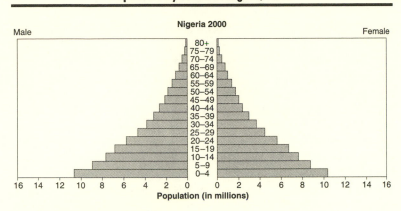

Source: U.S. Census Bureau, *International Data Base.*

FIGURE 4.7
Population Pyramid for Sweden, 2000

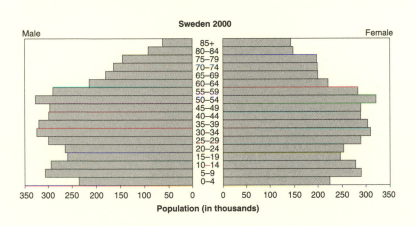

Source: U.S. Census Bureau, *International Data Base.*

was ever the case in Europe—and consequently, population continues to grow rapidly in the developing world.

Finally, Figures 4.6 and 4.7 are two examples of "population pyramids." Such pyramids are used by demographers to illustrate age structures. A pyramid with the classic shape, tapering from a narrow top to a wide bottom, indicates a population in which fertility rates are high and the total number of people is growing. The largest "cohorts"—groups of people born in a given span of years (usually five years)—are the youngest; the smallest cohorts are the oldest. Male and female populations are shown on the left- and right-hand sides of the graph, respectively. Figure 4.6 is the population pyramid for Nigeria in 2000, and it is typical of a developing country with high fertility, one that is far from having completed its demographic transition. Many nations of Africa, Asia, and Latin America have similar population pyramids.

Figure 4.7 gives the population pyramid for Sweden in 2000 and is typical of many European and East Asian nations. Because fertility has been declining for some time in Sweden, the youngest cohort is *not* the largest. Far from it. The largest cohort actually consists of Swedes born between 50 and 54 years ago. As fertility rates decline around the world in coming decades, the global age structure will gradually come to resemble Sweden's more than Nigeria's. (Even Nigeria's population pyramid will evolve away from its current shape and more toward the "barrel shape" of the developed nations.)

5

Documents

The documents included in this chapter represent important statements, projections, reports, and warnings on the subject of population. Space limitations require an extensive use of excerpts, but in each case the key points and flavor of the full document are conveyed. The starting point for debate on population, everyone agrees, is Malthus's *Essay on the Principle of Population* (often abbreviated to *Essay on Population*), published in 1798. The real core of Malthus's demographic argument is presented in the first two chapters.

Essay on Population (1798)

Chapter 1

...I think I may fairly make two postulata.

First, That food is necessary to the existence of man.

Secondly, That the passion between the sexes is necessary, and will remain nearly in its present state.

These two laws, ever since we have had any knowledge of mankind, appear to have been fixed laws of our nature, and, as we have not hitherto seen any alteration in them, we have no right to conclude that they will ever cease to be what they now are, without an immediate act of power in that Being who first arranged the system of the universe, and for the advantage of his creatures, still executes, according to fixed laws, all its various operations. ...

Assuming then my postulata as granted, I say, that the power of population is indefinitely greater than the power in the earth to produce subsistence for man.

Population, when unchecked, increases in a geometrical ratio. Subsistence increases only in an arithmetical ratio. A slight acquaintance with numbers will show the immensity of the first power in comparison of the second.

By that law of our nature which makes food necessary to the life of man, the effects of these two unequal powers must be kept equal.

This implies a strong and constantly operating check on population from the difficulty of subsistence. This difficulty must fall somewhere and must necessarily be severely felt by a large portion of mankind.

Through the animal and vegetable kingdoms, nature has scattered the seeds of life abroad with the most profuse and liberal hand. She has been comparatively sparing in the room and the nourishment necessary to rear them. The germs of existence contained in this spot of earth, with ample food and ample room to expand in, would fill millions of worlds in the course of a few thousand years. Necessity, that imperious all pervading law of nature, restrains them within the prescribed bounds. The race of plants and the race of animals shrink under this great restrictive law. And the race of man cannot, by any efforts of reason, escape from it. Among plants and animals its effects are waste of seed, sickness, and premature death. Among mankind, misery and vice. The former, misery, is an absolutely necessary consequence of it. Vice is a highly probable consequence, and we therefore see it abundantly prevail; but it ought not, perhaps, to be called an absolutely necessary consequence. The ordeal of virtue is to resist all temptation to evil.

This natural inequality of the two powers of population and of production in the earth, and that great law of our nature which must constantly keep their effects equal, form the great difficulty that to me appears insurmountable in the way to the perfectibility of society. All other arguments are of slight and subordinate consideration in comparison of this. I see no way by which man can escape from the weight of this law which pervades all animated nature. No fancied equality, no agrarian regulations in their utmost extent, could remove the pressure of it even for a single century. And it appears, therefore, to be decisive against the possible existence of a society, all the members of which should live in ease, happiness, and comparative leisure, and feel no anxiety about providing the means of subsistence for themselves and families.

Consequently, if the premises are just, the argument is conclusive against the perfectibility of the mass of mankind.

I have thus sketched the general outline of the argument, but I will examine it more particularly, and I think it will be found that experience, the true source and foundation of all knowledge, invariably confirms its truth.

Chapter 2

I said that population, when unchecked, increased in a geometrical ratio, and subsistence for man in an arithmetical ratio.

Let us examine whether this position be just.

I think it will be allowed, that no state has hitherto existed (at least that we have any account of) where the manners were so pure and simple, and the means of subsistence so abundant, that no check whatever has existed to early marriages; among the lower classes, from a fear of not providing well for their families; or among the higher classes, from a fear of lowering their condition in life. Consequently in no state that we have yet known has the power of population been left to exert itself with perfect freedom.

Whether the law of marriage be instituted or not, the dictate of nature and virtue seems to be an early attachment to one woman. Supposing a liberty of changing in the case of an unfortunate choice, this liberty would not affect population till it arose to a height greatly vicious; and we are now supposing the existence of a society where vice is scarcely known.

In a state therefore of great equality and virtue, where pure and simple manners prevailed, and where the means of subsistence were so abundant that no part of the society could have any fears about providing amply for a family, the power of population being left to exert itself unchecked, the increase of the human species would evidently be much greater than any increase that has been hitherto known.

In the United States of America, where the means of subsistence have been more ample, the manners of the people more pure, and consequently the checks to early marriages fewer, than in any of the modern states of Europe, the population has been found to double itself in twenty-five years.

This ratio of increase, though short of the utmost power of population, yet as the result of actual experience, we will take as our rule; and say,

That population, when unchecked, goes on doubling itself every twenty-five years, or increases in a geometrical ratio.

Let us now take any spot of earth, this Island for instance, and see in what ratio the subsistence it affords can be supposed to increase. We will begin with it under its present state of cultivation.

If I allow that by the best possible policy, by breaking up more land, and by great encouragements to agriculture, the produce of this Island may be doubled in the first twenty-five years, I think it will be allowing as much as any person can well demand.

In the next twenty-five years, it is impossible to suppose that the produce could be quadrupled. It would be contrary to all our knowledge of the qualities of land. The very utmost that we can conceive is that the increase in the second twenty-five years might equal the present produce. Let us then take this for our rule, though certainly far beyond the truth, and allow that by great exertion, the whole produce of the Island might be increased every twenty-five years, by a quantity of subsistence equal to what it at present produces. The most enthusiastic speculator cannot suppose a greater increase than this. In a few centuries it would make every acre of land in the Island like a garden.

Yet this ratio of increase is evidently arithmetical.

It may be fairly said, therefore, that the means of subsistence increase in an arithmetical ratio.

Let us now bring the effects of these two ratios together.

The population of the Island is computed to be about seven millions; and we will suppose the present produce equal to the support of such a number. In the first twenty-five years the population would be fourteen millions, and the food being also doubled, the means of subsistence would be equal to this increase. In the next twenty-five years the population would be twenty-eight millions, and the means of subsistence only equal to the support of twenty-one millions. In the next period, the population would be fifty-six millions, and the means of subsistence just sufficient for half that number. And at the conclusion of the first century the population would be one hundred and twelve millions and the means of subsistence only equal to the support of thirty-five millions, which would leave a population of seventy-seven millions totally unprovided for.

A great emigration necessarily implies unhappiness of some kind or other in the country that is deserted. For few persons will leave their families, connections, friends, and native land, to seek a settlement in untried foreign climes, without some strong subsisting causes of uneasiness where they are, or the hope of some great advantages in the place to which they are going.

But to make the argument more general, and less interrupted by the partial views of emigration, let us take the whole earth, instead of one spot, and suppose that the restraints to population were universally removed. If the subsistence for man that the earth affords was to be increased every twenty-five years by a quantity equal to what the whole world at present produces, this would allow the power of production in the earth to be absolutely unlimited, and its ratio of increase much greater than we can conceive that any possible exertions of mankind could make it.

Taking the population of the world at any number, a thousand millions, for instance, the human species would increase in the ratio of—1, 2, 4, 8, 16, 32, 64, 128, 256, 512, etc. and subsistence as—1, 2, 3, 4, 5, 6, 7, 8, 9, 10, etc. In two centuries and a quarter, the population would be to the means of subsistence as 512 to 10; in three centuries as 4096 to 13; and in two thousand years the difference would be almost incalculable, though the produce in that time would have increased to an immense extent.

No limits whatever are placed to the productions of the earth; they may increase for ever and be greater than any assignable quantity; yet still the power of population being a power of a superior order, the increase of the human species can only be kept commensurate to the increase of the means of subsistence by the constant operation of the strong law of necessity acting as a check upon the greater power.

The effects of this check remain now to be considered.

Among plants and animals the view of the subject is simple. They are all impelled by a powerful instinct to the increase of their species, and this instinct is interrupted by no reasoning or doubts about providing for their offspring. Wherever therefore there is liberty, the power of increase is exerted; and the superabundant effects are repressed afterwards by want of room and nourishment, which is common to animals and plants, and among animals, by becoming the prey of others.

The effects of this check on man are more complicated.

Impelled to the increase of his species by an equally powerful instinct, reason interrupts his career and asks him whether he may not bring beings into the world for whom he cannot provide the means of subsistence. In a state of equality, this would be the simple question. In the present state of society, other considerations occur. Will he not lower his rank in life? Will he not subject himself to greater difficulties than he at present feels? Will he not be obliged to labour harder? And if he has a large family, will his utmost exertions enable him to support them? May he not see his offspring in rags and misery, and clamouring for bread that he cannot give them? And may he not be reduced to the grating necessity of forfeiting his independence, and of being obliged to the sparing hand of charity for support? ...

The theory on which the truth of this position depends appears to me so extremely clear that I feel at a loss to conjecture what part of it can be denied.

That population cannot increase without the means of subsistence is a proposition so evident that it needs no illustration.

That population does invariably increase where there are the means of subsistence, the history of every people that have ever existed will abundantly prove.

And that the superior power of population cannot be checked without producing misery or vice, the ample portion of these too bitter ingredients in the cup of human life and the continuance of the physical causes that seem to have produced them bear too convincing a testimony.

World Population Plan of Action, Bucharest, 1974

Three international conferences on population have been held under the auspices of the United Nations, at ten-year intervals, beginning in 1974. The first one took place in Bucharest, Romania. Official representatives from the developed and the developing nations strongly disagreed on how to frame the world's population problems and how to tackle them. Less developed nations thought the emphasis should be placed on speeding up their economic development; such development would result, almost automatically, in an easing or elimination of population pressures. The richer countries, however, preferred a more limited policy focus. They wanted to see *quantitative goals* set by national population policymakers (item 37) and considered family-planning programs to be the appropriate instrument for achieving such goals. In spite of this fundamental discord, the conference was able to adopt a plan of action that remains today the cornerstone of international population policy.

A. Background to the Plan

... 2. The formulation of international strategies is a response to universal recognition of the existence of important problems in the world and the need for concerted national and international action to achieve their solution. Where trends of population growth, distribution and structure are out of balance with social, economic and environmental factors, they can, at certain stages of development, create additional difficulties for the achievement of sustainable development. Policies whose aim is to affect population trends must not be considered substitutes for socio-economic development policies but as being integrated with those policies in order to facilitate the solution of certain problems facing both developing and developed countries and to promote a more balanced and rational development.

3. Throughout history the rate of growth of world population averaged only slightly above replacement levels. The recent increase in the growth rate began mainly as a result of the decline in mortality during the past few centuries, a decline that has accelerated significantly during recent decades. The inertia of social structures and the insufficiency of economic progress, especially when these exist in the absence of profound socio-cultural changes, partly explain why in the majority of developing countries the decline in mortality has not been accompanied by a parallel decline in fertility. Since about 1950, the world population growth rate has risen to 2 per cent a year. If sustained, this will result in a doubling of the world's population every 35 years. However, national rates of natural growth range widely, from a negative rate to well over 3 per cent a year.

4. The consideration of population problems cannot be reduced to the analysis of population trends only. It must also be borne in mind that the present situation of the developing countries originates in the unequal processes of socio-economic development which have divided peoples since the beginning

of the modern era. This inequity still exists and is intensified by lack of equity in international economic relations with consequent disparity in levels of living. ...

6. While the right of couples to have the number of children they desire is accepted in a number of international instruments, many couples in the world are unable to exercise that right effectively. In many parts of the world, poor economic conditions, social norms, inadequate knowledge of effective methods of family regulation and the unavailability of contraceptive services result in a situation in which couples have more children that they desire or feel they can properly care for. In certain countries, on the other hand, because of economic or biologic factors, problems of involuntary sterility and of subfecundity exist, with the result that many couples have fewer children than they desire. Of course, the degree of urgency attached to dealing with each of these two situations depends upon the prevailing conditions within the country in question.

7. Individual reproductive behavior and the needs and aspirations of society should be reconciled. In many developing countries, and particularly in the large countries of Asia, the desire of couples to achieve large families is believed to result in excessive national population growth rates and Governments are explicitly attempting to reduce those rates by implementing specific policy measures. On the other hand, some countries are attempting to increase desired family size, if only slightly. ...

B. Principles and Objectives of the Plan

14 (c) Population and development are interrelated: population variables influence development variables and are also influenced by them; thus the formulation of a World Population Plan of Action reflects the international community's awareness of the importance of population trends for socio-economic development, and the socio-economic nature of the recommendations contained in this Plan of Action reflects its awareness of the crucial role that development plays in affecting population trends;

(d) Population policies are constituent elements of socio-economic development policies, never substitutes for them: while serving socioeconomic objectives, they should be consistent with internationally and nationally recognized human rights of individual freedom, justice and the survival of national, regional and minority groups;

(e) Independently of the realization of economic and social objectives, respect for human life is basic to all human societies;

(f) All couples and individuals have the basic right to decide freely and responsibly the number and spacing of their children and to have the information, education and means to do so; the responsibility of couples and individuals in the exercise of this right takes into account the needs of their living and future children, and their responsibilities towards the community;

(g) The family is the basic unit of society and should be protected by appropriate legislation and policy;

(h) Women have the right to complete integration in the development process, particularly by means of an equal access to education and equal participation in social, economic, cultural and political life. In addition, the necessary measures should be taken to facilitate this integration with family responsibilities which should be fully shared by both partners. ...

C. Recommendations for Action

... 27. This Plan of Action recognizes the variety of national goals with regard to fertility and does not recommend any world family-size norm.

28. This Plan of Action recognizes the necessity of ensuring that all couples are able to achieve their desired number and spacing of children and the necessity of preparing the social and economic conditions to achieve that desire. ...

37. In the light of the principles of this Plan of Action, countries which consider their birth rates detrimental to their national purposes are invited to consider setting quantitative goals and implementing policies that may lead to the attainment of such goals by 1985. Nothing herein should interfere with the sovereignty of any Government to adopt or not to adopt such quantitative goals. ...

41. Governments should ensure full participation of women in the educational, social, economic and political life of their countries on an equal basis with men. It is recommended that:

(a) Education for girls as well as boys should be extended and diversified to enable them to contribute more effectively in rural and urban sectors, as well as in the management of food and other household functions;

(b) Women should be actively involved both as individuals and through political and non-governmental organizations, at every stage and every level in the planning and implementation of development programs, including population policies;

(c) The economic contribution of women in households and farming should be recognized in national economies;

(d) Governments should make a sustained effort to ensure that legislation regarding the status of women complies with the principles spelled out in the Declaration on the Elimination of Discrimination against Women and other United Nations declarations, conventions and international instruments, to reduce the gap between law and practice through effective implementation, and to inform women at all socio-economic levels of their rights and responsibilities.

42. Equal status of men and women in the family and in society improves the overall quality of life. This principle of equality should be fully realized in family planning where each spouse should consider the welfare of the other members of the family.

43. Improvement of the status of women in the family and in society can contribute, where desired, to smaller family size, and the opportunity for women to plan births also improves their individual status. ...

68. This Plan of Action recognizes that economic and social development is a central factor in the solution of population problems. National efforts of developing countries to accelerate economic growth should be assisted by the entire international community. The implementation of the International Development Strategy for the Second United Nations Development Decade, and the Declaration and the Program of Action on the New International Economic Order as adopted at the sixth special session of the General Assembly should lead to a reduction in the widening gap in levels of living between developed and developing countries and would be conducive to a reduction in population growth rates particularly in countries where such rates are high.

Program of Action of the International Conference on Population and Development, Cairo, 1994

More clearly than in 1974 (Bucharest) or 1984 (Mexico City), the 1994 population conference in Cairo situated population policy-making within a broader context of all-round human development. Governments were urged to take the necessary steps to ensure the provision of reproductive health services to all their citizens, to broaden opportunities for women, and to equalize educational opportunities for girls and boys. There was an implicit recognition that high fertility rates, where they still occur, are unlikely to be reduced, or reduced sufficiently to ease population pressures, until women achieve a fuller measure of empowerment in their personal and social lives. Much behind-the-scenes negotiating was needed to achieve a final consensus on this document, with Nafis Sadik, head of the UNFPA and Secretary-General of the ICPD, playing an important mediating role.

Chapter 1 Preamble

… 1.3. The world population is currently estimated at 5.6 billion. While the rate of growth is on the decline, absolute increments have been increasing, currently exceeding 86 million persons per annum. Annual population increments are likely to remain above 86 million until the year 2015.

1.4. During the remaining six years of this critical decade, the world's nations by their actions or inactions will choose from among a range of alternative demographic futures. The low, medium and high variants of the United Nations population projections for the coming 20 years range from a low of 7.1 billion people to the medium variant of 7.5 billion and a high of 7.8 billion. The difference of 720 million people in the short span of 20 years exceeds the current population of the African continent. Further into the future, the projections diverge even more significantly. By the year 2050, the United Nations projections range from 7.9 billion to the medium variant of 9.8 billion and a high of 11.9 billion. Implementation of the goals and objectives contained in the present 20-year Program of Action, which address many of the fundamental population, health, education and development challenges facing the entire human community, would result in world population growth during this period and beyond at levels below the United Nations medium projection. …

1.8. Over the past 20 years, many parts of the world have undergone remarkable demographic, social, economic, environmental and political change. Many countries have made substantial progress in expanding access to reproductive health care and lowering birth rates, as well as in lowering death rates and raising education and income levels, including the educational and economic status of women. While the advances of the past two decades in areas such as increased use of contraception, decreased maternal mortality, implemented sustainable development plans and projects and enhanced educational programs provide a basis for optimism about successful implementation of the present Program of Action, much remains to be accomplished. The world as a whole has changed in ways that create important new opportunities for addressing population and development issues. Among the most significant are the major shifts in attitude among the world's people and their leaders in regard to reproductive health, family planning and population growth, resulting, *inter alia*, in the new comprehensive concept of reproductive health, including family planning and sexual health, as defined in the present Program of Action. A particularly encouraging trend has been the strengthening of political commitment to population-related policies and family-planning programs by many Governments. In this regard, sustained economic growth in the context of sustainable development will enhance the ability of countries to meet the pressures of expected population growth; will facilitate the demographic transition in countries where there is an imbalance between demographic rates and social, economic and environmental goals; and will permit the balance and integration of the population dimension into other development-related policies.

1.9. The population and development objectives and actions of the present Program of Action will collectively address the critical challenges and interrelationships between population and sustained economic growth in the context of sustainable development. In order to do so, adequate mobilization of resources at the national and international levels will be required as well as new and additional resources to the developing countries from all available funding mechanisms, including multilateral, bilateral and private sources. Financial resources are also required to strengthen the capacity of national, regional, subregional and international institutions to implement this Program of Action. ...

1.11. Intensified efforts are needed in the coming 5, 10 and 20 years, in a range of population and development activities, bearing in mind the crucial contribution that early stabilization of the world population would make towards the achievement of sustainable development. The present Program of Action addresses all those issues, and more, in a comprehensive and integrated framework designed to improve the quality of life of the current world population and its future generations. The recommendations for action are made in a spirit of consensus and international cooperation, recognizing that the formulation and implementation of population-related policies is the responsibility of each country and should take into account the economic, social and environmental diversity of conditions in each country, with full respect for the various religious and ethical values, cultural backgrounds and philosophical convictions of its people, as well as the shared but differentiated responsibilities of all the world's people for a common future. ...

1.13. Many of the quantitative and qualitative goals of the present Program of Action clearly require additional resources, some of which could become available from a reordering of priorities at the individual, national and international levels. However, none of the actions required—nor all of them combined—is expensive in the context of either current global development or military expenditures. A few would require little or no additional financial resources, in that they involve change in lifestyles, social norms or government policies that can be largely brought about and sustained through greater citizen action and political leadership. But to meet the resource needs of those actions that do require increased expenditures over the next two decades, additional commitments will be required on the part of both developing and developed countries. This will be particularly difficult in the case of some developing countries and some countries with economies in transition that are experiencing extreme resource constraints.

Chapter 2 Principles

... *Principle 4.* Advancing gender equality and equity and the empowerment of women, and the elimination of all kinds of violence against women, and ensuring women's ability to control their own fertility, are cornerstones of population- and development-related programs. The human rights of women and the girl child are an inalienable, integral and indivisible part of universal human rights. The full and equal participation of women in civil, cultural, economic, political and social life, at the national, regional and international levels, and the eradication of all forms of discrimination on grounds of sex, are priority objectives of the international community.

Principle 5. Population-related goals and policies are integral parts of cultural, economic and social development, the

principal aim of which is to improve the quality of life of all
people.

Principle 6. Sustainable development as a means to ensure
human well-being, equitably shared by all people today and in
the future, requires that the interrelationships between population, resources, the environment and development should be
fully recognized, properly managed and brought into harmo-
nious, dynamic balance. To achieve sustainable development
and a higher quality of life for all people, States should reduce
and eliminate unsustainable patterns of production and consumption and promote appropriate policies, including population-related policies, in order to meet the needs of current generations without compromising the ability of future generations
to meet their own needs. ...

Principle 8. Everyone has the right to the enjoyment of the
highest attainable standard of physical and mental health.
States should take all appropriate measures to ensure, on a basis
of equality of men and women, universal access to health-care
services, including those related to reproductive health care,
which includes family planning and sexual health. Reproductive health-care programs should provide the widest range of
services without any form of coercion. All couples and individuals have the basic right to decide freely and responsibly the
number and spacing of their children and to have the information, education and means to do so. ...

Principle 10. Everyone has the right to education, which
shall be directed to the full development of human resources,
and human dignity and potential, with particular attention to
women and the girl child. Education should be designed to
respect for human rights and fundamental freedoms, including
those relating to population and development. The best interests of the child shall be the guiding principle of those responsible for his or her education and guidance; that responsibility
lies in the first place with the parents.

Chapter 3 Interrelationships between Population, Sustained Economic Growth and Sustainable Development

... 3.14 Efforts to slow down population growth, to reduce
poverty, to achieve economic progress, to improve environmental protection, and to reduce unsustainable consumption and

production patterns are mutually reinforcing. Slower population growth has in many countries bought more time to adjust to future population increases. This has increased those countries' ability to attack poverty, protect and repair the environment, and build the base for future sustainable development. Even the difference of a single decade in the transition to stabilization levels of fertility can have a considerable positive impact on quality of life.

3.15 Sustained economic growth within the context of sustainable development is essential to eradicate poverty. Eradication of poverty will contribute to slowing population growth and to achieving early population stabilization. Investments in fields important to the eradication of poverty, such as basic education, sanitation, drinking water, housing, adequate food supply and infrastructure for rapidly growing populations, continue to strain already weak economies and limit development options. The unusually high number of young people, a consequence of high fertility rates, requires that productive jobs be created for a continually growing labor force under conditions of already widespread unemployment. The numbers of elderly requiring public support will also increase rapidly in the future. Sustained economic growth in the context of sustainable development will be necessary to accommodate those pressures.

Chapter 4 Gender Equality, Equity and Empowerment of Women

... 4.1 The empowerment and autonomy of women and the improvement of their political, social, economic and health status is a highly important end in itself. In addition, it is essential for the achievement of sustainable development. The full participation and partnership of both women and men is required in productive and reproductive life, including shared responsibilities for the care and nurturing of children and maintenance of the household. In all parts of the world, women are facing threats to their lives, health and well-being as a result of being overburdened with work and of their lack of power and influence. In most regions of the world, women receive less formal education than men, and at the same time, women's own knowledge, abilities and coping mechanisms often go unrecognized. The power relations that impede women's attainment of healthy and fulfilling lives operate at many levels of society, from the most personal to the highly public. Achieving change requires policy and program actions that will improve women's access to secure livelihoods and economic resources, alleviate their extreme responsibilities with regard to housework, remove legal impediments to their participation in public life, and raise social awareness through effective programs of education and mass communication. In addition, improving the status of women also enhances their decision-making capacity at all levels in all spheres of life, especially in the area of sexuality and reproduction. This, in turn, is essential for the long-term success of population programs. Experience shows that population and development programs are most effective when steps have simultaneously been taken to improve the status of women. . . .

Chapter 7 Reproductive Rights and Reproductive Health

. . . 7.12 The aim of family-planning programs must be to enable couples and individuals to decide freely and responsibly the number and spacing of their children and to have the information and means to do so and to ensure informed choices and make available a full range of safe and effective methods. The success of population education and family-planning programs in a variety of settings demonstrates that informed individuals everywhere can and will act responsibly in the light of their own needs and those of their families and communities. The principle of informed free choice is essential to the long-term success of family-planning programs. Any form of coercion has no part to play. In every society there are many social and economic incentives and disincentives that affect individual decisions about child-bearing and family size. Over the past century, many Governments have experimented with such schemes, including specific incentives and disincentives, in order to lower or raise fertility. Most such schemes have had only marginal impact on fertility and in some cases have been counterproductive. Governmental goals for family planning should be defined in terms of unmet needs for information and services. Demographic goals, while legitimately the subject of government development strategies, should not be imposed on family-planning providers in the form of targets or quotas for the recruitment of clients.

7.13 Over the past three decades, the increasing availability of safer methods of modern contraception, although still in some respects inadequate, has permitted greater opportunities

for individual choice and responsible decision-making in matters of reproduction throughout much of the world. Currently,
about 55 per cent of couples in developing regions use some
method of family planning. This figure represents nearly a five-
fold increase since the 1960s. Family-planning programs have
contributed considerably to the decline in average fertility rates
for developing countries, from about six to seven children per
woman in the 1960s to about three to four children at present.
However, the full range of modern family-planning methods
still remains unavailable to at least 350 million couples world
wide, many of whom say they want to space or prevent another
pregnancy. Survey data suggest that approximately 120 million
additional women world wide would be currently using a modern family-planning method if more accurate information and
affordable services were easily available, and if partners,
extended families and the community were more supportive. ...

7.16 All countries should, over the next several years,
assess the extent of national unmet need for good-quality family-planning services and its integration in the reproductive
health context, paying particular attention to the most vulnerable and underserved groups in the population. All countries
should take steps to meet the family-planning needs of their
populations as soon as possible and should, in all cases by the
year 2015, seek to provide universal access to a full range of
safe and reliable family-planning methods and to related reproductive health services which are not against the law. The aim
should be to assist couples and individuals to achieve their
reproductive goals and give them the full opportunity to exercise the right to have children by choice.

Population Growth, Resource Consumption, and a Sustainable World: Joint Statement by the Royal Society of London and the U.S. National Academy of Sciences, February 1992

This statement was issued in advance of the UN conference on
the environment held in Rio de Janeiro in June 1992. It points to
the environmental burden imposed on the Earth by "each additional human being," and the indisputable fact that "the recent
expansion of the human population" has accelerated the "pace of

environmental change." Science and technology have a role to play in meeting the challenges posed by this change, but equally important are global policies to promote, among other things, a "more rapid stabilization of world population."

World population is growing at the unprecedented rate of almost 100 million people every year, and human activities are producing major changes in the global environment. If current predictions of population prove accurate and patterns of human activity on the planet remain unchanged, science and technology may not be able to prevent either irreversible degradation of the environment or continued poverty for much of the world. The following joint statement, prepared by the Officers of the Royal Society of London and the United States National Academy of Sciences, reflects the judgment of a group of scientists knowledgeable about the historic contributions of science and technology to economic growth and environmental protection. It also reflects the shared view that sustainable development implies a future in which life is improved worldwide through economic development, where local environments and the biosphere are protected, and science is mobilized to create new opportunities for human progress. ...

World Population

In its 1991 report on world population, the United Nations Population Fund (UNFPA) states that population growth is even faster than forecast in its report of 1984. Assuming nevertheless that there will in the future be substantial and sustained falls in fertility rates, the global population is expected in the UN's mid-range projection to rise from 5.4 billion in 1991 to 10 billion in 2050. This rapid rise may be unavoidable; considerably larger rises must be expected if fertility rates do not stabilize at the replacement level of about 2.1 children per woman. At present, about 95 percent of this growth is in the less developed countries (LDCs); the percentage of global population that live in the LDCs is projected to increase from 77 percent in 1990 to 84 percent in 2020.

The Environment

Although there is a relationship between population, economic activity, and the environment, it is not simple. Most of the environmental changes during the twentieth century have been a product of the efforts of humans to secure improved standards of food, clothing, shelter, comfort, and recreation. Both developed and developing countries have contributed to environmental degradation. Developed countries, with 85 percent of the world's gross national product and 23 percent of its population, account for the majority of mineral and fossil-fuel consumption. One issue alone, the increases in atmospheric carbon dioxide, has the potential for altering global climate with significant consequences for all countries. The prosperity and technology of the developed countries, however, give them the greater possibilities and the greater responsibility for addressing environmental problems.

In the developing countries the resource consumption per capita is lower, but the rapidly growing population and the pressure to develop their economies are leading to substantial and increasing damage to the local environment. This damage comes by direct pollution from energy use and other industrial activities, as well as by activities such as clearing forests and inappropriate agricultural practices.

The Reality of the Problem

Scientific and technological innovations, such as in agriculture, have been able to overcome many pessimistic predictions about resource constraints affecting human welfare. Nevertheless, the present patterns of human activity accentuated by population growth should make even those most optimistic about future scientific progress pause and reconsider the wisdom of ignoring these threats to our planet. Unrestrained resource consumption for energy production and other uses, especially if the developing world strives to achieve living standards based on the same levels of consumption as the developed world, could lead to catastrophic outcomes for the global environment.

Some of the environmental changes may produce irreversible damage to the earth's capacity to sustain life. Many species have already disappeared, and many more are destined to do so. Man's own prospects for achieving satisfactory living standards are threatened by environmental deterioration, especially in the poorest countries where economic activities are most heavily dependent upon the quality of natural resources.

If they are forced to deal with their environmental and resource problems alone, the LDCs face overwhelming challenges. They generate only 15 percent of the world's GNP, and have a net cash outflow of tens of billions of dollars per year. Over 1 billion people live in absolute poverty, and 600 million on the margin of starvation. And the LDCs have only 6–7 percent of the world's active scientists and engineers, a situation that makes it very difficult for them to participate fully in global or regional schemes to manage their own environment.

In places where resources are administered effectively, population growth does not inevitably imply deterioration in the quality of the environment. Nevertheless, each additional human being requires natural resources for sustenance, each produces by-products that become part of the ecosystem, and each pursues economic and other activities that affect the natural world. While the impact of population growth varies from place to place and from one environmental domain to another, the overall pace of environmental changes has unquestionably been accelerated by the recent expansion of the human population.

International Action

There is an urgent need to address economic activity, population growth, and environmental protection as interrelated issues. The forthcoming UN Conference on Environment and Development, to be held in Brazil, should consider human activities and population growth, in both the developing and developed worlds, as crucial components affecting the sustainability of human society. Effective family planning, combined with continued economic and social development in the LDCs, will help stabilize fertility rates at lower levels and reduce stresses to the global environment. At the same time, greater attention in the developed countries to conservation, recycling, substitution and efficient use of energy, and a concerted program to start mitigating further buildup of greenhouse gases will help to ease the threat to the global environment.

Unlike many other steps that could be taken to reduce the rate of environmental changes, reductions in rates of population growth can be accomplished through voluntary measures. Surveys in the developing world repeatedly reveal large amounts of unwanted childbearing. By providing people with the means to control their own fertility, family planning programs have major possibilities to reduce rates of population growth and hence to arrest environmental degradation. Also, unlike many other potential interventions that are typically specific to a particular problem, a reduction in the rate of population growth would affect many dimensions of environmental changes. Its importance is easily underestimated if attention is focused on one problem at a time.

The Contributions of Science

What are the relevant topics to which scientific research can make mitigating contributions? These include: development of new generations of safe, easy to use, and effective contraceptive agents and devices; development of environmentally benign alternative energy sources; improvements in agricultural production and food processing; further research in plant and animal genetic varieties; further research in biotechnology relating to plants, animals, and preservation of the environment; improvements in public health, especially through development of effective drugs and vaccines for malaria, hepatitis, AIDS, and other infectious diseases causing immense human burdens. Also needed is research on topics such as: improved land-use practices to prevent ecological degradation, loss of topsoil, and desertification of grasslands; better institutional measures to protect watersheds and groundwater; new technologies for waste disposal, environmental remediation, and pollution control; new materials that reduce pollution and the use of hazardous substances during their life cycle; and more effective regulatory tools that use market forces to protect the environment.

Greater attention also needs to be given to understanding the nature and dimension of the world's biodiversity. Although we depend directly on biodiversity for sustainable productivity, we cannot even estimate the numbers of species of organisms—plants, animals, fungi, and microorganisms—to an order of magnitude. We do know, however, that the current rate of reduction in biodiversity is unparalleled over the past 65 million years. The loss of biodiversity is one of the fastest moving aspects of global change, is irreversible, and has serious consequences for the human prospect in the future.

What are the limits of scientific contributions to the solution of resource and environmental problems? Scientific research and technological innovation can undoubtedly mitigate these stresses and facilitate a less destructive adaptation of a growing population to its environment. Yet, it is not prudent to rely on science and technology alone to solve problems created by rapid population growth, wasteful resource consumption, and harmful human practices.

Conclusions

The application of science and technology to global problems is a key component of providing a decent standard of living for a majority of the human race. Science and technology have an especially important role to play in developing countries in helping them to manage their resources effectively and to participate fully in worldwide initiatives for common benefit. Capabilities in science and technology must be strengthened in LDCs as a matter of urgency through joint initiatives from the developed and developing worlds. But science and technology alone are not enough. Global policies are urgently needed to promote more rapid economic development throughout the world, more environmentally benign patterns of human activity, and a more rapid stabilization of world population.

The future of our planet is in the balance. Sustainable development can be achieved, but only if irreversible degradation of the environment can be halted in time. The next 30 years may be crucial.

Warning to Humanity, November 18, 1992

Later in the same year as the joint statement from the Royal Society and the National Academy of Sciences (see previous item), the Union of Concerned Scientists issued their own statement. It was more ominous in tone and content than the earlier statement, cautioning that if there were not a "great change in our stewardship of the earth," the unavoidable consequence would be "vast human misery" and a planet "irretrievably mutilated." Blunt language was used to warn developed countries of the harmful effects of their "overconsumption" and pollution, and to warn the developing countries of the environmental damage, poverty, and unrest that *they* will experience if their populations "go unchecked." The statement was signed by over 1,500 scientists, including half of the living Nobel laureates in the sciences.

Human beings and the natural world are on a collision course. Human activities inflict harsh and often irreversible damage on the environment and on critical resources. If not checked, many of our current practices put at serious risk the future that we wish for human society and the plant and animal kingdoms, and may so alter the living world that it will be unable to sustain life in the manner that we know. Fundamental changes are urgent if we are to avoid the collision our present course will bring about.

The Environment

The environment is suffering critical stress;

The atmosphere

Stratospheric ozone depletion threatens us with enhanced ultra-violet radiation at the earth's surface, which can be damaging or lethal to many life forms. Air pollution near ground level, and acid precipitation, are already causing widespread injury to humans, forests and crops.

Water resources

Heedless exploitation of depletable ground water supplies endangers food production and other essential human systems. Heavy demands on the world's surface waters have resulted in serious shortages in some 80 countries, containing 40% of the world's population. Pollution of rivers, lakes and ground water further limits the supply.

Oceans

Destructive pressure on the oceans is severe, particularly in the coastal regions which produce most of the world's food fish. The total marine catch is now at or above the estimated maximum sustainable yield. Some fisheries have already shown signs of collapse. Rivers carrying heavy burdens of eroded soil into the seas also carry industrial, municipal, agricultural, and livestock waste—some of it toxic.

Soil

Loss of soil productivity, which is causing extensive land abandonment, is a widespread byproduct of current practices in agriculture and animal husbandry. Since 1945, 11% of the earth's vegetated surface has been degraded—an area larger than India and China combined—and per capita food production in many parts of the world is decreasing.

Forests
Tropical rain forests, as well as tropical and temperate dry forests, are being destroyed rapidly. At present rates, some critical forest types will be gone in a few years and most of the tropical rain forest will be gone before the end of the next century. With them will go large numbers of plant and animal species.

Living Species
The irreversible loss of species, which by 2100 may reach one-third of all species now living, is especially serious. We are losing the potential they hold for providing medicinal and other benefits, and the contribution that genetic diversity of life forms gives to the robustness of the world's biological systems and to the astonishing beauty of the earth itself.

Much of this damage is irreversible on a scale of centuries or permanent. Other processes appear to pose additional threats. Increasing levels of gases in the atmosphere from human activities, including carbon dioxide released from fossil fuel burning and from deforestation, may alter climate on a global scale. Predictions of global warming are still uncertain—with projected effects ranging from tolerable to very severe—but the potential risks are very great.

Our massive tampering with the world's interdependent web of life—coupled with the environmental damage inflicted by deforestation, species loss, and climate change—could trigger widespread adverse effects, including unpredictable collapses of critical biological systems whose interactions and dynamics we only imperfectly understand.

Uncertainty over the extent of these effects cannot excuse complacency or delay in facing the threat.

Population
The earth is finite. Its ability to absorb wastes and destructive effluent is finite. Its ability to provide food and energy is finite. Its ability to provide for growing numbers of people is finite. And we are fast approaching many of the earth's limits. Current economic practices which damage the environment, in both

developed and underdeveloped nations, cannot be continued without the risk that vital global systems will be damaged beyond repair.

Pressures resulting from unrestrained population growth put demands on the natural world that can overwhelm any efforts to achieve a sustainable future. If we are to halt the destruction of our environment, we must accept limits to that growth. A World Bank estimate indicates that world population will not stabilize at less than 12.4 billion, while the United Nations concludes that the eventual total could reach 14 billion, a near tripling of today's 5.4 billion. But, even at this moment, one person in five lives in absolute poverty without enough to eat, and one in ten suffers serious malnutrition.

No more than one or a few decades remain before the chance to avert the threats we now confront will be lost and the prospects for humanity immeasurably diminished.

Warning

We the undersigned, senior members of the world's scientific community, hereby warn all humanity of what lies ahead. A great change in our stewardship of the earth and the life on it is required, if vast human misery is to be avoided and our global home on this planet is not to be irretrievably mutilated.

What we must do

Five inextricably linked areas must be addressed simultaneously:

1. We must bring environmentally damaging activities under control to restore and protect the integrity of the earth's systems we depend on.

    We must, for example, move away from fossil fuels to more benign, inexhaustible energy sources to cut greenhouse gas emissions and the pollution of our air and water. Priority must be given to the development of energy sources matched to third world needs—small scale and relatively easy to implement.

    We must halt deforestation, injury to and loss of agricultural land, and the loss of terrestrial and marine plant and animal species.
2. We must manage resources crucial to human welfare more effectively.

We must give high priority to efficient use of energy, water, and other materials, including expansion of conservation and recycling.
3. We must stabilize population. This will be possible only if all nations recognize that it requires improved social and economic conditions, and the adoption of effective, voluntary family planning.
4. We must reduce and eventually eliminate poverty.
5. We must ensure sexual equality, and guarantee women control over their own reproductive decisions.

The developed nations are the largest polluters in the world today. They must greatly reduce their overconsumption, if we are to reduce pressures on resources and the global environment. The developed nations have the obligation to provide aid and support to developing nations, because only the developed nations have the financial resources and the technical skills for these tasks.

Acting on this recognition is not altruism, but enlightened self-interest: whether industrialized or not, we all have but one lifeboat. No nation can escape from injury when global biological systems are damaged. No nation can escape from conflicts over increasingly scarce resources. In addition, environmental and economic instabilities will cause mass migrations with incalculable consequences for developed and undeveloped nations alike.

Developing nations must realize that environmental damage is one of the gravest threats they face, and that attempts to blunt it will be overwhelmed if their populations go unchecked. The greatest peril is to become trapped in spirals of environmental decline, poverty, and unrest, leading to social, economic and environmental collapse.

Success in this global endeavor will require a great reduction in violence and war. Resources now devoted to the preparation and conduct of war—amounting to over $1 trillion annually—will be badly needed in the new tasks and should be diverted to the new challenges.

A new ethic is required—a new attitude towards discharging our responsibility for caring for ourselves and for the earth. We must recognize the earth's limited capacity to provide for us. We must recognize its fragility. We must no longer allow it to be ravaged. This ethic must motivate a great movement, convince reluctant leaders and reluctant governments and reluctant peoples themselves to effect the needed changes.

The scientists issuing this warning hope that our message will reach and affect people everywhere.

We need the help of many.

We require the help of the world community of scientists—natural, social, economic, political;

We require the help of the world's business and industrial leaders;

We require the help of the world's religious leaders; and

We require the help of the world's peoples.

We call on all to join us in this task.

National Security Study Memorandum 200 (December 10, 1974) Subject: Implications of Worldwide Population Growth for U.S. Security and Overseas Interests

Essential reading for anyone seeking to understand U.S. international population policy in the late twentieth century is National Security Study Memorandum 200 (NSSM 200), a study President Nixon ordered from his National Security Council in early 1974. The aim was to assess the possible impacts on U.S. security interests from continued rapid growth of world population over the coming quarter-century. The final report of nearly 200 pages was submitted in December 1974 to Nixon's successor, President Ford; it remained a classified document until 1989. Typically for the time period, it expressed great concern about impending "massive famines." Other possible risks from population growth abroad included chronic unemployment, food riots, sectarian violence, revolutions, and counter-revolutionary coups. U.S. assistance might enable less-developed countries to lower their population growth rates. The following excerpts are from the executive summary.

World Demographic Trends

1. World population growth since World War II is quantitatively and qualitatively different from any previous epoch in human history. The rapid reduction in death rates, unmatched by corresponding birth rate reductions, has brought total

growth rates close to 2 percent a year, compared with about 1 percent before World War II, under 0.5 percent in 1750–1900, and far lower rates before 1750. The effect is to double the world's population in 35 years instead of 100 years. Almost 80 million are now being added each year, compared with 10 million in 1900.

2. The second new feature of population trends is the sharp differentiation between rich and poor countries. Since 1950, population in the former group has been growing at 0 to 1.5 percent per year, and in the latter at 2.0 to 3.5 percent (doubling in 20 to 35 years). Some of the highest rates of increase are in areas already densely populated and with a weak resource base. ...

Adequacy of World Food Supplies

5. Growing populations will have a serious impact on the need for food, especially in the poorest, fastest growing LDCs. While under normal weather conditions and assuming food production growth in line with recent trends, total world agricultural production could expand faster than population, there will nevertheless be serious problems in food distribution and financing, making shortages, even at today's poor nutrition levels, probable in many of the larger, more populous LDC regions. Even today 10 to 20 million people die each year due, directly or indirectly, to malnutrition. Even more serious is the consequence of major crop failures which are likely to occur from time to time.

6. The most serious consequence for the short and middle term is the possibility of massive famines in certain parts of the world, especially the poorest regions. World needs for food rise by 2.5 percent or more per year (making a modest allowance for improved diets and nutrition) at a time when readily available fertilizer and well-watered land is already largely being utilized. Therefore, additions to food production must come mainly from higher yields. Countries with large population growth cannot afford constantly growing imports, but for them to raise food output steadily by 2 to 4 percent over the next generation or two is a formidable challenge. Capital and foreign exchange requirements for intensive agriculture are heavy, and are aggravated by energy cost increases and fertilizer scarcities and price rises. The institutional, technical, and economic problems of

transforming traditional agriculture are also very difficult to overcome.

7. In addition, in some overpopulated regions, rapid population growth presses on a fragile environment in ways that threaten longer-term food production: through cultivation of marginal lands, overgrazing, desertification, deforestation, and soil erosion, with consequent destruction of land and pollution of water, rapid siltation of reservoirs, and impairment of inland and coastal fisheries.

Minerals and Fuel

8. Rapid population growth is not in itself a major factor in pressure on depletable resources (fossil fuels and other minerals), since demand for them depends more on levels of industrial output than on numbers of people. On the other hand, the world is increasingly dependent on mineral supplies from developing countries, and if rapid population frustrates their prospects for economic development and social progress, the resulting instability may undermine the conditions for expanded output and sustained flows of such resources.

9. There will be serious problems for some of the poorest LDCs with rapid population growth. They will increasingly find it difficult to pay for needed raw materials and energy. Fertilizer, vital for their own agricultural production, will be difficult to obtain for the next few years. Imports for fuel and other materials will cause grave problems which could impinge on the U.S., both through the need to supply greater financial support and in LDC efforts to obtain better terms of trade through higher prices for exports. ...

Economic Development and Population Growth

10. Rapid population growth creates a severe drag on rates of economic development otherwise attainable, sometimes to the point of preventing any increase in per capita incomes. In addition to the overall impact on per capita incomes, rapid population growth seriously affects a vast range of other aspects of the quality of life important to social and economic progress in the LDCs. ...

15. The universal objective of increasing the world's standard of living dictates that economic growth outpace popula-

tion growth. In many high population growth areas of the world, the largest proportion of GNP is consumed, with only a small amount saved. Thus, a small proportion of GNP is available for investment—the "engine" of economic growth. Most experts agree that, with fairly constant costs per acceptor, expenditures on effective family planning services are generally one of the most cost effective investments for an LDC country seeking to improve overall welfare and per capita economic growth. We cannot wait for overall modernization and development to produce lower fertility rates naturally since this will undoubtedly take many decades in most developing countries, during which time rapid population growth will tend to slow development and widen even more the gap between rich and poor. ...

Political Effects of Population Factors

19. The political consequences of current population factors in the LDCs—rapid growth, internal migration, high percentages of young people, slow improvement in living standards, urban concentrations, and pressures for foreign migration—are damaging to the internal stability and international relations of countries in whose advancement the U.S. is interested, thus creating political or even national security problems for the U.S. In a broader sense, there is a major risk of severe damage to world economic, political, and ecological systems and, as these systems begin to fail, to our humanitarian values.

20. The pace of internal migration from countryside to over-swollen cities is greatly intensified by rapid population growth. Enormous burdens are placed on LDC governments for public administration, sanitation, education, police, and other services, and urban slum dwellers (though apparently not recent migrants) may serve as a volatile, violent force which threatens political stability.

21. Adverse socio-economic conditions generated by these and related factors may contribute to high and increasing levels of child abandonment, juvenile delinquency, chronic and growing underemployment and unemployment, petty thievery, organized brigandry, food riots, separatist movements, communal massacres, revolutionary actions and counter-revolutionary coups. Such conditions also detract from the environment needed

to attract the foreign capital vital to increasing levels of economic growth in these areas. If these conditions result in expropriation of foreign interests, such action, from an economic viewpoint, is not in the best interests of either the investing country or the host government.

22. In international relations, population factors are crucial in, and often determinants of, violent conflicts in developing areas. Conflicts that are regarded in primarily political terms often have demographic roots. Recognition of these relationships appears crucial to any understanding or prevention of such hostilities.

General Goals and Requirements for Dealing with Rapid Population Growth

23. The central question for world population policy in the year 1974, is whether mankind is to remain on a track toward an ultimate population of 12 to 15 billion—implying a five to seven-fold increase in almost all the underdeveloped world outside of China—or whether (despite the momentum of population growth) it can be switched over to the course of earliest feasible population stability—implying ultimate totals of 8 to 9 billions and not more than a three or four-fold increase in any major region.

24. What are the stakes? We do not know whether technological developments will make it possible to feed over 8, much less 12 billion people in the 21st century. We cannot be entirely certain that climatic changes in the coming decade will not create great difficulties in feeding a growing population, especially people in the LDCs who live under increasingly marginal and more vulnerable conditions. There exists at least the possibility that present developments point toward Malthusian conditions for many regions of the world.

25. But even if survival for these much larger numbers is possible, it will in all likelihood be bare survival, with all efforts going in the good years to provide minimum nutrition, and utter dependence in the bad years on emergency rescue efforts from the less populated and richer countries of the world. In the shorter run—between now and the year 2000—the difference between the two courses can be some perceptible material gain in the crowded poor regions, and some improvement in the rel-

ative distribution of intra-country per capita income between rich and poor, as against permanent poverty and the widening of income gaps. A much more vigorous effort to slow population growth can also mean a very great difference between enormous tragedies of malnutrition and starvation as against only serious chronic conditions.

Policy Recommendations

26. There is no single approach which will "solve" the population problem. The complex social and economic factors involved call for a comprehensive strategy with both bilateral and multilateral elements. At the same time actions and programs must be tailored to specific countries and groups. Above all, LDCs themselves must play the most important role to achieve success.

27. Coordination among the bilateral donors and multilateral organizations is vital to any effort to moderate population growth. Each kind of effort will be needed for worldwide results. ...

29. While specific goals in this area are difficult to state, our aim should be for the world to achieve a replacement level of fertility (a two-child family on the average) by about the year 2000. This will require the present 2 percent growth rate to decline to 1.7 percent within a decade and to 1.1 percent by 2000. Compared to the U.N. medium projection, this goal would result in 500 million fewer people in 2000 and about 3 billion fewer in 2050. Attainment of this goal will require greatly intensified population programs. A basis for developing national population growth control targets to achieve this world target is contained in the World Population Plan of Action.

30. The World Population Plan of Action is not self-enforcing and will require vigorous efforts by interested countries, U.N. agencies and other international bodies to make it effective. U.S. leadership is essential. The strategy must include the following elements and actions:

... Concentration on key countries. Assistance for population moderation should give primary emphasis to the largest and fastest growing developing countries where there is special U.S. political and strategic interest. Those countries are: India, Bangladesh, Pakistan, Nigeria, Mexico, Indonesia, Brazil, the Philippines, Thailand, Egypt, Turkey, Ethiopia and Colombia.

Together, they account for 47 percent of the world's current population increase. ...

For its own merits and consistent with the recommendations of the World Population Plan of Action, priority should be given in the general aid program to selective development policies in sectors offering the greatest promise of increased motivation for smaller family size. In many cases pilot programs and experimental research will be needed as guidance for later efforts on a larger scale. The preferential sectors include:

- Providing minimal levels of education, especially for women;
- Reducing infant mortality, including through simple low-cost health care networks;
- Expanding wage employment, especially for women;
- Developing alternatives to children as a source of old age security;
- Increasing income of the poorest, especially in rural areas, including providing privately owned farms;
- Education of new generations on the desirability of smaller families. ...

Global Trends 2015: A Dialogue about the Future with Nongovernment Experts (2000)

In the fall of 1999, the U.S. intelligence community undertook a year-long series of consultations with experts in and out of government, to try to envision the major forces that would shape the world of 2015. Workshops and conferences were held. A report was drafted, widely reviewed, and, on December 18, 2000, released. (In a departure from normal intelligence-community practice, the report was posted on the CIA's website!) In some ways, Global Trends 2015 (GT-2015) is comparable to NSSM 200 (1974), although now population is viewed as just one of the "drivers" likely to affect global stability and U.S. interests in 2015.

Over the past 15 months, the National Intelligence Council (NIC), in close collaboration with US Government specialists and a wide range of experts outside the government, has worked to identify major drivers and trends that will shape the world of 2015.

The key drivers identified are: (1) Demographics, (2) Natural resources and environment, (3) Science and technology, (4) The global economy and globalization, (5) National and international governance, (6) Future conflict, (7) The role of the United States.

Demographics

World population in 2015 will be 7.2 billion, up from 6.1 billion in the year 2000, and in most countries, people will live longer. Ninety-five percent of the increase will be in developing countries, nearly all in rapidly expanding urban areas. Where political systems are brittle, the combination of population growth and urbanization will foster instability. Increasing lifespans will have significantly divergent impacts.

- In the advanced economies—and a growing number of emerging market countries—declining birthrates and aging will combine to increase health care and pension costs while reducing the relative size of the working population, straining the social contract, and leaving significant shortfalls in the size and capacity of the work force.
- In some developing countries, these same trends will combine to expand the size of the working population and reduce the youth bulge—increasing the potential for economic growth and political stability. ...

Population Trends

The world in 2015 will be populated by some 7.2 billion people, up from 6.1 billion in the year 2000. The rate of world population growth, however, will have diminished from 1.7 percent annually in 1985, to 1.3 percent today, to approximately 1 percent in 2015.

Increased life expectancy and falling fertility rates will contribute to a shift toward an aging population in high-income developed countries. Beyond that, demographic trends will sharply diverge. More than 95 percent of the increase in world population will be found in developing countries, nearly all in rapidly expanding urban areas.

- India's population will grow from 900 million to more than 1.2 billion by 2015; Pakistan's probably will swell from 140 million now to about 195 million.
- Some countries in Africa with high rates of AIDS will experience reduced population growth or even declining populations despite relatively high birthrates. In South Africa, for example, the population is projected to drop from 43.4 million in 2000 to 38.7 million in 2015.
- Russia and many post-Communist countries of Eastern Europe will have declining populations. As a result of high mortality and low birthrates, Russia's population may drop from its current 146 million to as low as 130 to 135 million in 2015, while the neighboring states of Central Asia will experience continued population growth. In Japan and West European countries such as Italy and Spain, populations also will decline in the absence of dramatic increases in birthrates or immigration.
- North America, Australia, and New Zealand, the traditional magnets for migrants, will continue to have the highest rates of population growth among the developed countries, with annual population growth rates between 0.7 percent and 1.0 percent.

Divergent Aging Patterns

In developed countries and many of the more advanced developing countries, the declining ratio of working people to retirees will strain social services, pensions, and health systems. Governments will seek to mitigate the problem through such measures as delaying retirement, encouraging greater participation in the work force by women, and relying on migrant workers. Dealing effectively with declining dependency ratios is likely to require more extensive measures than most governments will be prepared to undertake. The shift towards a greater proportion of older voters will change the political dynamics in these countries in ways difficult to foresee.

At the same time, "youth bulges" will persist in some developing countries, notably in Sub-Saharan Africa and a few countries in Latin America and the Middle East. A high proportion of young people will be destabilizing, particularly when combined with high unemployment or communal tension. ...

Movement of People

Two major trends in the movement of people will characterize the next 15 years—urbanization and cross-border migration—each of which poses both opportunities and challenges.

Growth in Mega-Cities

The ratio of urban to rural dwellers is steadily increasing. By 2015 more than half of the world's population will be urban. The number of people living in mega-cities—those containing more than 10 million inhabitants—will double to more than 400 million.

- Urbanization will provide many countries the opportunity to tap the information revolution and other technological advances.
- The explosive growth of cities in developing countries will test the capacity of governments to stimulate the investment required to generate jobs and to provide the services, infrastructure, and social supports necessary to sustain livable and stable environments.

[Migration]

Divergent demographic trends, the globalization of labor markets, and political instability and conflict will fuel a dramatic increase in the global movement of people through 2015. Legal and illegal migrants now account for more than 15 percent of the population in more than 50 countries. These numbers will grow substantially and will increase social and political tension and perhaps alter national identities even as they contribute to demographic and economic dynamism.

States will face increasing difficulty in managing migration pressures and flows, which will number several million people annually. Over the next 15 years, migrants will seek to move:

- To North America primarily from Latin America and East and South Asia.

- To Europe primarily from North Africa and the Middle East, South Asia, and the post-Communist states of Eastern Europe and Eurasia.
- From the least to the most developed countries of Asia, Latin America, the Middle East, and Sub-Saharan Africa.

For high-income receiving countries, migration will relieve labor shortages and otherwise ensure continuing economic vitality. EU countries and Japan will need large numbers of new workers because of aging populations and low birthrates. Immigration will complicate political and social integration: some political parties will continue to mobilize popular sentiment against migrants, protesting the strain on social services and the difficulties in assimilation. European countries and Japan will face difficult dilemmas in seeking to reconcile protection of national borders and cultural identity with the need to address growing demographic and labor market imbalances.

For low-income receiving countries, mass migration resulting from civil conflict, natural disasters, or economic crises will strain local infrastructures, upset ethnic balances, and spark ethnic conflict. Illegal migration will become a more contentious issue between and among governments.

For low-income sending countries, mass migration will relieve pressures from unemployed and underemployed workers and generate significant remittances. Migrants will function as ethnic lobbies on behalf of sending-country interests, sometimes supporting armed conflicts in their home countries, as in the cases of the Albanian, Kurdish, Tamil, Armenian, Eritrean, and Ethiopian diasporas. At the same time, emigration increasingly will deprive low-income sending countries of their educated elites. An estimated 1.5 million skilled expatriates from developing countries already are employed in high-income countries. This brain drain from low-income to high-income countries is likely to intensify over the next 15 years. ...

Food

Driven by advances in agricultural technologies, world food grain production and stocks in 2015 will be adequate to meet the needs of a growing world population. Despite the overall adequacy of food, problems of distribution and availability will remain.

- The number of chronically malnourished people in conflict-ridden Sub-Saharan Africa will increase by more than 20 percent over the next 15 years.
- The potential for famine will still exist where the combination of repressive government or internal conflict and persistent natural disasters prevents or limits relief efforts, as in Somalia in the early 1990s and North Korea more recently.
- Donors will become more reluctant to provide relief when the effort might become embroiled in military conflict. ...

Major Regions

The following snapshots of individual regions result from our assessment of trends and from estimates by regional experts as to where specific nations will be in 15 years. To make these judgments, we have distilled the views expressed by many outside experts in our conferences and workshops. The results are intended to stimulate debate, not to endorse one view over another. ...

Although population growth rates in *South Asia* will decline, population still will grow by nearly 30 percent by 2015. India's population alone will grow to more than 1.2 billion. Pakistan's projected growth from 140 million to about 195 million in 2015 will put a major strain on an economy already unable to meet the basic needs of the current population. The percentage of urban dwellers will climb steadily from the current 25–30 percent of the population to between 40–50 percent, leading to continued deterioration in the overall quality of urban life. Differential population growth patterns will exacerbate inequalities in wealth. Ties between provincial and central governments throughout the region will be strained. ...

Demographic pressures also will affect the economic performance and political cohesiveness of [*Russia and Eurasia*]. Because of low birthrates and falling life expectancy among males, the populations of the Slavic core and much of the Caucasus will continue to decline; Russian experts predict that the country's population could fall from 146 million at present to 130–135 million by 2015. At the other end of the spectrum, the Central Asian countries will face a growing youth cohort that will peak around 2010 before resuming a more gradual pattern of population growth. ...

A key driver for the *Middle East* over the next 15 years will be demographic pressures, specifically how to provide jobs, housing, public services, and subsidies for rapidly growing and increasingly urban populations. By 2015, in much of the Middle East populations will be significantly larger, poorer, more urban, and more disillusioned. In nearly all Middle Eastern countries, more than half the population is now under 20 years of age. These populations will continue to have very large youth cohorts through 2015, with the labor force growing at an average rate of 3.1 percent per year. The problem of job placement is compounded by weak educational systems producing a generation lacking the technical and problem-solving skills required for economic growth. ...

The interplay of demographics and disease—as well as poor governance—will be the major determinants of *Africa's* increasing international marginalization in 2015. Most African states will miss out on the economic growth engendered elsewhere by globalization and by scientific and technological advances. Only a few countries will do better, while a handful of states will have hardly any relevance to the lives of their citizens. As Sub-Saharan Africa's multiple and interconnected problems are compounded, ethnic and communal tensions will intensify, periodically escalating into open conflict, often spreading across borders and sometimes spawning secessionist states. ...

The aging of the population and low birthrates will be major challenges to *European* prosperity and cohesion. Greater percentages of state budgets will have to be allocated to the aging, while, at the same time, there will be significant, chronic shortages both of highly skilled workers in IT and other professions and unskilled workers in basic services. Legal and illegal immigration will mitigate labor shortages to a limited extent but at a cost in terms of social friction and crime. As EU governments grapple with immigration policy and European and national identity, anti-immigrant sentiment will figure more prominently in the political arena throughout Western Europe. ...

Latin America's demographics will shift markedly—to the distinct advantage of some countries—helping to ease social strains and underpin higher economic growth. During the next 15 years, most countries will experience a substantial slowdown in the number of new jobseekers, which will help reduce unemployment and boost wages. But not all countries will enjoy these shifts; Bolivia, Ecuador, Guatemala, Honduras, Nicaragua, and Paraguay will still face rapidly increasing populations in need of work. ...

Pressures for legal and illegal migration to the *United States* and regionally will rise during the next 15 years. Demographic factors, political instability, personal insecurity, poverty, wage differentials, the growth of alien-smuggling networks, and wider family ties will propel more Latin American workers to enter the United States. El Salvador, Guatemala, Honduras, and Nicaragua will become even greater sources of illegal migrants. In Mexico, declining population growth and strong economic prospects will gradually diminish pressures to seek work in the United States, but disparities in living standards, US demand for labor, and family ties will remain strong pull factors. Significant political instability during a transition process in Cuba could lead to mass migration.

- The growth of Central American and Mexican alien-smuggling networks will exacerbate problems along the US border.

World Population Estimates and Projections (1998)

The next two documents present recent UN estimates of where world population is headed in the twenty-first and twenty-second centuries. First, we have an excerpt from *Briefing Packet: World Population Estimates and Projections, 1998 Revision,* which was posted on the Internet in advance of the publication of the official *World Population Prospects* for 1998. It summarizes key findings from that report, including the high-, medium-, and low-variant estimates of world population for 2050, as well as specific projections for the most populous countries in 2050, and details on the demographic impact AIDS will have in coming decades.

... Between 1995 and 2000 the world population is growing at 1.33 percent per year, adding an average of 78 million persons each year. In the mid 21st century world population will be in the range of 7.3 to 10.7 billion, depending on the assumed future fertility trends. In the medium variant, the world population reaches 8.9 billion in 2050. ...

The mid-1998 world population stood at 5,901 million, with 4,719 million (80 per cent) in the less developed regions and 1,182 million (20 per cent) in the more developed regions. Asia accounted for 3,585 million, i.e., 61 per cent of the world total. During the last two years, Africa's population (749 million in 1998) became larger than Europe's (729 million). The population of Latin America and the Caribbean is estimated at 504 million, and that of Northern America at 305 million.

The world population is growing at 1.33 per cent per year between 1995 and 2000, which is significantly less than the peak growth rate of 2.04 per cent in 1965–1970, and less than the rate of 1.46 per cent in 1990–1995. The annual population increment also declined from its peak of 86 million in 1985–1990 to the current 78 million. It will further decline gradually to 64 million in 2015–2020, and then sharply to 30 million in 2045–2050.

In the medium-fertility variant, it is projected that the annual population growth rate will continue declining from 1.33 per cent in 1995–2000 to 0.34 per cent in 2045–2050. From 1804, when the world passed the 1 billion mark, it took 123 years to reach 2 billion people in 1927, 33 years to attain 3 billion in 1960, 14 years to reach 4 billion in 1974, 13 years to attain 5 billion in 1987 and 12 years to reach 6 billion in 1999. It will take 14 years to reach 7 billion in 2013, 15 years to reach 8 billion in 2028, and, with the slowing down of population growth, it will take 26 years to reach 9 billion, in 2054.

According to the high-fertility variant, the annual population growth rate will decrease more slowly, reaching 0.87 per cent per year in 2045–2050. The low-fertility variant results in a rapid decline of annual rate of population change, to a negative value of –0.23 per cent per year in the middle of the 21st century. The population in 2050 will be 10.7 billion according to the high variant and 7.3 billion according to the low variant.

Ninety-seven per cent of the world population increase takes place in the less developed regions. Every year the population of Asia is increasing by 50 million, the population of Africa by 17 million, and that of Latin America and the Caribbean by nearly 8 million. Africa has the highest growth rate among all major areas (2.36 per cent). Middle Africa, Eastern Africa and Western Africa have growth rates of 2.5 per cent and over. Europe, on the other hand, has the lowest growth rate

(0.03 per cent), with a negative rate of –0.2 per cent in Eastern Europe.

Sixty per cent of the world population increase is contributed by only 10 countries, with 21 per cent contributed by India and 15 per cent by China (see Table 5.1).

TABLE 5.1
Top Ten Contributors to World Population Growth, 1995–2000
(net annual additions in thousands)

No.	Country	Net addition	Percent	Cumulative percent
1	India	15,999	20.6	20.6
2	China	11,408	14.7	35.3
3	Pakistan	4,048	5.2	40.5
4	Indonesia	2,929	3.8	44.2
5	Nigeria	2,511	3.2	47.5
6	United States	2,267	2.9	50.4
7	Brazil	2,154	2.8	53.1
8	Bangladesh	2,108	2.7	55.9
9	Mexico	1,547	2.0	57.9
10	Philippines	1,522	2.0	59.8
	Subtotal	46,494	59.8	59.8
	World total	77,738	100.0	100.0

Source: United Nations Population Division of the Department of Economic and Social Affairs of the United Nations Secretariat. 1999. *World Population Prospects: The 1998 Revision,* vol. 1, *Comprehensive Tables.* New York: United Nations.

Currently 2 out of 5 people in the world live in either China (1,256 million) or India (982 million). There are eight other countries with a population over 100 million: the United States of America, Indonesia, Brazil, Pakistan, Russian Federation, Japan, Bangladesh and Nigeria. According to the medium-fertility variant projection, by the year 2050 eight additional countries will have exceeded the 100 million mark: Ethiopia, the Democratic Republic of Congo, Mexico, Philippines, Viet Nam, Iran, Egypt and Turkey (see Table 5.2). The ranking will be somewhat different; India will then be the most populated country (1,529 million) followed by China (1,478 million), the United States of America (349 million) and Pakistan (346 million).

According to the medium variant, by 2045–2050, 56 countries will experience a negative population growth, including all European countries, Japan and China. The population of the more developed regions as a group is expected to reach a peak

TABLE 5.2
Countries with a Population over 100 Million, 1998 and 2050
(population in millions, medium variant)

	1998				2050	
1	China	1,256		1	India	1,529
2	India	982		2	China	1,478
3	United States	274		3	United States	349
4	Indonesia	206		4	Pakistan	346
5	Brazil	166		5	Indonesia	312
6	Pakistan	148		6	Nigeria	244
7	Russian Federation	147		7	Brazil	244
8	Japan	126		8	Bangladesh	213
9	Bangladesh	125		9	Ethiopia	170
10	Nigeria	106		10	Democratic Republic of Congo	160
				11	Mexico	147
				12	Philippines	131
				13	Viet Nam	127
				14	Russian Federation	122
				15	Iran	115
				16	Egypt	115
				17	Japan	105
				18	Turkey	101

Source: United Nations Population Division of the Department of Economic and Social Affairs of the United Nations Secretariat. 1999. *World Population Prospects: The 1998 Revision,* vol. 1, *Comprehensive Tables.* New York: United Nations.

of 1,617 million in 2020, then it will start a gradual decline and by 2050 will be 2 per cent smaller than in 1998. By contrast, the population of the less developed regions will increase by 64 per cent, from 4,719 million in 1998 to 7,754 million in 2050. The fastest population growth will take place in Africa: its population will more than double during the first half of the 21st century; and Africa's share in the world population growth will increase from the current 22 per cent to 55 per cent in 2045–2050.

Different demographic growth rates lead to a redistribution of the world population among major geographic areas and groups of countries. While in 1950, Europe and North America accounted for 28.5 per cent of the world population, their share of the world total decreased to 17.5 in 1998, and it will further decline to 11.5 per cent in 2050. Conversely, the world population share of Africa increased from 8.8 per cent in 1950 to 12.7 per cent in 1988 and is projected to reach 19.8 per cent in 2050.

The shares of Asia and Latin America are relatively more stable at approximately 60 and 10 per cent, respectively. All projection variants yield similar results with respect to the distribution of the world population (see Table 5.3).

TABLE 5.3
Population of the Major Regions of the World, 1950, 1998, and 2050
(population in millions, medium variant)

	1950	1998	2050
World	2,521	5,901	8,909
More developed regions	813	1,182	1,155
Less developed regions	1,709	4,719	7,754
Africa	221	749	1,766
Asia	1,402	3,585	5,268
Europe	547	729	628
Latin America and Caribbean	167	504	809
North America	172	305	392
Oceania	13	30	46

Source: United Nations Population Division of the Department of Economic and Social Affairs of the United Nations Secretariat. 1999. *World Population Prospects: The 1998 Revision,* vol. 1, *Comprehensive Tables.* New York: United Nations.

The United Nations Population Division considered the demographic impact of AIDS in 34 countries with a population of at least 1 million and an adult HIV prevalence of 2 per cent or more, or with very large infected adult populations. Among these countries, 29 are in Sub-Saharan Africa, three are in Asia (Cambodia, India and Thailand) and two in Latin America and the Caribbean (Brazil and Haiti). Of the 30 million persons currently infected by HIV in the world, 26 million (85 per cent) reside in these 34 countries.

The *1998 Revision* shows a devastating toll from AIDS with respect to mortality and population loss. In the 29 African countries in which the impact of AIDS was studied, life expectancy at birth is projected to decrease to 47 years in 1995–2000 whereas it would have expected to have reached 54 years, in the absence of the AIDS epidemic, a loss of 7 years. The demographic impact of AIDS is even more dramatic when one focuses on the hardest hit countries, for example the 9 countries with an adult HIV prevalence of 10 per cent or more: Botswana, Kenya, Malawi, Mozambique, Namibia, Rwanda, South Africa, Zambia and Zimbabwe. In these countries the average life expectancy at birth is estimated to reach 48 years in 1995–2000 whereas it would have been expected to reach 58 years in the absence of AIDS, a loss of 10 years. By 2010–2015, the average life expectancy at birth in these countries is projected to reach only 47 years, instead of 64 years in the absence of AIDS: 17 years of life expectancy lost to AIDS.

Even in the worst cases, the toll of AIDS is not expected to lead to declines of population, because fertility in these countries is high. In the hardest-hit country, Botswana, with an adult HIV/AIDS prevalence of 25 per cent, the population in 2025 is expected to be 23 per cent smaller than what it would have been in the absence of AIDS. Nevertheless, the population is still expected to nearly double between 1995 and 2050.

According to the *1998 Revision*, 61 countries of the world exhibit a total fertility rate (TFR) in 1995–2000 at or below the level of 2.1 children per woman, which is the level necessary for the replacement of generations. The combined population of those 61 countries (2.6 billion in 1998) amounts to 44 per cent of the global population.

In practically all countries of the more developed regions, fertility is currently significantly below 2.1. In 20 of these countries the TFR has stayed at below-replacement level for more than two decades. In the 1980s–1990s fertility has decreased to levels below replacement in several countries from the less developed regions, including all countries in the populous region of Eastern Asia (except Mongolia). Consequently, in its medium variant, the *1998 Revision* assumes that fertility in these countries will not return to replacement level within the time horizon of the projections, i.e., until 2050.

The *1998 Revision* for the first time presents estimated and projected numbers of octogenarians, nonagenarians and centenarians, for all countries of the world. In 1998, 66 million persons were aged 80 or over, that is, about 1 of every 100 persons. That proportion was 5 times higher in the more developed regions than in the less developed regions (3.0 versus 0.6 per cent). Among them, 6.4 million were aged 90 years or over, and about 135 thousand are estimated to be aged 100 or over. The population aged 80 or over is projected to increase almost 6-fold and reach 370 million in 2050. The number of centenarians is projected to increase 16-fold to reach 2.2 million.

As a result of the combined effects of the decrease in fertility and the increase in life expectancy, the population of the world is becoming older, with a diminishing proportion of children, aged less than 15 years, and an increase of older persons, aged 60 or over. Overall in the world there are still three times as many children (30 per cent) as older persons (10 per cent).

However, in the more developed regions, in 1998 the number of older persons exceeded that of children for the first time. Italy has the oldest population, with 60 per cent more older persons than children. Greece, Japan, Spain and Germany have between 50 per cent and 40 per cent more older persons than children. By the year 2050, in the medium variant, in the more developed regions there will be more than twice as many older persons as children.

In the less developed regions, the proportion of older persons will increase from 8 to 21 per cent between 1998 and 2050, while that of children will decrease from 33 to 20 per cent. For the world as a whole, the proportion aged 60 or over will increase from the current 10 per cent to 22 per cent in 2050, while the proportion aged less than 15 will decrease from 30 per cent to 20 per cent. By the year 2050, there will be more older persons than children in the world.

UN Long-Range World Population Projections (1998)

No demographer is going to stake his or her reputation on the accuracy of population projections extending 150 years into the future. At the same time, most people will admit to being fascinated by the possibility of a global population in 2150 of 256 billion, or, at the low end of the range of estimates, just 3.2 billion (about half the current population). What becomes unmistakably clear in the truly long-range estimates that the United Nations generates periodically is that even small variations in fertility or mortality rates can, over the long run, have an enormous impact on national or world population levels.

The long-range projections prepared by the United Nations Population Division include several scenarios of population growth for the world and its major areas over the period 1995–2150. The *medium scenario* assumes that fertility in all major areas stabilizes at replacement level around 2050; the *low scenario* assumes that fertility is half a child lower than in the medium scenario; and the *high scenario* assumes that fertility is half a child higher than in the medium scenario. The *constant scenario* maintains fertility constant during 1995–2150 at the level estimated for 1990–1995, and the *instant-replacement scenario* makes fertility drop instantly to replacement level in 1995 and remain at that level thereafter. The key findings yielded by these projection scenarios are the following:

World population rises from 5.7 billion persons in 1995 to 9.7 billion persons in 2150 according to the medium scenario and, assuming that fertility remains at replacement level thereafter, world population nearly stabilizes at a level just above 10 billion after 2200.

Future population size is sensitive to small but sustained deviations of fertility from replacement level. Thus, the low scenario results in a declining population that reaches 3.2 billion in 2150 and the high scenario leads to a growing population that rises to 24.8 billion by 2150.

If the fertility of major areas is kept constant at 1995 levels, the world population soars to 256 billion by 2150, 169 billion of whom live in Africa.

If fertility remains at replacement level starting in 1995, the world population rises from 5.7 billion persons in 1995 to 9.3 billion persons in 2150, 400 million less than according to the medium scenario.

All scenarios result in significant shifts in the geographical distribution of the world population. According to the medium scenario, the share of Africa doubles (passing from 12 per cent of the world population in 1995 to 24 per cent in 2150), whereas that of China is reduced by a third (from 22 per cent in 1995 to 14 per cent in 2150) and that of Europe by more than half (from 13 per cent to 5 per cent).

By 2150 in the medium scenario about a third of the world population lives in China and India; about a quarter in the rest of Asia; another quarter in Africa; less than one in ten persons live in Europe and North America; and about the same proportion live in Latin America and the Caribbean.

The low, medium and high scenarios all result in significant shifts of the age distribution toward older ages. According to the medium scenario, the share of persons aged 0–14 declines from 30 per cent in 1995 to 18 per cent in 2150, whereas the share of persons aged 60 or over rises from 10 per cent to 30 per cent over the same period.

Increasing longevity is expected to have a moderate impact on population increase over the long-term. If longevity does not increase after 2050, the world population reaches 8.6 billion by 2150 instead of the 9.7 billion reached under the assumption of declining mortality in the medium scenario.

Census Bureau Projects Doubling of Nation's Population by 2100

Like the United Nations, the United States issues long-range population projections. Before January 2000, however, the Census Bureau had never projected U.S. population levels to the end of the twenty-first century. Advocates for population stabilization cannot be encouraged by what the Census Bureau foresees, as detailed in this press release of January 13, 2000: the "middle" or maximum-likelihood forecast puts U.S. population in one hundred years at 571 million, or about *twice* the current population.

The nation's resident population could more than double in this century, according to national population projections to the year 2100 released today by the Commerce Department's Census Bureau.

According to the projections, the nation's resident population, 273 million on July 1, 1999, is projected to reach 404 million in 2050 and 571 million in 2100. These results are based on middle-level assumptions regarding population growth during the century.

"Even though childbearing levels in the United States remain quite close to the level needed only to replace the population, the increasing number of potential parents and continued migration from abroad would be sufficient to add nearly 300 million people during the next century," said Census Bureau analyst Frederick W. Hollmann. "Because the Hispanic and Asian and Pacific Islander populations in the U.S. are younger than the nation as a whole and because they continue to receive international migrants, these populations will become increasingly prominent."

The data also show lowest and highest alternative projections. The lowest series projects population growth to 314 million in 2050 and then a decline to 283 million in 2100. The highest projects 553 million people in 2050 and 1.2 billion in 2100.

The projections do not take into account possible future changes in the way people report their race and ethnicity and, because of the length of time covered and other uncertainties, they are considered less reliable for the latter part of the century.

According to the middle series projections, the Hispanic population (of any race) would triple from 31.4 million in 1999 to 98.2 million in 2050. By 2005, Hispanics may become the nation's largest minority group. The percentage of Hispanics in the total population could rise from 12 percent in 1999 to 24 percent in 2050.

The Asian and Pacific Islander population, meanwhile, would more than triple, from 10.9 million in 1999 to 37.6 million in 2050. Its percentage of the total population would rise from 4 percent now to 9 percent in 2050.

According to the projections, the non-Hispanic White and African-American populations would increase more slowly than the other groups. The non-Hispanic White population would rise from 196.1 million in 1999 to 213.0 million in 2050, a 9 percent increase. Its share of the total population would decline, however, from 72 percent in 1999 to 53 percent in 2050.

The African-American population, according to the projections, would rise from 34.9 million in 1999 to 59.2 million in 2050, a 70-percent increase; under this scenario, the African-American share of the total population would increase slightly, from 13 percent to 15 percent.

Between 1999 and 2050, the total number of foreign-born would more than double, increasing from 26.0 million to 53.8 million. The proportion of the nation's population that is foreign-born may rise from 10 percent in 1999 to 13 percent in 2050.

The population age 65 and over would grow from 34.6 million in 1999 to 82.0 million in 2050, a 137 percent increase. The projections also show an especially rapid surge in the elderly population as the surviving "baby boomers" pass age 65; in the year 2011, baby boomers (those born between 1946 and 1964) will begin turning 65. Between 2011 and 2030, the number of elderly would rise from 40.4 million (13 percent of the population) to 70.3 million (20 percent of the population).

The projections show that the number of children under 18 would increase from 70.2 million in 1999 to 95.7 million in 2050. However, their share of the nation's population would decline slowly, falling from 26 percent in 1999 to 24 percent in 2050.

The projections are based on assumptions about future childbearing, mortality and migration. The level of childbearing among women for the middle series is assumed to remain close to present levels, with differences by race and Hispanic origin diminishing over time. Mortality is assumed to decline gradually with less variation by race and Hispanic origin than at present. International migration is assumed to vary over time and decrease generally relative to the size of the population.

This is the first time that the Census Bureau has projected the population to 2100 and the first time it includes information on the foreign-born population. The projections are presented by age, sex, race and Hispanic origin. ... (See Table 5.4.)

TABLE 5.4
Total U.S. Resident Population (millions): Middle,
Lowest, and Highest Series, 1999–2100

Year	Lowest	Middle	Highest
1999	272.7	272.8	273.0
2025	308.2	337.8	380.4
2050	313.5	403.7	552.8
2075	304.0	480.5	809.2
2100	282.7	571.0	1,182.4

Source: Population Projections Program, Population Division, U.S. Census Bureau.

HIV Epidemic Restructuring Africa's Population (October 31, 2000)

The grim effects of HIV/AIDS on the population of the continent most affected by the pandemic are detailed in this *Worldwatch Issue Alert*, No. 10, by Lester Brown. Although the realities of higher death rates and shortening life expectancies are undeniably bleak, there is some hope for the future in the successful AIDS-prevention programs of countries like Uganda and Zambia.

The HIV epidemic raging across Africa is a tragedy of epic proportions, one that is altering the region's demographic future. It is reducing life expectancy, raising mortality, lowering fertility, creating an excess of men over women, and leaving millions of orphans in its wake.

This year began with 24 million Africans infected with the virus. In the absence of a medical miracle, nearly all will die before 2010. Each day, 6,000 Africans die from AIDS. Each day, an additional 11,000 are infected.

The epidemic has proceeded much faster in some countries than in others. In Botswana, 36 percent of the adult population is HIV-positive. In Zimbabwe and Swaziland, the infection rate is 25 percent. Lesotho is at 24 percent. In Namibia, South Africa, and Zambia, the figure is 20 percent. In none of these countries has the spread of the virus been checked.

Life expectancy, a sentinel indicator of economic progress, is falling precipitously. In Zimbabwe, without AIDS, life expectancy in 2010 would be 70 years, but with AIDS, it is expected to fall below 35 years. Botswana's life expectancy is projected to fall from 66 years to 33 years by 2010. For South Africa, it will fall from 68 years to 48 years. And for Zambia, from 60 to 30 years. These life expectancies are more akin to those of the Middle Ages than of the modern age.

The demography of this epidemic is not well understood simply because, in contrast to most infectious diseases, which take their heaviest toll among the elderly and the very young, this virus takes its greatest toll among young adults. The effect on mortality is most easily understood. In the absence of a low-cost cure, infection leads to death. The time from infection until death for adults in Africa is estimated at 7 to 10 years.

This means that Botswana can expect to lose the 36 percent of its adult population that is HIV-positive within this decade, plus the additional numbers who will be infected within the next year or two. The HIV toll, plus normal deaths among adults, means that close to half of the adults in Botswana today will be dead by 2010. Other countries with high infection rates, such as South Africa, Swaziland, and Zimbabwe, will likely lose nearly a third of their adults by 2010.

Adults are not the only ones dying from AIDS. In Africa, infants of mothers who are HIV-positive have a 30 to 60 percent chance of being born with the virus. Their life expectancy is typically less than 2 years. Many more infants acquire the virus through breastfeeding. Few of them will reach school age.

Thus far, attention has focused on the effect of rising mortality on future population trends, but the virus also reduces fertility. Research is limited, but early evidence indicates that from the time of infection onward, fertility among infected women slowly declines. By the time symptoms of AIDS appear, women are 70 percent less likely to be pregnant than those who are not infected.

Females are infected at an earlier age than males because they have sexual relations with older men who are more likely to be HIV-positive. Female infection rates are also higher than those of males. Among 15- to 19-year-olds, five times as many females are infected as males. Because they are infected so early in life, many women will die before completing their reproductive years, further reducing births.

A demographically detailed study in Kisumu, Kenya, found that 8 percent of 15-year-old girls are HIV-positive. For 16-year-olds, the figure is 18 percent; and by age 19, it is 33 percent. Among the 19-year-olds, the average age of infection was roughly 17 years. With a life expectancy of perhaps nine years after infection, the average woman in this group will die at age 26, long before her child-bearing years are over.

Much work remains to be done in analyzing the effects of the HIV epidemic on fertility, but we do know that with other social traumas, such as famine, the effect of fertility decline on population size can equal the effect of rising mortality. For example, in the 1959–61 famine in China, some 30 million Chinese starved to death, but the actual reduction in China's population as a result of the famine was closer to 60 million.

The reasons are well understood. In a famished population, the level of sexual activity declines, many women stop ovulating, and even the women who do conceive often abort spontaneously. In a prolonged famine, the fall in births can contribute as much to the population decline as the rise in mortality. How much the HIV epidemic will eventually reduce fertility no one knows.

One thing is known: The wholesale death of young adults in Africa is creating millions of orphans. By 2010, Africa is expected to have 40 million orphans. Although Africa's extended family system is highly resilient and capable of caring for children left alone when parents die, it will be staggered by this challenge. There is a real possibility that millions of orphans will become street children, trying to survive by whatever means they can.

Africa is also facing a gender imbalance, a unique shortage of women. After wars, countries often face a severe shortage of males, as Russia did after World War II. This epidemic, however, is claiming more females than males in Africa, promising a future where men will outnumber women 11 to 9. This will leave many males either destined to bachelorhood or forced to migrate to countries outside the region in search of a wife.

The demographic effects of the HIV epidemic on Africa will be visible for generations to come. Until recently, the official projections at the United Nations indicated continuing population growth in all countries in Africa. Now this may be changing as the United Nations acknowledges that populations could decline in some countries. If the new U.N. biennial update of world population numbers and projections, due out before the end of this year, includes the full effect of the epidemic on fertility as well as on mortality, it will likely show future population declines for many African countries, including Botswana, Zimbabwe, South Africa, and Zambia.

There are many unknowns in the effects of the HIV epidemic on the demographic equation. Will health care systems, overwhelmed by AIDS victims, be able to meet the need for basic health care? How will the loss of so many adults in rural communities affect food security? What will be the effect on fertility of women surrounded by death? What will be the social effects of the missing generation of young adults unable to rear their children or to care for their parents?

Even though the HIV epidemic may claim more lives in Africa than World War II claimed worldwide, the epidemic is simply not being given the priority it deserves either within the countries most affected or within the international community. The challenge is to reduce the number of new infections as rapidly as possible. Nothing should deter societies from this goal.

One of the earliest countries hit by the epidemic, Uganda, has become a model for other countries as the infected share of its adult population has dropped from 14 percent in the early 1990s to 8 percent in 2000, a dramatic achievement. In Zambia, which has mobilized the health, education, agricultural, and industrial sectors, plus church groups, in the effort to curb the spread of the virus, the infected share of young females in some cities has dropped by nearly half since 1993. Zambia may soon turn the HIV tide. If all African countries can do what Uganda has done and what Zambia appears to be doing—namely, reduce the number of new infections below that of AIDS deaths—they may set the stage for ending this history-altering epidemic.

References

Brown, Lester R. 2000. "HIV Epidemic Restructuring Africa's Population." *Worldwatch Issue Alert No. 10* (October 31, 2000). Washington, DC: Worldwatch Institute.

Kendall, Henry. 1992. "World Scientists' Warning to Humanity." Cambridge, Mass.: Union of Concerned Scientists. Accessible at http://www.ucsusa.org/resources/warning.html.

Malthus, Thomas Robert. 1993 (1798). *An Essay on the Principle of Population*. Edited by Geoffrey Gilbert for Oxford World's Classics. New York: Oxford University Press.

Population Division of the Department of Economic and Social Affairs of the United Nations Secretariat. 2000. *Long-Range World Population Projections: Based on the 1998 Revision.*

Population Division of the Department of Economic and Social Affairs of the United Nations Secretariat. 1999. *World Population Prospects: The 1998 Revision,* vol. I, *Comprehensive Tables.*

Population Division of the Department of Economic and Social Affairs of the United Nations Secretariat. 1995. *Programme of Action Adopted at the International Conference on Population and Development, Cairo, 5–13 September 1994.*

Population Division of the Department of Economic and Social Affairs of the United Nations Secretariat. 1975. *World Population Plan of Action, Report of the United Nations World Population Conference, Bucharest, 19–20 August 1974.*

U.S. Bureau of the Census. 2000. "Census Bureau Projects Doubling of Nation's Population by 2100." Press release, January 13, 2000.

U.S. National Intelligence Council. 2000. *Global Trends 2015: A Dialogue about the Future with Nongovernment Experts.* Accessible at http://www.cia.gov/cia/publications/globaltrends2015/globaltrends2015.pdf.

U.S. National Security Council. 1974. *National Security Study Memorandum 200: Implications of Worldwide Population Growth for U.S. Security and Overseas Interests.* Washington, D.C. NSC classified document (declassified 7/3/89).

6

Directory of Organizations

Organizations, agencies, and institutes concerned with world population, either directly or indirectly, now number in the many hundreds. Virtually every country on Earth has a government agency or department charged with keeping an accurate count of its population, and that is just *one* of the ways governments are involved with population. At the same time there is a whole universe of private research institutes, advocacy organizations, university research centers, and international agencies with an interest in population. It would be impossible to list all such organizations in this chapter—and fortunately unnecessary, since most of those chosen for inclusion have on their websites a links feature that will quickly generate a large number of related websites. The usual caveat applies here: websites are not eternal. For various reasons they are sometimes relocated or renamed or simply disappear.

Carrying Capacity Network (CCN)
2000 P Street, NW, Suite 240
Washington, DC 20036
(202) 296-4548
Fax: (202) 296-4609
ccn@us.net
http://www.carryingcapacity.org

Carrying Capacity Network (CCN) is one of a number of advocacy organizations seeking to educate the public and influence policymakers in the direction of slower population growth. Most of the network's attention is focused on U.S. population. It has on its board of advisers the former senator Gaylord Nelson (an original sponsor of Earth Day in 1970), the biodiversity expert Thomas Lovejoy, and other environmental activists. CCN's mission statement declares its interest in "national revitalization, immigration reduction, economic sustainability, and resource conservation." Its strongest policy interest, however, seems to be immigration into the United States, which it considers to be excessive. (In stressing the substantial net costs of immigration, it relies heavily on studies done by Donald Huddle, an emeritus professor at Rice University.) CCN subscribes to the view, often associated with ecologist Paul Ehrlich, that citizens of the industrially advanced nations have a much more damaging impact, per capita, on the environment than those in less industrialized nations; hence the emphasis on slowing population growth in the United States.

Publications: CCN puts out a variety of studies and documents, all listed on its website. The *Carrying Capacity Briefing Book* is a veritable tome (2,500 pages!) that compiles scores of articles and op-ed pieces regarding population. A similar compilation, the *Immigration Briefing Book,* is also available for purchase. The "Network Bulletin" goes out to new members, giving them the latest information on U.S. population issues, while "Focus" carries longer, more scholarly articles. CCN also underwrites Carrying Capacity Research Issues Series that explores the costs of additional population and its impact on American quality of life.

Center for Migration Studies
209 Flagg Place
Staten Island, NY 10304-1199
Fax: (718) 667-4598
CMSFT@aol.com
http://www.cmsny.org

Founded in 1964 and incorporated in 1969, the Center for Migration Studies (CMS) is a nonprofit educational institute devoted to the study of all aspects of migration. It prides itself on taking an independent approach to the study of the demographic, political, economic, historical, and pastoral aspects of migration. (Currently being developed in association with CMS is the J. B. Scalabrini Pastoral Institute, the goal of which will be to meet the pastoral needs of immigrant newcomers to the United States.) The main but not exclusive focus of CMS is on immigration into the United States, and this includes the special needs of refugees. The center sponsors an annual National Legal Conference on Immigration and Refugee Policy in Washington, D.C.

Publications: CMS publishes the quarterly *International Migration Review*, considered to be the leading journal in the field; it covers all aspects of human mobility. Also published by CMS is a bimonthly magazine, *Migration World*, which is directed to those who are "socially and pastorally involved with immigrants and refugees." *In Defense of the Alien* makes available each year the proceedings of the conference mentioned above. A free biannual newsletter, *CMS Newsletter*, reports on recent or upcoming activities, publications, and conferences.

Federation for American Immigration Reform (FAIR)
1666 Connecticut Avenue, NW
Washington, DC 20009
(202) 328-7004
Fax: (202) 387-3447
info@fairus.org
http://www.fairus.org

The Federation for American Immigration Reform (FAIR) makes no bones about where it stands on immigration: it wants *less* of it. Given the importance of immigration to current and future levels of U.S. population, it makes sense to become acquainted with national organizations that have an interest in the issue. FAIR seeks to reduce and then eliminate illegal immigration; it would also have the United States cut legal immigration to more "reasonable" and "moderate" (although unspecified) levels. A nonprofit, nonpartisan organization with a nationwide membership of over 70,000, FAIR tries to influence public policy in various ways: running ads during political campaigns, testifying in Congress, making its spokespersons available for interviews in the media, doing grassroots organizing, and even litigating in court. The organization was founded in 1978. Its national advisory board includes former senator Eugene McCarthy, former Colorado governor Richard Lamm, and Paul and Anne Ehrlich.

Publications: FAIR circulates a monthly newsletter called *Immigration Report* to its members. (To others, the cost is $25 annually, but contents are downloadable from the website.) The more frequently updated "e-zine" called the *Stein Report*—FAIR's director is Dan Stein—offers current news stories and links to other relevant organizations and sites. Several immigration-related booklets are available, including the *Environmentalist's Guide to a Sensible Immigration Policy*. FAIR maintains a bulletin board at its website featuring items it thinks will interest visitors and giving them an opportunity to respond. Bear in mind, however, that FAIR makes no pretense of giving both sides of the issue: it is firmly opposed to the continuation of what it calls "mass migration" into the United States.

International Center for Migration, Ethnicity and Citizenship
65 Fifth Avenue, Room 230
New York, NY 10003
(212) 229-5399
Fax: (212) 989-0504
icmec@newschool.edu
http://www.newschool.edu/icmec

Founded in 1993 at the New School for Social Research (since renamed the New School University) in New York City, the International Center for Migration, Ethnicity and Citizenship is devoted to scholarly research on the causes of large-scale international migration and on the most appropriate policy responses. It provides a forum for debate and reflection on migration matters by scholars, public officials, journalists, and members of the NGO community. Although it takes a strong interest in the *causes* of heavy migration flows, such as the breakup of multiethnic societies and the instabilities attending the end of the Cold War, it is equally interested in the reception given newcomers in the host countries. The center's activities include sponsorship of seminars in New York City and Washington, D.C., the Refugee Forum held in New York City (jointly with several other organizations), a summer institute cohosted by the United States Information Agency, conferences and symposia on policy issues related to migration, ethnicity, and citizenship, and several e-mail discussion lists.

Publications: The center puts out a semiannual newsletter, *Epi-Center*, which reviews recent activities of the center and announces upcoming events. It also sponsors a series of working papers, which are abstracted online and can be ordered for a small fee.

International Organization for Migration
17 Route des Morillons
C.P. 71
CH-1211 Geneva 19
Switzerland
Phone: 41-22-7179111
Fax: 41-22-7986150
info@iom.int
http://www.iom.int

Demographers consider international migration an important part of the study of world population, and the International Organization for Migration (IOM), an international agency founded in 1953 (under an earlier name), dedicates itself to assisting refugees and internally displaced persons all over the world. By now it has helped 11 million people, including Indo-Chinese refugees, Kurds in northern Iraq, East Timorese refugees, and various populations displaced by the breakdown of the former Yugoslavia. Assistance can take the form of moving threatened people from their homeland to safer places abroad, repatriation of people who had earlier fled their homelands, or simply assistance to people who have lost food and shelter where they are, as in the case of the Honduran victims of Hurricane Mitch in 1998. Besides offering technical assistance to governments facing migration challenges, the IOM tries to advance the public's understanding of migration issues, encourage economic and social development through migration, and uphold the dignity and welfare of migrants. Its website offers online information on a variety of migration issues, such as trafficking in migrants, migrant rights, migration-relevant reports and resolutions of the United Nations, and reference information.

Publications: The IOM publishes a quarterly refereed journal, *International Migration*, which tackles both theoretical and empirical migration issues from the perspectives of economists, political scientists, demographers, sociologists, and others. Three other quarterly publications (essentially newsletters) are *Trafficking in Migrants, Migration and Health*, and *IOM News*. Twice a year the IOM puts out its *IOM Latin American Migration Journal* (English/Spanish). Finally, the IOM sponsors the publication of various books, surveys, and studies on migration that are listed on their website.

Negative Population Growth (NPG)
1717 Massachusetts Avenue, NW
Washington, DC 20036
(202) 667-8950
Fax: (202) 667-8953
npg@npg.org
http://www.npg.org

Negative Population Growth (NPG) calls itself "the leading voice in the population awareness movement." It is quite explicit about its long-term goal: to see the population of the United States *decline* to a level of 150 million, through voluntary incentives for smaller families and tighter immigration policies. Immigration, NPG believes, should be held to 100,000 annually—far below its current rate. With a smaller national population, ecosystems would be less strained, resources less depleted, and people's quality of life better. Headquartered in the nation's capital, NPG attempts to influence the political elite and shape public opinion. Its website features a population news listserve, a variety of NPG publications, population clocks for both the United States and the world, polling numbers for public attitudes about population, and links to other organizations concerned with population, immigration, and the environment.

Publications: NPG publishes a semiannual newsletter for its members (over 18,000), and at its website has a variety of special reports and position papers available for downloading.

Population Action International (PAI)
1300 19th Street, NW, Second Floor
Washington, DC 20036
(202) 557-3400
Fax: (202) 728-4177
pai@popact.org
http://www.populationaction.org

Population Action International (PAI) is a relatively small, privately funded organization that seeks to build public support for policies and programs that can slow population growth, particularly in developing countries. The policies advocated by PAI are generally in line with the program of action adopted by the International Conference on Population and Development (in Cairo, 1994), such as universal access to family-planning services, improved health care for women, and more gender equality. PAI lobbies Congress both directly and indirectly to enlarge U.S. funding of international population efforts; it also interacts with the United Nations and other international agencies on matters related to population. It arranges seminars, briefings, and roundtables, and maintains an informative website with links to like-minded organizations and downloadable policy briefs on various population issues. PAI was established in 1965 as the Population Crisis Committee. It is funded entirely by foundations (Rockefeller, Packard, Pew, Rasmussen, and others) and individuals.

Publications: PAI publishes a variety of fact sheets, occasional papers, wall charts, and books, all listed on their website.

Population Communications International (PCI)
777 United Nations Plaza
New York, NY 10017
(212) 687-3366
Fax: (212) 661-4188
pciny@population.org
http://www.population.org

Since 1985, Population Communications International (PCI) has been producing country-specific soap operas, both for radio and television, which convey messages of positive decision-making in regard to sex, reproductive health, gender roles, and family-planning. Decades ago, Albert Bandura, a psychologist at Stanford University, developed a theory of social learning that has become the basis for this ambitious approach to population policy. The overall purpose is to change behavior in ways that conform to the goals established at the Cairo conference in 1994 (International Conference on Population and Development). PCI works with local partner organizations on four continents to research and produce programs that are tailored to the specific cultural values of each country. It also helps evaluate, systematically, the impact of the programs. A recent five-year study found that, in Tanzania, people living in the areas to which a PCI radio drama was broadcast altered their sexual behavior in ways that were significantly helpful for HIV/AIDS prevention.

Publications: In 1998, PCI began offering a monthly online news digest, "Global Intersections," summarizing recent developments in the areas of population and development, sexual and reproductive health, and the environment. It is intended mainly for journalists, but would be of interest to educators as well.

Population Council
1 Dag Hammarskjold Plaza
New York, NY 10017
(212) 339-0500
Fax: (212) 755-6052
pubinfo@popcouncil.org
http://www.popcouncil.org

For almost half a century, the Population Council has funded and conducted research on reproductive health, fertility regulation, and family-planning. With a worldwide staff of almost 500 and an annual budget of over $75 million, it is an institution of global influence. In developing countries, it collaborates with governments and nongovernmental organizations to enhance the quality of family-planning programs. It sponsors research in over 40 developing countries, mainly in Africa and Asia, and maintains regional offices in Mexico City, Cairo, Dakar, Nairobi, and Bangkok. Through a program of awards, fellowships, training, and collaborations, it works to increase professional expertise in the developing nations. Although the Population Council sponsors and publishes research on family structure, gender relations, and other social-demographic issues, it is probably better known to the public for having developed the Norplant contraceptive device and several modern versions of the intrauterine device (IUD). In recent years it has stepped into a void left by the major U.S. pharmaceutical companies and sponsored the introduction of the so-called abortion pill RU 486. (The drug has recently become available to American women.) The council is also pursuing the development of other contraceptive techniques, such as patches and implants. External funding for the Population Council comes from governments, NGOs, corporations, individuals, and foundations. The council was founded in 1952 by John D. Rockefeller III.

Publications: Population Briefs is a quarterly research newsletter for population specialists, with coverage of demographic and reproductive news and updates on the achievements of council-sponsored programs. *Studies in Family Planning* is a peer-reviewed bimonthly journal with articles and commentary on family-planning programs in (mainly) Africa and Asia. *Population and Development Review* has been a leading quarterly journal of demography since 1975. Scholarly yet readable, it explores economic, political, and sociological aspects of population, present and past.

The Population Institute
107 Second Street, NE
Washington, DC 20002
(800) 787-0038
Fax: (202) 544-0068
web@populationinstitute.org
http://www.populationinstitute.org

The Population Institute, established in 1969 and long headed by Werner Fornos, advocates and educates on the subject of population. It seeks to provide leadership in raising awareness of the need for global population stabilization, whether in the classroom, in the press, or in Congress. It strongly supports U.S. assistance to international family-planning programs. Its own funding comes from foundations, corporations, and individuals, but not from the government. As part of its effort to heighten awareness of the population issue, the institute sponsors a variety of programs and campaigns, including its Educate America Campaign, World Population Awareness Week, Global Media Awards, Future Leaders of the World Program, and others. The Global Media Awards are given out annually to journals and journalists judged to have achieved excellence in their population reporting. The institute boasts a network of 100,000 volunteers who work to support its aims.

Publications: The Population Institute publishes POPLINE, a bimonthly newspaper covering developments in the population field. It goes out, at no charge, to legislators, the media, and advocates. Also issued by the institute is a Twenty-first Century Monograph series ($7.50 each) that focuses on the linkages between population and literacy, food, environment, health, and women's empowerment.

Population Reference Bureau
1875 Connecticut Avenue, NW, Suite 520
Washington, DC 20009
(202) 483-1100

Fax: (202) 328-3937
popref@prb.org
http://www.prb.org

Founded in 1929, the Population Reference Bureau (PRB) is the premier population organization in the United States, with a well-earned reputation for producing clear, accurate, and timely population information, both for the United States and the rest of the world. By describing itself as a "nonprofit, *nonadvocacy* organization" (emphasis added), PRB hints at one of the ways it differs from several other groups with the word "population" in their titles: it draws no policy conclusions from the data it presents. Nor does it do any lobbying to advance a political or social agenda. Its concern is only with the facts. Yet PRB is heavily committed to research, education, and outreach, abroad and at home. Its professional staff monitors and reports on trends in population and a range of social issues that are linked to population, such as crime, aging, the status of minorities, and the environment. PRB provides technical services to governments and nongovernmental organizations. It runs seminars, training courses, and briefings to assist various audiences in understanding population issues. It is a resource for the print and broadcast media, and its comprehensive library makes it a valuable resource for scholars and researchers as well. PRB has an active interest in education, making available a wide array of curricular materials to teachers, especially at the middle and high school levels.

Publications: PRB publishes the highly useful *World Population Data Sheet (WPDS)* in booklet or wall-poster format. For every country and region of the world the *WPDS* presents the most recent data on the birth rate, death rate, life expectancy, total fertility rate, population projections (to the years 2025 and 2050), and much more. The quarterly *Population Bulletin* covers various population topics in depth; they can be either U.S.-related or international in scope. *Population Today* is the PRB newsletter. *PRB Reports on America*, published quarterly, deals with important U.S. population issues and their impact on society.

Union of Concerned Scientists
2 Brattle Square
Cambridge, MA 02238
(617) 547-5552
Fax: (617) 864-9405

ucs@ucsusa.org
http://www.ucusa.org

The Union of Concerned Scientists (UCS) was founded at MIT in 1969 and now boasts a membership of scientists and concerned citizens in excess of 70,000. Its interests are broad, falling into five main categories: agriculture, arms control, energy, global resources, and transportation. The population issue comes under the heading of global resources. UCS believes that population growth can be linked to environmental degradation, including loss of biodiversity, global warming, and ozone depletion; it seeks to communicate the scientific basis of this belief not only to the public but to policymakers. In 1995 it established the Sound Science Initiative, under which participating scientists agreed to write op-ed pieces and letters to editors on current issues as they arose. In the population area, this has meant identifying and explaining population-environment linkages, as well as writing to members of Congress in opposition to cuts in U.S. funding of international family-planning efforts.

Publications: UCS's quarterly magazine *Nucleus* covers the full range of issues in which the organization takes an interest. At its website are several fact sheets and frequently asked questions relating to such topics as "population misperceptions," "population and environment," and "population policy." A few printed reports on population can be ordered from UCS.

United Nations Population Fund (UNFPA)
220 East 42nd Street
New York, NY 10017
(212) 297-5000
Fax: (212) 370-0201
hq@unfpa.org
http://www.unfpa.org

A UN agency created in 1969, the United Nations Population Fund (UNFPA) is the world's largest multilateral source of funding for family-planning programs. Its mission is to "support the right of couples and individuals to decide freely and responsibly the number and spacing of their children and to have the information and means to do so." That is its mandate under the Program of Action adopted in 1994 at the International Conference on Population and Development (ICPD), held in Cairo. The

UNFPA works toward the goals of lower maternal and child mortality, universal access to primary education for children of both sexes, and universal access to reproductive health care, especially for women. It offers technical and financial assistance to developing countries as they design and implement their own national population programs. UNFPA funding comes from contributions of governments that are separate from their normal UN dues. The United States was a key supporter of the UNFPA at its inception, but in recent years domestic political factors have made that support unpredictable. The United States made no contribution in 1999; in 2000, it contributed $25 million, well below earlier levels of support. Japan currently provides the most funding of any nation.

Publications: From 1978 onward, the annual *State of World Population* has presented in-depth reports on selected population issues, such as urbanization, population and the environment, and, in 1999, the "world of six billion." UNFPA also publishes two periodicals: the general-interest quarterly, *Populi*, with news, features, and analysis of population issues, and the bimonthly *Dispatches*, which summarizes recent UNFPA projects all over the world. Both periodicals are available in English, French, or Spanish, in paper copy or downloadable from the Internet.

United States Bureau of the Census
International Programs Center
Washington, DC 20233-8860
Fax: (301) 457-3033
ipc@census.gov
http://www.census.gov/ipc/www

Those who think the job of the U.S. Census Bureau is limited to counting Americans every ten years should think again. It is true that the bureau has long produced population estimates for virtually every locality in the United States, from the states and counties to metropolitan areas and Puerto Rican *municipios*. (It also produces tremendous quantities of data on U.S. income, poverty, health, and education.) But probably of most interest to those studying world population is the International Programs Center (IPC), where a wealth of demographic information on all the world's countries and regions can be obtained either in print or online. Much of this information is free; the rest is available at modest cost either from the bureau itself (Atlanta office) or from the Government Printing Office in Washington. At the heart of the IPC's data-gathering work is something called the International Data Base (IDB), a computerized data bank covering demographic and socioeconomic indicators for 227 countries and areas of the world. Online, one can tap into this statistical storehouse in creative ways, such as ordering up a customized table on infant mortality rates, male and female, in the less developed countries from 1985 to 2000. Information is also available on fertility rates, migration, marital status, family-planning, literacy, and labor force activity for most nations, and in many cases the data extend back to 1950. There is an option for downloading the data to one's own computer.

Publications: The IPC issues a multitude of technical reports and papers, many on an occasional basis, all indexed at their website. Their main publication, however, is the *World Population Profile*, which comes out biennially. The most recent is for 1998.

Worldwatch Institute
1776 Massachusetts Avenue, NW
Washington, DC 20036-1904
(202) 452-1999
Fax: (202) 296-7365
worldwatch@igc.apc.org

Worldwatch Institute is one of the best-known environmentalist organizations in the world, with population one of its abiding concerns. The continuing focus on population was underscored with the publication in 1999 of *Beyond Malthus: Nineteen Dimensions of the Population Challenge*, coauthored by the institute's founder and longtime president, Lester Brown. Worldwatch monitors a number of global environmental threats, from ozone depletion to agricultural topsoil erosion and the potential exhaustion of oceanic fish stocks. It sees its mission as one of providing such information and analysis, on a regular basis, in order to promote a more sustainable world economy. Its research findings, produced by a knowledgeable staff of 32, are highly readable and routinely find their way into mainstream media outlets. Worldwatch is supported financially by such foundations as Ford, Hewlett, MacArthur, Rockefeller, and Packard.

Publications: The institute's flagship publication is *State of the World*, published annually since 1984. Each year Worldwatch identifies and analyzes in depth ten issues of significance for a sustainable future. Another annual book published by World-watch is *Vital Signs,* which, since 1992, has laid out a variety of key trends for the economy and environment both graphically and in text. Other publications include the bimonthly magazine *World Watch,* a series of *Worldwatch Papers* (over 150 titles), and a number of environmental books, including the *Worldwatch Reader on Global Environmental Issues,* compiled from *World Watch* magazine. News briefs, press releases, and issue alerts also pour forth continuously from the institute.

Zero Population Growth (ZPG)
1400 16th Street, NW, Suite 320
Washington, DC 20036
(202) 332-2200; 1-800-POP-1956
Fax: (202) 332-2302
info@zpg.org
http://www.zpg.org

Zero Population Growth (ZPG) promotes the achievement of a sustainable balance between the planet's resources and its population. One of its founders in 1968 was Paul Ehrlich, author of *The Population Bomb.* As a nonprofit organization, ZPG advocates positions on a wide range of issues, from the global to the local. It lobbies Congress, engages in publicity campaigns, and provides curricular materials for schools at all levels. Its Campus Outreach Program arranges presentations and workshops on college campuses. The ZPG website offers many reports on population-related issues, including a Congressional Report Card.

Publications: The bimonthly *ZPG Reporter* covers various population matters in the news. The *Campus Activist Newsletter,* issued five times a year, is addressed to an audience of college-age activists. It features columns written by students. Both publications are downloadable from the ZPG website.

7

Print Resources

In the age of the Internet, one's first impulse in trying to get answers to population-related questions would be to go online. That is not necessarily a bad idea (see the websites listed in Chapter 8), but there are many *print* resources, too, which can provide quick answers to questions and sometimes much fuller explorations of issues than will be found at the typical website. A well-stocked university or public library ought to have most of the works listed below. They have been placed in two categories. In the first group are books that deal with one or more of the following: history, population policy, the optimistic ("cornucopian") and pessimistic ("doomsayer") viewpoints, immigration, and personal reflections on population issues. In the second category are works that generally are published on an annual or biennial schedule to reflect the latest population data. At this writing, all the books or booklets listed are in print; the ISBN numbers are for paperback editions whenever that is an option.

Monographs

Borjas, George J. *Heaven's Door: Immigration Policy and the American Economy.* Princeton, NJ: Princeton University Press, 1999. 263 pages. ISBN 0-691-05966-7.

This book has been much praised, and deservedly so, for the clarity it brings to the issue of U.S. immigration policy. Borjas, who as a boy in the early 1960s was a refugee from Castro's Cuba and who now teaches public policy at Harvard's Kennedy School of Government, takes a clear-eyed view of the costs and benefits of immigration to various concerned parties—native-born Americans, immigrants themselves, and those left behind in the sending countries. He insists that the facts about immigration, in themselves, tell us nothing about the direction in which we should go with policy. We must first answer some important questions about whose interests we rank highest and what kinds of changes we are willing to tolerate in the slicing of the economic pie as a result of immigration. Borjas argues that the current wave of immigrants (around a million a year) is massive enough that we are justified in calling this era the "Second Great Migration" in U.S. history. What troubles Borjas and others are the low education levels and skills of the recent arrivals, which intensify competition for low-skill, low-wage jobs in the United States and thus harm the least-skilled native workers. In its current pattern, he argues, immigration is tending to shift income away from native workers toward business owners and consumers. The kind of immigration reform he proposes would favor the entry of skilled workers, and lower the overall annual quota of immigration to about half a million.

Bouvier, Leon F., and Jane T. Bertrand. *World Population: Challenges for the Twenty-first Century.* Santa Ana, CA: Seven Locks Press, 1999. 214 pages. ISBN 0-929765-66-4.

The basic plan of this book is to review demographic patterns and shifts that occurred in the late twentieth century and then assess their probable impact on populations in the twenty-first century. But in execution the book turns out to be a loosely organized set of reflections and speculations on population, presented in a lively, engaging prose style, and tilted toward a U.S. readership. The authors, professors in the fields of demography and international health at Tulane University, are alert to the long-term consequences of low fertility in the developed nations and high fertility in the rest of the world. The most notable effect of this fertility differential will be mounting immigration pressure on the developed nations. (Bouvier has written on this before.) For the United States, the recommended policy is two-fold: first, resist the rising immigration pressures and hold the numbers of immigrants to more manageable, or assimilable, levels; and second, do what it takes to insure that those who immigrate are given the fullest opportunity to advance themselves socially and economically into the mainstream of American life. Encouraging lower birth rates in the developing countries is the other side of the policy. The authors strongly favor generous funding for such efforts.

Brown, Lester R., Gary Gardner, and Brian Halweil. *Beyond Malthus: Nineteen Dimensions of the Population Challenge.* New York: W. W. Norton, 1999. 167 pages. ISBN 0-393-31906-7.

The Worldwatch Institute has issued this study as the latest in its Environmental Alert Series. (Two earlier volumes in the series, also authored or coauthored by Lester Brown, sounded some of the same themes: *Full House* and *Who Will Feed China?*) Even though worldwide population growth has slowed, it has certainly not become a nonissue. In the years ahead, we can expect difficulties with each of the following dimensions of human well-being: grain production, fresh water supplies, biodiversity, energy, oceanic fish catches, meat production, infectious diseases, cropland acreage, forests, climate change, materials for construction and other uses, urbanization, protected wildlife areas, and waste disposal, as well as the more socially defined issues of jobs, housing, education, internal and international conflict, and income levels. An emerging concern, spelled out in the book's final and longest chapter, is that countries stressed by the effects of rapid population increase—what the authors call "demographic fatigue"—may slide backward into an earlier demographic stage, where mortality and fertility rates both remain at high levels. The HIV/AIDS epidemic is contributing in Africa to the worst cases of demographic fatigue. Given the long list of topics covered here, and the relatively short length of the book, truly in-depth analysis can hardly be expected. But important questions are raised, and for those who want to dig deeper, there are footnotes to be followed up.

Caplow, Theodore, Louis Hicks, and Ben J. Wattenberg. *The First Measured Century: An Illustrated Guide to Trends in America, 1900–2000.* Washington, DC: American Enterprise Institute Press, 2001. 308 pages. ISBN 0-84474138-8.

This book presents a host of demographic, economic, and social trends for the United States across the twentieth century using the format of a short essay on one page and a related graph on the facing page. Of the fifteen chapters, at least three are directly relevant to the study (or teaching) of U.S. population trends: population, family, and health. To give a sense of the breadth of coverage, the population chapter includes these topics: total population, population growth rate, life expectancy, changing age structure, centenarians, geographic distribution, urban-rural breakdown, national origins of immigrants, the proportion of foreign-born and minorities in the total U.S. population, and the ethnic composition of the ten largest U.S. cities. The book is a companion volume to the PBS documentary of the same title, although the authors stress that it "does not re-package the television program into a coffee-table picture book" (p. xiii). It includes far more information than could possibly be presented in a TV program, and in a much more retrievable form. A subject index and footnote section make the book even more useful. One of the authors, Ben J. Wattenberg of the American Enterprise Institute, has built a reputation as an acute observer of U.S. and world population trends. His 1987 book *The Birth Dearth* was one of the first efforts to outline the social and political consequences of declining fertility in the West.

Castles, Stephen, and Mark J. Miller. *The Age of Migration: International Population Movements in the Modern World.* New York: Guilford Press, 1993. 306 pages. ISBN 0-89862-248-4.

This book, by an Australian sociologist and an American political scientist, offers a good all-around treatment of the international migration process, stressing the way that migration creates (or enlarges) ethnic minorities in the countries of destination, and thus alters both the social and political dynamic within those countries. Other broad tendencies of recent years include the globalization and acceleration of migration: more and more countries are becoming involved, at higher rates of migratory flow. Also observable, say the authors, is a kind of flexibility of reasons for migrating, so that a particular flow, or "chain," that begins for one reason (say, for political asylum) can sustain itself for quite different reasons (economic advancement, for example, or family reunification). These reasons can greatly complicate the task of governments in formulating migration policy. There is a chapter on the history of international migration before 1945, another on migration since 1945, and an interesting chapter comparing the migration experiences of Germany and Australia. What does not get much attention here (nor in most books) is migration within the developing world.

Cohen, Joel. *How Many People Can the Earth Support?* New York: W. W. Norton, 1995. 532 pages. ISBN 0-393-03862-9.

This study of the Earth's carrying capacity has become a modern classic. Cohen tackles the title question with gusto but also with the care and precision of a man schooled in the rigors of the scientific method. He demonstrates that there are many ways to speculate about the maximum human population of our planet, and many ways to translate those speculations into hard numbers. Cohen has examined every approach thoroughly; his book is packed with data, graphs, analysis, and quotations. Yet he retains a healthy skepticism about the entire exercise, as evident in his "Law of Prediction," which states: "The more confidence someone places in an unconditional prediction of what will happen in human affairs, the less confidence you should place in that prediction" (p. 134). The key conclusion of the book is captured in the title of the penultimate chapter: "Entering the Zone." It opens with these sobering words: "The human population of the Earth now travels in the zone where a substantial fraction of scholars have estimated upper limits on human population size" (p. 367). It is unlikely that Cohen's work will be superseded any time soon.

Cook, Noble David. *Born to Die: Disease and New World Conquest (1492–1650).* Cambridge: Cambridge University Press, 1998. 272 pages. ISBN 0-521-62730-3.

One of the most interesting (if saddening) ways to learn about demographic processes is to study historical episodes of drastic population change. A particularly striking case, vividly rendered in *Born to Die*, is that of European contact with the indigenous peoples of the Western Hemisphere. Europeans arrived in waves, beginning in 1492, and made it clear wherever they went, from Hudson Bay to the southernmost tip of South America, that they intended to subdue local Amerindian populations—by force if necessary. But all too often, force was *not* needed because the infectious diseases brought in by the "conquerors" effectively did the conquering. The Aztecs, Incas, and other indigenous peoples could not resist what they had never been exposed to: smallpox, typhus, measles, influenza, malaria, yellow fever, and plague. The resulting pandemic and depopulation almost defy comprehension. Cook knows his subject well, having written on it several times before.

Eberstadt, Nicholas. *Prosperous Paupers and Other Population Problems.* New Brunswick, NJ: Transaction Publishers, 2000. 272 pages. ISBN 1-56000-423-1.

Of special interest in this book is the revised article, "What If It's a World Population *Implosion*? Speculations about Global *De-*Population," which first appeared in *The Public Interest* in 1997. Eberstadt explores the full implications of a continued trend toward lower fertility around the world, which could spell a rapid graying of populations, significant shifts in the population shares of countries and continents, changes in the work force, potential crises in the support of the elderly, and a transformation in the traditional idea of family. Many people in the future may have no siblings, aunts, uncles, cousins, nieces, or nephews, but only direct ancestors and single offspring. Eberstadt likes to take the demographic road "less traveled by"; the eleven essays in this volume, ten of them revised or reprinted from other places, constitute an alternative take on many of the major population issues of the day. Few of them will win approval from population activists or the "global [population] policy apparatus," which, in Eberstadt's view, is reflexively antinatalist.

Evans, L. T. *Feeding the Ten Billion: Plants and Population Growth.* Cambridge: Cambridge University Press, 1998. 247 pages. ISBN 0-521-64685-5.

The author, a distinguished plant physiologist, wrote this book in part to update the sort of question Malthus was posing two centuries ago. How will we manage to feed the population we expect to have by the middle of the twenty-first century? (The UN now expects slightly less than *nine* rather than ten billion people, but the question is still there.) Getting to the answer involves a long journey through centuries of scientific discoveries and developments. Fortunately Evans has a knack for making science palatable. Among his conclusions: we will need to depend on agricultural research just as much in the future as we have in the past, and the bulk of the increased food production of the coming half-century will need to be achieved in Asia and Africa.

Homer-Dixon, Thomas. *Environment, Scarcity, and Violence.* Princeton, NJ: Princeton University Press, 1999. 253 pages. ISBN 0-691-02794-3.

Thomas Homer-Dixon, a political scientist at the University of Toronto, fears that one version of the Malthusian nightmare—too many people, resulting in human dislocation, distress, and even death—may have begun to be realized in several parts of the world. Homer-Dixon's version links population growth to rising pressures on renewable resources such as forests, fresh water supplies, and croplands, and ultimately, in the presence of other kinds of social and political stress, to the outbreak of violence. Societies with stable governments, educated citizens, and efficient markets have often been able to overcome resource pressures with innovations. But when those advantages are lacking, one sees the breakdown of civil order, whether in the form of ethnic conflict, urban disorders, or insurrection. Homer-Dixon's theorizing is never crude and never without empirical support. (His examples are drawn from Mexico, Africa, and other places.) The threats he identifies appear substantial, especially in light of the dependence half the world's people place on local renewable resources for their well-being. The book's extensive footnoting and bibliography will allow readers to pursue this important topic in several directions.

Homer-Dixon, Thomas, and Jessica Blitt. *Ecoviolence: Links among Environment, Population, and Security.* Lanham, MD: Rowman & Littlefield, 1998. 238 pages. ISBN 0-8476-8870-4.

This highly readable volume reports the findings of a major 1994–1996 research effort, the Project on Environment, Population, and Security, sponsored by the University of Toronto and the American Association for the Advancement of Science. Under the direction of, and guided by the theoretical framework laid out by, Thomas Homer-Dixon, researchers conducted case studies of violence in five places around the world where resource scarcities seemed to play a major role: Chiapas (Mexico), Gaza, South Africa, Pakistan, and Rwanda. Chapters dealing with each of those conflicts constitute the core of the book, with a "Theoretical Overview" at the beginning and a brief "Key Findings" chapter at the end of the book. Unfortunately, this is probably as good a place as any to preview tomorrow's headlines from those parts of the world where population is expanding rapidly against tight resource constraints.

Isbister, John. *The Immigration Debate: Remaking America.* West Hartford, CN: Kumarian Press, 1996. 262 pages. ISBN 1-56549-053-3.

Given the facts that (1) the United States currently accepts more immigrants each year than all other countries in the world combined and (2) long-term projections of U.S. population growth are heavily influenced by this flow of immigration, books on the subject that are balanced and thoughtful are very welcome. This one, by a Princeton-trained economist who teaches at the University of California, Santa Cruz, addresses the economic, political, historical, and moral aspects of immigration in prose that is clear enough for any general reader. One of the issues Isbister focuses on is whether the labor market skills of recent immigrants have deteriorated in comparison with earlier immigrants; the issue has been hotly debated by professional economists and, as the author makes clear, remains unsettled. An interesting final chapter rehearses the ethical arguments both for and against an open border policy. Overall, Isbister sees more long-term rewards than risks—though he concedes the risks—in maintaining the current high rate of immigration into the United States.

Jain, Anrudh (ed.). *Do Population Policies Matter? Fertility and Politics in Egypt, India, Kenya, and Mexico.* New York: Population Council, 1998. 203 pages. ISBN 0-87834-091-2.

This volume explores in depth the political and historical contexts within which population policies in four countries have been formulated, implemented, and evaluated. For anyone who may naively have thought that a country's transition from high to low fertility was a simple process, these essays will prove eye-opening. Many stakeholders have an input into the design of population programs, be they women's groups, NGOs, government bureaucracies, donor countries, religious leaders, academics and other policy elites, the media, or the medical establishment. The authors of these four case studies are mainly sociologists and economists. Anrudh Jain, of the Population Council in New York, provides an overview chapter on "population policies that matter" and a short concluding chapter on the future of population policies.

Lee, James Z., and Wang Feng. *One Quarter of Humanity: Malthusian Mythology and Chinese Realities, 1700–2000.* Cambridge, MA: Harvard University Press, 1999. 272 pages. ISBN 0-674-63908-1.

From as early as the eighteenth century, Western observers have believed that Chinese demographic behavior differed from that of Europeans. One sees this in the writings of the economists

Adam Smith and Thomas Malthus (with Malthus mainly crib-
bing from Smith). Lee and Feng's book makes clear that, while
Malthus and others got many details wrong, their assertion of
distinctive Chinese population practices was fundamentally correct. From 1700 to the present, Chinese strategies for regulating
population have included high rates of abortion and female
infanticide, low male rates of marriage, low fertility within marriage, and high rates of adoption. Given China's status as the
world's most populous nation, and given the controversy over its
one-child policy, this book will be of interest to many readers.

Livi-Bacci, Massimo. *A Concise History of World Population*, 2d
ed. Malden, MA: Blackwell, 1997. 249 pages. ISBN 0-631-20455-5.

This selective survey of the theory, biology, history, and policy of
world population is by one of Europe's leading demographers.
Livi-Bacci builds an analytical framework within which human
populations are seen as making compromises between forces of
constraint and forces of choice. *Constraining* factors include climate, disease, limited food and energy supplies, and environmental quality; the *choices* for man include flexible strategies of
marriage and reproduction, defense from disease, and migration
from less to more favorable locations. This conceptual framework
comes to life in chapters that explore historical episodes of demographic expansion and decline, as well as contemporary examples
of population dynamics. Some of the graphs are tricky enough to
challenge the uninitiated, but the main lines of argument are clear
enough even without graphs. In its discussion of the current
world situation, the book lingers much longer on India and China
than Africa, which serves to remind us that Livi-Bacci has written
a concise, not a *complete*, account of world population.

Malthus, Thomas Robert. *An Essay on the Principle of Population* [1798]. Ed. Geoffrey Gilbert. Reprinted in the Oxford
World's Classics series. New York: Oxford University Press. 1999.
172 pages. ISBN 0-19-283747-8.

This volume is where all the controversy began. Malthus laid out
the basic questions in their starkest terms: How quickly can populations grow? How fast can food supplies be increased? And
what forces will constrain population within the available stock
of resources? The picture Malthus painted in 1798 was fairly grim
(famine and pestilence) but not without hints of a humane way

out of the dilemma. He understood that humankind's capacity for altering behavior in light of probable future consequences makes us different from other animals. He also understood the importance of government policies, for good or ill, in influencing people's reproductive choices. This essay is required reading for anyone who wants to see how the terms of the ongoing population debate were set two centuries ago. There are other paperback editions on the market but this one features an up-to-date editorial introduction, a list of suggested readings, the original text as it appeared in 1798, a set of explanatory notes, and a topical index.

Mazur, Laurie Ann (ed.). *Beyond the Numbers: A Reader on Population, Consumption, and the Environment.* Washington, DC: Island Press, 1994. 444 pages. ISBN 1-55963-299-2.

This reader achieves such a high standard of quality that it probably has several more years of use in the classroom. The individual readings—some reprinted from other places, some solicited for this book—are organized into sections focused on population and consumption, family-planning, reproductive health and rights, population and gender, population and religion, immigration, and the link between population and national security. What distinguishes this volume from some others on the market is the emphasis on social rather than environmental aspects of population; thus *Beyond the Numbers* would be highly suitable as a supplement in a social studies course, at the high school or college level. One regrettable oversight is the absence, in the section on population and religion, of any serious commentary on Islam. Many of the nations still experiencing rapid population growth are Muslim, and religion surely plays as strong a role in the family-planning of those places as Christianity does in other places.

McKibben, Bill. *Maybe One: A Case for Smaller Families.* New York: Plume, 1999. 254 pages. ISBN 0-452-28092-3.

McKibben wrote a rueful book called *The End of Nature*, in which he examined the irreversible impact human beings are having on the natural world. There is no longer any corner of the planet so remote, he found, as to be able to escape the effects of human activity. Nothing is truly "natural" (untainted by humanity) anymore, including the climate. *Maybe One* can be seen as a companion volume, or even a logical sequel, to the earlier book.

What, after all, could make more sense to anyone deeply committed to preserving the wondrous diversity of creation than a deliberate restraint on childbearing? Essentially, this is a book about how and why an intelligent, thoughtful couple (the McKibbens) chose to have only one child. It explores the varied reasons for that personal decision as well as the social and economic consequences to be anticipated—not all of them positive—if *many* people made the same decision. While McKibben is careful not to insist that the one-child idea is right for everyone, he will leave most readers convinced that the choice he and his wife made was an honorable one, and that, with the environment in its present condition, there is a great deal to be said for it.

O'Grada, Cormac. *Black '47 and Beyond: The Great Irish Famine in History, Economy, and Memory.* Princeton: Princeton University Press, 1999. 302 pages. ISBN 0-691-01550-3.

One cannot claim a good understanding of the dynamics of world population, past and present, without giving some attention to the millions of lives that have, as Malthus put it, been "mowed down by the scythe of famine." History knows no famine more famous, or traumatic to the nation involved, than the Great Irish Famine of the 1840s, brought on by the failure of the all-important potato crop. The human cost to Ireland was one-eighth of its population dead and a huge further loss through emigration. Much has been written about all this, including an earlier study by O'Grada, but this new work offers a fresh look at every aspect of the famine. The author compares the severity of the Irish famine to some of the notable famines of the twentieth century, assesses the predictability (or unpredictability) of this famine, examines its agonizingly lengthy course, asks how adequate or inadequate was the English response, and finds A. K. Sen's theory of famines—that they are the result of inadequate entitlements—only partially useful in explaining the Irish debacle.

Peterson, Peter G. *Gray Dawn: How the Coming Age Wave Will Transform America—and the World.* New York: Times Books, 1999. 288 pages. ISBN 0812990692.

Almost everywhere in the world, populations on average are growing older—markedly so in Europe and Japan. Peter Peterson's book takes a hard look at the difficulties this "graying" of the age structure will pose and some possible ways to mitigate them. The main problem is that workers are choosing to leave the labor force earlier than they used to, are living *longer* than they used to, and are saving less than they need to. How, then, will they be able to afford a long, comfortable retirement? Solutions such as reduced pension benefits to the elderly, higher ages for receiving state pensions (like Social Security), or higher taxes on the working generation will be, to say the least, unpopular. Maybe unacceptable. Peterson offers a number of proposals for dealing with the problem, for example, encouraging more saving by workers and later retirements. The author is a former chairman of Lehman Brothers.

Population. Opposing Viewpoints series. San Diego: Greenhaven Press, 2000. 224 pages. ISBN 0-73770291-5.

The Opposing Viewpoints series has long been a mainstay of college classrooms where discussion and debate are fostered. Students are presented with short essays on both sides of controversial issues so that they can exercise critical thinking and decide for themselves which side has the stronger argument. In the newly released population volume, the four thematic questions addressed are: "The Historical Debate: Is There a Population Problem?" "How Will Population Grow in the Twenty-first Century?" "How Serious a Problem Is Overpopulation?" and "Can Nations Control Population without Violating Individuals' Reproductive Freedom?" For each of these questions, an individual pamphlet may be ordered in lieu of the full volume (at lower cost). Opposing points of view are expressed in each pamphlet.

Rohe, John F. *A Bicentennial Malthusian Essay: Conservation, Population and the Indifference to Limits.* Traverse City, MN: Rhodes & Easton, 1997. 189 pages. ISBN 1-890394-00-9.

John Rohe, a self-described "small-town lawyer in northern Michigan," offers a somewhat quirky personal take on the legacy and relevance of Malthus in today's world. Most chapters are headed by a quotation from Malthus's 1798 *Essay on Population*, but it is impossible to know in what direction they will go from there. The underlying theme is that we tend, all too often, to ignore the limits of our resource and technology base—and do so at our own peril.

Rostow, Walt W. *The Great Population Spike and After: Reflections on the Twenty-first Century.* New York: Oxford University Press, 1998. 228 pages. ISBN 0-19-511691-7.

This book is not *mainly* about population, but it illustrates how the assumptions we make about population can be fundamental to how we envision our economic future. Its author, Walt Rostow, has been a student of economic growth for decades. Here he asks whether the demographic trends we see around us in the world today, particularly the slowdown toward zero and even negative population growth in the industrialized nations, are moving us toward economic stagnation or whether economic growth is destined to continue. His answers are mainly optimistic. He sees no reason why revolutionary technological advances should not continue to occur, as they have with some regularity since the eighteenth century. The population-focused reader can easily skim through Rostow's concluding speculations on the subject of U.S. international responsibilities in the complicated world we are entering.

Sarre, Philip, and John Blunden. *An Overcrowded World?* New York: Oxford University Press, 1995. 279 pages. ISBN 0-19-874189-8.

One could build a college course around this fascinating text. Indeed the book was conceived and is currently used as part of an Open University course in Britain called "The Shape of the World: Explorations in Human Geography." It features chapters on the social and economic meaning of "nature" (or "wilderness"); the interaction of populations and natural environment in Africa; the long-term population experience of Europe (including its demographic transition); the extraction, substitution, renewal, and recycling of natural resources; concerns about mineral extraction as a basis for economic development; and a short summing-up chapter on sustainability. At the back of every chapter is a list of references. Most chapters also feature excerpts from other sources that are uniformly well-chosen. Rarely does one find population set so meaningfully into a larger cultural and geographic context.

Sen, Amartya K. *Development as Freedom.* New York: Alfred A. Knopf, 1999. 366 pages. ISBN 0-375-40619-0.

Everything the Nobel Prize–winning economist Amartya Sen writes on the subject of population and poverty is worth reading.

This book is not *primarily* about population, but two chapters deal explicitly and lucidly with it. Chapter 7, "Famines and Other Crises," restates what Sen has been arguing for many years (see especially his 1981 book, *Poverty and Famines*), that famines are not a simple matter of excess population in relation to food production. The Malthusian perspective is simplistic, as it ignores the fact that "the ability to acquire food has to be *earned*" (p. 162). Thus, it is a lack of earnings or other monetary entitlements that put people at risk of hunger or starvation, and this becomes the key not only to explaining but to preventing famine. Chapter 9, "Population, Food and Freedom," finds the global food-production picture fairly encouraging and argues strongly against any form of coercion in family-planning programs. Coercion can be less effective than its advocates believe, ethical issues aside. Sen is no fan of China's one-child policy, but he strongly admires what has been accomplished in the southern Indian state of Kerala, in terms of lowered fertility, higher literacy, and the empowerment of women.

Sen, Gita, Adrienne Germain, and Lincoln C. Chen (eds.). *Population Policies Reconsidered: Health, Empowerment, and Rights.* Cambridge, MA: Harvard University Press, 1994. 280 pages. ISBN 0-674-69003-6.

Population policy as it was once conceived is dead. Notions of population *control*, with explicit goals, targets, or quotas, have been abandoned in most countries. At the international level, as seen at the Cairo International Conference on Population and Development in 1994, and at the academic and intellectual level, the new paradigm stresses women's health and empowerment. Less is heard about demographic issues, more about honoring human rights. Women's perspectives are being voiced, almost for the first time, in discussions about population. The new approach gets a vigorous airing in this volume of seventeen essays, written and cowritten by thirty scholars, activists, and practitioners from various fields. All are committed to rethinking the subject of population. This affordable paperback brings readers up to date on that effort. The prose—academically dense in places—is punctuated with boxes, figures, and tables. One of the editors, Gita Sen, has earned a reputation as a leading international women's rights activist; she cofounded and remains active in Development Alternatives with Women for a New Era

(DAWN), a network of advocates for women's causes in the developing world.

Simon, Julian. *The Ultimate Resource 2.* Princeton, NJ: Princeton University Press, 1998. 778 pages. ISBN 0-691-00381-5.

When Julian Simon published the earlier edition of this book (same title without the 2) in 1981, it was met with considerable skepticism by environmental activists and most academic demographers. Economists were more favorably impressed, and the business media, for example, the *Wall Street Journal* and *Fortune* magazine, unanimously so. That, essentially, is where things stand two decades later. Simon's optimistic views about the long-term impact of population on the economy and environment—most notably, his view that natural resources are *not* becoming scarcer over time—got an extensive hearing during the 1980s and 1990s. They are not as easily dismissed today as they once were. The "ultimate resource" in the Simon worldview is human ingenuity, something that always increases with human numbers. Population growth *can* pose short-term scarcity problems, but over time new solutions are found, and ultimately people live better than before. Simon delights in confounding and refuting his Malthusian opponents with humor, statistics, and a crisp prose style. The book, despite its length, is not a scholarly tome. Rather, it is a collection of thematically linked essays, many of them keyed to provocative questions like "Are Humans Causing Species Holocaust?" and "Do Humans Breed Like Flies?" The paperback version of *The Ultimate Resource 2* was issued in 1998; the hardcover version preceded it in 1996.

Teitelbaum, Michael S., and Jay Winter. *A Question of Numbers: High Migration, Low Fertility, and the Politics of National Identity.* New York: Hill and Wang, 1998. 290 pages. ISBN 0-8090-7781-7.

This book examines how the combination of declining fertility and rising immigration—trends that have become entrenched during the period 1965–1995—are affecting not just the demography but the very sense of national identity of the industrialized nations in Europe and North America. The result in one country after another has been, at best, heated debate and political dispute, at worst, violence directed against immigrant minorities. The book presents case studies of Germany, France, Britain,

Yugoslavia, the former Soviet Union, Romania, Canada, and the United States. It also takes up the issues of refuge- and asylum-seeking migration and Islamic fundamentalism as a factor in Western attitudes toward immigrants from Muslim nations. One cannot read this book without concluding that "population politics" is going to be with us for a long time to come.

Tiffen, M., et al. *More People, Less Erosion: Environmental Recovery in Kenya.* Chichester, NY: J. Wiley, 1994. 326 pages. ISBN 0471941433.

The story this book tells will bolster the spirits of demographic optimists. It chronicles the remarkable recovery of an arid part of Kenya, the Machakos District, from the 1930s to 1990 —a period of time in which the local population increased five-fold. Through systematic efforts to conserve water and soil, partly through Asian-style terracing of the hillsides, the district was able to achieve environmental sustainability in spite of its growing population. The good news from Machakos is somewhat tempered by the low-density conditions that prevailed there initially, but readers are still likely to be impressed by what could be achieved under a program based on the implementation of sound agricultural and conservation technologies.

Tobias, Michael. *World War III: Population and the Biosphere at the End of the Millennium.* New York: Continuum, 1998. 296 pages. ISBN 0-8264-1085-5.

This book is like no other. Tobias has traveled the world, taking in the sights and smells of overpopulation, overconsumption, and environmental devastation. There are chapters on China, India, Indonesia, and Africa, in each case detailing the environmental disruption and degradation occurring in part because of expanding human numbers. The so-called developed nations do not escape his scorn. In a chapter titled "The Price of Development," Japan, the United States, Netherlands, and Italy are among the nations found to have paid a terrible environmental price for their material progress. Tobias is prone to slip into rhetorical overdrive, as when he bemoans the "mindless vandalism wreaked by humans on the scale of a planetary cancer" (p. 203). But he also has a keen eye for the telling detail, a genuine passion for nature in all of its splendid—and tenuous—diversity, and a proselytizer's determination to open readers' eyes to the problem and the solution, both of which are *us.*

Weeks, John R. *Population: An Introduction to Concepts and Issues,* 7th ed. Belmont, CA: Wadsworth, 1998. 673 pages. ISBN 0-534-55305-2.

This clear and comprehensive treatment of demography (the study of population) sets the standard for college textbooks on the subject. Weeks, a demographer at San Diego State University, has a knack for expressing complex ideas in relatively straight-forward (sometimes funny and folksy) ways. The graphs, tables, and maps are well-chosen and clearly explained, and the data are as timely as circumstances will allow. There are chapters on the basic demographic processes—mortality, fertility, migration—as well as on population structure and characteristics; population, development, and the environment; population policy; and demographics, which is the term for practical applications of population data in business, social, and political planning. Throughout the text, Canada and Mexico are brought into the discussion as nations to which the U.S. population experience can be compared. Readers of the present volume are especially directed to chapter 1, "An Introduction to the World's Popula-tion." At the ends of chapters are "Suggested Readings" and "Websites of Interest."

Handbooks, Yearbooks, and Data Sheets

Haupt, Arthur, and Thomas T. Kane. *The Population Reference Bureau's Population Handbook,* 4th ed. Washington, DC: Popu-lation Reference Bureau, 1997. 80 pages. ISBN 0-917136-09-8.

This useful little handbook features short chapters on all the stan-dard demographic concepts and measures: age and sex composi-tion, fertility, mortality, morbidity, nuptiality, migration, race and ethnicity, households and families, urbanization, and population change. Examples are given for all the main concepts; they are tilted toward the United States but do not exclude other coun-tries. The contrasts can be most instructive; for example, the crude birth rate for the United States in 1995 is given as 15 per 1,000 population, while in Italy it was 9 per 1,000 and in Angola,

51 (p. 13). A fairly complete glossary of technical terms is provided in the appendix, as well as a listing of organizations—and websites—that can provide additional information on most population-related questions.

Population Reference Bureau. *The 2000 United States Population Data Sheet: The American Work Force.* Washington, DC: Population Reference Bureau, 2000.

This handy wall chart provides the basic demographic indicators for each state, for example, total population, its growth rate, population density, and percent of population under age 18 or over age 64. Every year the Population Reference Bureau (PRB) also focuses on a special topic; in 2000, it was the U.S. labor force. Detailed information by state is given on such variables as unemployment rate, percent of workers who are foreign-born, who are self-employed, who are union members, and so on. As with the following item, all the data can be obtained online from PRB but not in the same visually satisfying form.

Population Reference Bureau. *The 2000 World Population Data Sheet.* Washington, DC: Population Reference Bureau, 2000. ISSN 0085-8315.

Published annually, in both booklet and wall-chart formats, the *World Population Data Sheet* is an extraordinary resource for anyone interested in world population issues. For every country in the world, it gives the essential demographic statistics: population, birth and death rates, rate of natural increase, doubling time, infant mortality rate, total fertility rate, percent "young" and "old," life expectancy, percent of adults with HIV/AIDS, contraceptive use, GNP per capita, and more. Data are also given in aggregated form for the world, the more developed countries, the less developed countries, and the various regions, for example, Northern Africa, Eastern Africa, Middle Africa, and Southern Africa. There is no handier source of world population information than this.

United Nations. *1998 Demographic Yearbook/Annuaire Demographique 1998,* 50th ed. New York: United Nations Publications, 2000. 1,152 pages. ISBN 9210510895.

Issued annually by the United Nations and based on the data-gathering of its Population Division, the Demographic Yearbook is the "bible" of the international demographic community. Here in a single volume one can find summary population data for the world as a whole (back to 1950, on a decade basis), by continent, by subcontinent, and by individual nation. The data tables include crude birth and death rates, rates of natural increase, population densities, urban/rural residency patterns, and cross-tabulations by age and sex. In addition, there is detailed information for every nation on natality, fetal mortality, infant and maternal mortality, general mortality, nuptiality, and divorce. The yearbook is advertised as "comprehensive" and "definitive." It is both.

United Nations Population Division. *World Population Prospects: The 1998 Revision.* New York: United Nations, 1999. *Vol. I: Comprehensive Tables.* 627 pages. ISBN 92-1-151333-2. *Vol. II: Sex and Age.* 883 pages. ISBN 92-1-151332-4.

Since 1951 the UN's Population Division has issued world population projections every few years. (The intervals have been as long as six years, as short as two.) As might be expected, these estimates are the most widely referred to of any such attempts to forecast the world's demographic future. Low-, medium-, and high-fertility paths to the population of 2050 are presented, so people may decide for themselves which forecast seems most plausible. Specialists and the media generally confine their attention to the "medium" estimate; some, however, believe that recent declines in fertility around the world have been so unexpectedly large that more attention should be given to the UN's low-fertility estimate. Volume I offers detailed demographic projections for each country, region, and the whole world, to the year 2050. Volume II gives age and sex distributions for countries and regions back to 1950 and, on an estimated basis, forward to 2050 (on low-, medium-, and high-fertility assumptions). The highlights of the 1998 revision will be found in the documents chapter.

U.S. Bureau of the Census. *Statistical Abstract of the United States 1999: The National Data Book.* Washington, DC: Government Printing Office, 1999. ISBN 0934213739.

Issued annually by the Census Bureau since 1878 and now offered in both print and CD-ROM formats, the *Statistical Abstract* provides a wealth of demographic information for the United States. Sections 1 ("Population") and 2 ("Vital Statistics") contain over 100 pages of detailed statistics, covering everything from the most basic—total U.S. population by year—to the most specific, if not arcane, such as "Deaths and Death Rates for Injury by Firearms, by Race and Sex: 1980 to 1996." Vital statistics are presented in great detail: births, deaths, marriage, divorce, all categorized by the appropriate qualifiers, such as race, age, sex, cause, etc. The 1,000-plus fine-print pages of this volume fully justify the subtitle, "The National Data Book."

U.S. Bureau of the Census. *World Population Profile: 1998.* Report WP/98. Washington, DC: Government Printing Office, 1999.

The International Programs Center (IPC) of the U.S. Census Bureau prepares its own estimates and projections of world population, country by country, that do not necessarily coincide with those prepared by the United Nations. The differences are normally not large and need not be explained in detail here. (See the booklet, B-16 to B-18.) The heart of the *World Population Profile* consists of numerical tables on total population by country and age group, births, deaths, total fertility rates, life expectancies, and contraceptive prevalence, all given for 1998 and projected for the year 2025. Each issue of the *World Population Profile* also features a special section on a topic of demographic interest. The 1998 topic is HIV/AIDS in the developing world; in 1996 it was adolescent fertility and contraceptive practice in developing countries. By contrast with the UN's *Demographic Yearbook*, this publication seems designed to be as much an educational tool as a data source book. It has (brief) discussions of the history of world population, the main forces determining future population growth, trends in infant mortality, the demographic effects of migration, and much more.

8

Nonprint Resources

In this chapter we survey some of the nonprint sources of information on world population, a body of information that grows with every passing year. "Nonprint," for our purposes, means videotapes and websites. Many videotapes on the topic of population are now available. The actual or anticipated arrival of the six-billionth inhabitant of the planet on October 12, 1999, seems to have stimulated interest in the production of this kind of video. So, too, did the convening of the International Conference on Population and Development (ICPD) in Cairo in 1994. And several of the videos reviewed below take note of the bicentennial of the publication of Malthus's *Essay on Population* (1798), although only one is devoted entirely to Malthus and his ideas. Only videos produced since 1990 are included.

Videos

Decade of Decision
Date: 1994
Length: 14 minutes
Price: $95 (purchase), $20 (rental)
Source: Bullfrog Films
           PO Box 149
           Oley, PA 19547
           (800) 543-3764
           www.bullfrogfilms.com

Narrated by newscaster Walter Cronkite and produced by Population Action International, this succinct video makes the case that the brakes must be put on population momentum during the

1990s. It poses the population issue in standard Ehrlichian terms: in the poorer parts of the world, human numbers are increasing too rapidly; in the richer parts, per capita consumption is rising too rapidly. The main policy emphasis is placed on the provision of family-planning services to those who presently lack access to them. A study guide is available. Suitable for ages 12 to adult.

Dodging Doomsday: Life Beyond Malthus
Date: 1992
Length: 51 minutes
Price: $129 (purchase), $75 (rental)
Source: Films for the Humanities & Sciences
PO Box 2053
Princeton, NJ 08543-2053
(800) 257-5126
Fax: (609) 275-3767
custserv@films.com
www.films.com

This British (BBC) program features Paul Ehrlich as the persuasive spokesperson for the "gloomsters" and Julian Simon as the cheerful and equally convincing spokesperson for the "cornucopians." Other population experts weigh in on various aspects of population. A genuine radical, Maria Elena Hurtado, argues that "overpopulation" is a smokescreen for the problems created by unequal land distribution in many countries. Two key questions are central to this balanced and engaging video: is population growing too big for the Earth to sustain, and is population to blame for various social and environmental problems we currently face? It would be hard to find another video that raises as many population-linked issues—economic, environmental, and political—as "Dodging Doomsday."

Food or Famine?
Date: 1997
Length: 49 minutes each (two videos)
Price for both: $395 (purchase), $95 (rental)
Source: Filmakers Library
124 East 40th Street
New York, NY 10016
(212) 808-4980
Fax: (212) 808-4983

info@filmakers.com
www.filmakers.com

This two-part video tackles the issue of sustainable agriculture within a framework of concern to feed a growing global population. Experts seen on camera include Lester Brown of Worldwatch Institute, David Pimentel of Cornell University, Ismail Serageldin of International Agricultural Research, and Miguel Altieri of the University of California. Part 1 sets out the basic dilemma: modern "industrial" agriculture feeds billions of people but relies on pesticides, herbicides, and a process of plant selection and breeding that reduces diversity. The cost of monoculture is seen not only in a loss of the natural diversity of plants and soil organisms but also in worrisome rates of soil erosion. Yet there are positive developments to be seen in places such as Chile, California, and Canada, where some groups of farmers are following more organic and sustainable methods of agriculture with excellent results. Part 2 raises the larger issues of global population trends, loss of cropland to urban sprawl, degradation of existing farmlands, limits to water supply, and the shift toward higher-protein foods, all of which give reason to be concerned about the future. As in Part 1, the strength of the video is in the clear focus on important questions—and in the telling film footage, such as the Indian farmer who has just dynamited the bottom of his well, already 30 meters deep, to try and reach the receding water table. Although serious "Malthusian-type" questions are raised about humanity's capacity to feed our rising numbers without doing irreparable damage to the ecology, numerous examples of positive, environmentally friendly approaches are offered. Narrated by David Suzuki, this pair of videos would be best appreciated by those of college age or older.

Future in the Cradle

Date:	1996
Length:	22 minutes
Price:	$59.95 (purchase), $35.00 (rental) for institutions; lower rates for individuals
Source:	The Video Project
	PO Box 77188
	San Francisco, CA 94107-7188
	(800) 475-2638
	Fax: (415) 821-7204

video@videoproject.net
http://www.videoproject.net

This aptly titled video examines the world population issue through the lens of the International Conference on Population and Development held in 1994 in the "cradle of civilization," Cairo. Featured speakers include Nafis Sadik, Secretary-General of the conference; Timothy Wirth, U.S. representative to the conference; Paul Ehrlich, the well-known Stanford environmentalist; and David Brower of the Sierra Club. An interesting aspect of the video is its attention to the domestic U.S. political dimension of international family-planning and the significant shift of U.S. policy in 1993. The tilt of the program is clearly toward affirming the goals set at the Cairo conference, that is, making reproductive health services more widely available around the world and expanding educational and other opportunities for girls and women. Suitable for ages 14 and up.

The Grandchild Gap: The Effects of Low Birth Rates
Date: 1997
Length: 56 minutes
Price: $89.95
Source: Films for the Humanities & Sciences
             PO Box 2053
             Princeton, NJ 08543-2053
             (800) 257-5126
             Fax: (609) 275-3767
             custserv@films.com
             www.films.com

"The Grandchild Gap" offers a welcome break from the standard fare of population videos, which almost universally center on the rapid increase of world population. This video explores instead the emerging problem of *low* birth rates in Europe, a few east Asian nations, and the United States. Ben Wattenberg, senior scholar at the American Enterprise Institute, narrates. Also frequently on camera are Samuel Preston, a demographer at the University of Pennsylvania, and Andrew Cherlin, a sociologist at Johns Hopkins University. But equally compelling on screen are the ordinary young Italians and Americans who explain why they want to delay marriage and keep their number of children low. More poignant are the older people who express regret at not having any grandchildren, or even much *prospect* of grand-children. All the relevant background statistics are presented along the way, including fertility rates and "ideal" family size figures. (People in low-fertility countries seem uniformly to *want* more children than they end up having.) One long-term economic effect of the "birth dearth" will be the serious problem of supporting a disproportionately large retired generation from the work efforts of—and taxes paid by—a smaller generation. Wattenberg asks whether government can do anything to solve the problem and gets little encouragement from his experts. Much larger tax credits for children might increase the number of children people choose to have, or, as one expert suggests, might simply change the spacing of children. Immigration receives less attention than it should as a possible mitigating force, at least in the United States. The video should stimulate plenty of discussion in audiences of high school age and older.

How Much Is Enough?

Date: 1992
Length: 26 minutes
Price: $49 (purchase), $20 (rental)
Source: Bullfrog Films
             PO Box 149
             Oley, PA 19547
             (800) 543-3764
             www.bullfrogfilms.com

The last in a six-part documentary series, "How to Save the Earth," this video explores the twin problems of excess population and excess consumption, with an emphasis on practical solutions. It first looks at the poverty and pollution found in Mexico City, the world's second largest mega-city. Carmen Leyte, of the Mexican Family Planning Association (MEXFAM), notes the agency's success in helping change attitudes and behavior, and ultimately the population growth rate. Brief mention is made of similar successes in other countries. The focus then shifts to the issue of excess consumption in the richer nations, particularly in North America, where the environmental impact of population is magnified. Vicki Robin, of the New Road Map Foundation, describes a new ethic of "living better on less," or voluntary simplicity. Suitable for ages 12 to adult.

The Human Tide

Date:	1995
Length:	35 minutes
Price:	$350 (purchase), $65 (rental)
Source:	Filmakers Library
	124 East 40th Street
	New York, NY 10016
	(212) 808-4980
	Fax: (212) 808-4983
	info@filmakers.com
	www.filmakers.com

This video, narrated by David Suzuki for the Canadian television series "The Nature of Things," conveys a sense of urgency, of time running out, on the issue of world population. That is its strength, and it has a formidable cast of guest experts to drive home the crisis message: Paul Ehrlich, Nafis Sadik of the UN Population Fund (UNFPA), Lester Brown of Worldwatch Institute, Sharon Camp of the Population Crisis Committee, and Stephen Lewis, former Canadian ambassador to the United Nations. The video's weakness lies in its attempt to cover every single aspect of world population; in 35 minutes, that cannot be done. The issue that receives the fullest treatment is birth control—the adequate or inadequate access to it in various parts of the world, the cost, the different types and how research is expanding the range of choices, abortion, the politics of family-planning (mainly a domestic U.S. concern but with worldwide implications), and the need many see for the developed countries to be generous in funding the efforts developing countries are making to rein in their population growth. A striking fact is that in Ethiopia the cost of a year's supply of condoms (the best contraceptive choice where AIDS is a serious threat) is about one-third of annual income. On questions like the role of economic development in lowering fertility, the threatened loss of species and biodiversity, and the emerging problem of environmental refugees, this video has less to say than many others. Suitable for high school, college, and adult audiences.

Jam Packed

Date:	1997
Length:	29 minutes
Price:	$79.95 institutional, $39.95 nonprofit, individual

Source: The Video Project
PO Box 77188
San Francisco, CA 94107-7188
(800) 475-2638
Fax: (415) 821-7204
video@videoproject.net
http://www.videoproject.net

There is an MTV-like energy to this video, which is clearly aimed at a U.S. teenage audience. Narrated by Alexandra Paul, star of the popular TV show "Baywatch," it cuts back and forth between scenes of urban sprawl, African wildlife (threatened by human overpopulation), experts attesting to the urgency of slowing population growth, and candid statements by an unmarried young mother about the life-burdening effects of her accidental pregnancy. Much more emphasis is placed on the benefits of deferring sexual activity until marriage and on the threat to the environment from a wasteful American lifestyle than on the family-planning needs of less developed nations. Population Communications International, which produced the video, prides itself on careful preproduction research. They undoubtedly have concluded that the most effective way to engage American teens in global population issues is through the "up-close-and-personal" approach taken here. Available in both English and Spanish; teacher's guide included. Suitable for ages 12 and up.

The Legacy of Malthus

Date: 1994
Length: 52 minutes
Price: $150 (purchase), $75 (rental)
Source: Bullfrog Films
PO Box 149
Oley, PA 19547
(800) 543-3764
www.bullfrogfilms.com

The view that poverty is not a result of overpopulation but of a maldistribution of resources, within and among nations, informs this unusual video. The director, Deepa Dhanraj, quotes and then subverts the message of Malthus as well as those present-day agencies that seem to accept the Malthusian explanation of poverty (e.g., the Population Institute and the UNFPA). The destitution of nineteenth-century Scottish crofters is contrasted, through alternating segments, with that of poor villagers in India. In both cases, it is made clear that unequal access to the land is the real problem. There is no narration, leaving the viewer to draw his or her own conclusions. Marred by poor audio quality. Suitable for ages 15 to adult.

Mothers of Malappuram

Date:	1996
Length:	10 minutes
Price:	$95 (purchase), $25 (rental)
Source:	Bullfrog Films
	PO Box 149
	Oley, PA 19547
	(800) 543-3764
	www.bullfrogfilms.com

One of a six-video series called "Not the Numbers Game," this brief film deals with the shift in the Indian government's population policy from a top-down emphasis on numbers and targets to a wider emphasis on women's empowerment. (The new approach conforms with the recommendations issued at the ICPD in Cairo in 1994.) Raising female literacy has been a key to lowering fertility in Kerala, the southern Indian state featured here. Elsewhere in India, women are assuming positions of power in village *panchayat* assemblies, becoming "engines of social change." Improved health services are another part of the picture, since lower infant mortality rates lead to lower birth rates. An optimistic video with a clear message. Suitable for ages 15 to adult.

Paul Ehrlich and the Population Bomb

Date:	1996
Length:	60 minutes
Price:	$149 (purchase), $75 (rental)
Source:	Films for the Humanities & Sciences
	PO Box 2053
	Princeton, NJ 08543-2053
	(800) 257-5126
	Fax: (609) 275-3767
	custserv@films.com
	www.films.com

No one who has worried about world population at any time during the past 30 years could be unfamiliar with the name Paul

Ehrlich. This video gives Ehrlich a chance to speak at length on the issue that has made him a kind of environmental celebrity. It takes him from a youthful science enthusiast—his mother recalls his early interest in butterflies—through college and a research stint working with Eskimos around Hudson Bay, to his lifelong partnership with his wife, Anne, and his long career of teaching and ecological research at Stanford University. Considerable attention is paid to the sensational *Population Bomb* of 1968, which earned Ehrlich a visit, and then dozens of *re*visits, to the Johnny Carson Show. (In one scene, he is shown briefly debating Ben Wattenberg on that program.) There is film footage of poverty and starvation in Africa and India, and of the wasteful affluence of American consumption. A fair hearing is given to Ehrlich's arch-foe, the economist Julian Simon, who has argued at great length that life is getting better and better for most of the Earth's inhabitants, that it will continue to do so, and that a rising population is part of the reason why. Ehrlich's impatience with Simon, economists in general, and "creationists" is unmistakable in his salty comebacks to all of them. Suitable for high-school students and older audiences.

Population Six Billion

Date: 1999
Length: 56 minutes
Price: $129 (purchase), $75 (rental)
Source: Films for the Humanities & Sciences
             PO Box 2053
             Princeton, NJ 08543-2053
             (800) 257-5126
             Fax: (609) 275-3767
             custserv@films.com
             www.films.com

This video opens with a recitation of bad demographic news: rising global population poses serious problems in the areas of the environment, housing, migration, and water supplies; per-capita food production is now falling; there is an expanding pool of unemployed workers around the world. Over 100 countries face a doubled or tripled population by the year 2050. Kofi Annan, Secretary-General of the United Nations, warns of an overpopulated world. But here the focus shifts to three highly specific case studies of countries that have been facing rapid population growth and have been *doing* something to curb it. The three are Vietnam, Uganda, and Mexico. In all three, scenes of misery and destitution are intercut with scenes of sex education classes or private counseling sessions. In Vietnam, one learns that abortion is so common—costing less than $2—that it is relied upon as a form of birth control. (Vietnam does not offer sex education in its schools.) In Uganda, the issue of female genital mutilation is addressed in a forceful way. In Mexico, the *empowerment* of women is treated as a high priority in connection with family-planning. The tone is low-key throughout, but some material is adult enough that the video seems inappropriate for audiences below college level.

Setting the Grass Roots on Fire: Norman Borlaug and Africa's Green Revolution
Date: 2000
Length: 56 minutes
Price: $295 (purchase), $75 (rental)
Source: Filmakers Library
             124 East 40th Street
             New York, NY 10016
             (212) 808-4980
             Fax: (212) 808-4983
             info@filmakers.com
             www.filmakers.com

Population may not be in the title of this video but it is never far from the center of concern, since Norman Borlaug's motivation throughout a long career has been to avert hunger and famine through agricultural research. His initial plant-breeding success-es came in Mexico, as recounted in the video, but the real proof of a historic food-production breakthrough came on the Indian subcontinent during the 1960s and 1970s. (Borlaug won the Nobel Peace Prize in 1970.) At a late stage of his career—indeed he had already retired, *twice*—Borlaug was asked to apply his Green Revolution methods to Africa, a continent facing immense and almost hopeless odds against being able to feed its growing numbers. Partly under the urging of former president Jimmy Carter, he accepted the challenge. The contrast seen here between starving, cadaverous Ethiopians and happy, well-nourished chil-dren at a later date, after the Sasakawa-Global 2000 (SG 2000) program has been fully implemented, is moving—and convincing. The only skeptical moment permitted to intrude into this firmly upbeat version of Borlaug's life story is a mild confrontation between the scientist and a critic who questions the environmental impact of chemical fertilizers. (The response: fertilizers *can* pollute waterways when they are overused, but in Africa that is very unlikely, given the low doses applied. And in any case, is pollution a worse problem than starvation?) Suitable for ages 14 and up.

Six Billion and Beyond

Date:	1999
Length:	56 minutes
Price:	$225 (purchase), $75 (rental)
Source:	University of California Extension, Center for Media and Independent Learning
	2000 Center Street, Fourth Floor
	Berkeley, CA 94704-1223
	(510) 642–0460
	Fax: (510) 643–9271
	cmil@uclink.berkeley.edu
	http://www-cmil.unex.berkeley.edu/media/

The approach taken by this video is to portray young people in various countries—Mexico, Italy, Kenya, India, China, and the United States—as they face real-life choices concerning reproduction and consumption. It demonstrates the many linkages among human numbers, economic development, and the whole gamut of environmental concerns, and does so with considerable insight. In line with the emerging paradigm guiding population policy around the world, the video gives serious attention to matters of gender equity. It is most suitable for college courses and should stimulate lively discussion.

Sustainable Lives, Attainable Dreams

Date:	1994
Length:	28 minutes
Price:	$59.95 (purchase), $29.95 (rental)
Source:	The Video Project
	PO Box 77188
	San Francisco, CA 94107-7188
	(800) 475-2638
	Fax: (415) 821-7204

video@videoproject.net
http://www.videoproject.net

This well-produced video from the National Wildlife Federation explains how family-planning programs have helped slow population growth and—equally important—improve the lives of the people in three countries. In Indonesia, where the main island (Java) is smaller than Florida and yet supports a population of 110 million, the current policy is to promote two-child families in hopes of reaching replacement-level fertility by the year 2010. People from all parts of society—representing government, religion, and private enterprise—are shown cooperating to achieve the desired objective. In Kenya, where women have traditionally had fewer rights than men and indeed have been seen as "belonging to their husbands," the emphasis of family-planning programs has been on women's empowerment (with efforts to bring men along as willing partners). Sharp drops in fertility rates in a short period of time signal success and make Kenya an example for much of Africa. And in Mexico, programs like those offered by the Mexican Federation of Private Health and Community Development Associations (FEMAP), supported by funding from USAID, have promoted women's health and employment opportunities, not just "condoms and pills." The video makes the point (briefly) that the more developed nations have a responsibility to curb their consumption and share their resources. Stunning NASA images of the Earth from outer space underline the idea expressed by an astronaut that this is the only planet we have. Suitable for ages 11 to adult.

Time to Act
Date: 1998
Length: 16 minutes
Price: no charge to members
Source: Population Communications International
            777 United Nations Plaza
            New York, NY 10017-3521
            (212) 687-3366
            Fax: (212) 661-4188
            pciny@population.org
            www.population.org

This is an outreach and recruitment tool of Population Communications International (PCI). Beyond its self-promoting message, however, the program offers an interesting inside look at the planning, production, and popularity, as well as the positive impact, of the soap operas for which PCI has become famous. PCI stresses that its stories are locally researched, written, produced, and acted. Through both radio and television, these programs are reaching a wide audience. Seeing itself as an agent of change, PCI has developed partnerships with the World Health Organization, the United Nations Population Fund, the International Planned Parenthood Federation, and the National Wildlife Federation, among others. Suitable for ages 12 to adult.

Was Malthus Right? Population and Resources in the Twenty-first Century

Date:	1998
Length:	27 minutes
Price:	$129 (purchase), $75 (rental)
Source:	Films for the Humanities & Sciences
	PO Box 2053
	Princeton, NJ 08543-2053
	(800) 257-5126
	Fax: (609) 275-3767
	custserv@films.com
	www.films.com

This edition of the PBS program "Think Tank" raises a variety of questions about the relevance of Malthus's *Essay on Population* in a world of 6 billion rather than the 1 billion of 1798. The roundtable discussion, hosted by Ben Wattenberg, of the American Enterprise Institute, a Washington, D.C., think tank, includes Paul Demeny, a distinguished scholar at the Population Council in New York; Max Singer, a cofounder of the Hudson Institute; and Walter Reid, of the World Resources Council in Washington. The exchange of ideas ranges across various topics, from the exact nature of Malthus's population theory, to the debated links among population growth, resource depletion, and environmental degradation. Unlike most videos on population, this one consists of nothing but unrehearsed talk around a table, although the intellectual level (especially by television standards) is high. Suitable for college audiences and adults.

World Population
Date: 2000
Length: 7 minutes
Price: $29.95
Source: The Video Project
PO Box 77188
San Francisco, CA 94107-7188
(800) 475-2638
Fax: (415) 821-7204
video@videoproject.net
http://www.videoproject.net

The concept of this video is simple and stark: portray the history of world population with dots lighting up on a world map. Each dot represents a million people. At the starting date of 1 A.D. there are very few dots, mainly clustered in India and China. As the digital clock ticks away, the dots slowly multiply. The growth of population is almost imperceptible at first, but by the end it is visually dramatic, especially accompanied by the sound of a beating heart. Important epochs of world history, for example, "India's Golden Age," "Mayan Empire," and "Crusades," are noted with icons in a lower corner of the frame. (A 10-page activity guide provides further details on these historical eras, as well as discussion questions.) At the end, when population trends have been extrapolated to the year 2030, a simple message is offered: the quality of our environment in the future will be determined by the decisions we make about both population and consumption. Suitable for ages 12 to adult.

World Population Issues: How Many Is Too Many?
Date: 1998
Length: 27 minutes
Price: not available
Source: New Dimensions Media, Inc.
611 East State
Jacksonville, IL 62650
(800) 288-4456
Fax: (800) 242-2288
ndm@btsbbooks.com

This short video, produced by Classroom Videos, a company in British Columbia (Canada), covers all the basic points in an orderly fashion: world population trends, population growth rates, migration, population and resources, and programs of population control. It is particularly good on the basic population processes, for example, births minus deaths equals natural increase, and immigration minus emigration equals net migration—a part of total population change. The human cost of migration is vividly portrayed in footage of refugee camps in Rwanda. In addressing the issue of unequal access to resources, the video neatly contrasts Vietnam and Australia, a less developed country versus one that is more highly developed. American viewers will instantly identify with the Australian lifestyle, which is quite similar to that in the United States. In the segment on population control, which focuses on China's one-child policy, a tough moral and political question is raised: should government be able to tell people how many children to have? Suitable for grades 6 to 12.

World War III: The Population Explosion and Our Planet

Date:	1994
Length:	50 minutes
Price:	$89 (purchase), $39.95 (rental) for institutions; less for individuals
Source:	The Video Project
	PO Box 77188
	San Francisco, CA 94107-7188
	(800) 475-2638
	Fax: (415) 821-7204
	video@videoproject.net
	http://www.videoproject.net

Written, directed, and produced by Michael Tobias and based on a book of the same title, "World War III" is one of the most compelling presentations in recent years on the issue of global population growth and its repercussions. It opens with some basic facts about the current rate of population increase and where the numbers are headed, then turns to a country-by-country examination of the impact, especially on poverty and on the natural environment, of current trends. Kenya, India, China, and the United States are the four countries featured. The interviews are skillfully conducted and consistently engaging. The film footage alternates between breathtaking and wrenching. (The most suitable audience would probably be college-level or adult. "World War III" was originally produced for public television.) Perhaps the greatest strength of the video is its avoidance of hackneyed ideas. It raises unusually interesting questions, such as: Will economic prosperity in China lead to reduced fertility or just the opposite? Why did the falling Kenyan fertility rate *stop* falling? And why does the government of that country, which officially supports family-planning, not devote more resources to it? The answers are not simple—because the questions are good ones.

Population Websites

The Internet has become a sort of electronic almanac, offering information (and sometimes misinformation) on every topic imaginable. The subject of population is, for the most part, well served by the Internet. There are numerous reliable and up-to-date Internet sites that allow one to explore population issues in depth. Some are oriented to the environmental aspects of population, some to the family-planning aspects; some deal with population policy, and some are simply places to obtain demographic data. A number of websites offer several of these features at one location. Because so many sites provide links to other population-related websites, the following is a selective list.

Those sites that are data-oriented generally provide not only global population data but more detailed statistics by country, and often for the past and the projected future as well as the present. Some sites offer their data in multiple formats: downloadable files, wall charts, booklets, and CD-ROMs. Hardly anyone but a professional demographer requires data on a CD-ROM, so that particular resource is not covered here.

Alan Guttmacher Institute
http://www.agi-usa.org/home.html

This is the premier site for information on reproductive health, including contraception, pregnancy and birth, sexually transmitted diseases, and the law and public policy relating to reproduction. The institute is often the source of news stories in the mainstream media.

Carrying Capacity Network
http://www.carryingcapacity.org

This site invites one to think of overpopulation as a U.S. national issue. Its policy orientation is toward the limitation of further immigration into the United States.

Center for Immigration Studies
http://www.cis.org

Immigration is a key part of the population picture for a number of countries; for the United States it has become critical to present and future population trends. This website takes a decidedly unenthusiastic view of immigration's impact on the United States. Many studies of individual immigration issues are available either online or in print.

Family Planning Association of India
http://fpaindia.com

This website provides an example of the vital family-planning work that is being done around the world by nongovernmental organizations. More examples can be reached through links at the International Planned Parenthood Federation (IPPF) website.

The Hunger Site
http://www.thehungersite.com

The Hunger Site allows visitors to click on a button and make a free donation of staple food *every day* to hungry people overseas. The site is commercially sponsored. It does not attempt to make an analytical connection between hunger and population, but it could provoke interesting discussions about possible reasons for hunger.

International Planned Parenthood Federation
http://www.ippf.org

Comparable to the Alan Guttmacher Institute in its concerns but with more of an international and program orientation, the IPPF is another good source of information on reproductive health. There are links to all the member organizations that comprise the IPPF.

International Programs Center of U.S. Bureau of the Census
http://www.census.gov/ipc/www

This site is one of the best places to get reliable information about world population. The International Programs Center (IPC) and its predecessor agencies have been collecting and processing international demographic data for over 50 years. The site has a world population clock, an international data base (IDB) with current and historical data on national populations, a feature that permits one to view and print population pyramids for individual countries, and projections of future population trends by Census Bureau experts.

Julian Simon
http://www.bmgt.umd.edu/~jsimon

The late Julian Simon, who taught in the management program of the University of Maryland, was a powerful intellectual force in *support* of both population growth and immigration. At his personal home page are links to many of his writings, freely downloadable.

Migration News
http://migration.ucdavis.edu/mn

Started in 1993 by Philip Martin at the University of California, Davis, this site summarizes worldwide migration news, month by month, and offers an archive of past issues. It also provides an excellent set of links to other immigration sites grouped by these categories: academic, advocacy groups, government, and international organizations.

Negative Population Growth
http://www.npg.org

Negative Population Growth (NPG) has been worrying about overpopulation for several decades. Its website currently emphasizes *U.S.* problems, such as urban sprawl and deteriorating quality of life, caused (allegedly) by too rapid population growth, exacerbated by immigration. NPG offers a population news listserve at its site.

PopPlanet
http://www.popplanet.org

A new website, PopPlanet represents a collaboration between the Population Reference Bureau (PRB) and the National Council for

Science and the Environment. It looks at issues involving population, health, and the environment, with links to databases at PRB, the Census Bureau, and UN agencies. There are country "briefing books" on a select list of countries around the world.

Population Communications International
http://www.population.org

Population Communications International (PCI) is an organization that uses the media, especially TV and radio soap operas, to deliver messages about safe and responsible sexual behavior. Its website provides information about this new approach, including a "resource center" listing several videos and reports available from PCI, and a link to *Global Intersections*, a monthly online digest of population news (free).

The Population Council
http://www.popcouncil.org

The Population Council is perhaps the world's foremost organization devoted to reproductive health research. Its website has an entire section on reproductive health and family-planning, with authoritative coverage of such topics as emergency contraception, abortion, Norplant, and IUDs. But there is also a section on "Population and Social Policy," which indexes a series of Policy Research Division (PRD) Working Papers on such topics as urban growth, population and poverty, and policy options, all available online.

Population Institute
http://www.populationinstitute.org

At this website one may order booklets on population subjects (for a fee) and see the most recent issue of the institute's bimonthly newsletter *Popline*.

Population Reference Bureau
http://www.prb.org

This site offers the most complete and objective coverage of population on the Web. It is a splendid resource for students and teachers alike (the "Educators' Forum" supplies a number of tools for teachers). There are links to the online version of the *World Population Data Sheet*, the *U.S. Population Data Sheet*, the *Population Bul-*

letin, and *Population Today,* as well as press releases, a demographic glossary, and various reports focused mainly on U.S. population topics. There is also a link to PopNet, a website PRB maintains as a kind of gateway to global data on population, education, environment, gender, and economic variables. The information at the PopNet site comes from government sources, NGOs, university research centers, and other sources around the world.

Princeton University—Office of Population Research
http://opr.princeton.edu/resources

Among the twenty or so university population centers in the United States, Princeton's stands out as the oldest, and its website is perhaps the most useful, especially for those who have progressed beyond the basics of population study. Click on the "Internet Resources of Interest to Demographers" for a lengthy menu of demographic resources, including online publications.

Sierra Club
http://www.sierraclub.org

Although bitterly divided by internal battles over U.S. immigration policy in recent years, the Sierra Club has not distanced itself from the subject of population. Its website offers reports, fact sheets, and brochures on population, as well as a listserve and suggestions on how to get involved as an activist on population issues.

United Nations Population Fund
http://www.unfpa.org

This website gives access to online versions of the publications of the UN Population Fund, including the annual *State of World Population,* two periodicals, and a very informative "Population Issues Briefing Kit." The strong emphasis at the UNFPA is on the empowerment of women. That is in line with the deliberations and Program of Action finalized at the 1994 International Conference on Population and Development in Cairo.

World Health Organization
http://www.who.int/whosis

The World Health Organization (WHO) Statistical Information System site is the place to go for authoritative information on the extent and impact of diseases worldwide (including HIV/AIDS), mortality rates, and everything health-related. It has enormous depth of coverage on health issues, and, as a bonus, has links to world population estimates and projections, including those of the United Nations.

Worldwatch Institute
http://www.worldwatch.org

The Worldwatch site provides indexes and access to many of the organization's studies, Worldwatch Papers and Books, and "issue alerts," which come out two or three times per month. The well-known annual *State of the World* often features a chapter on, or related to, population trends. Worldwatch is one of the most respected sources of information on population, resources, and the environment.

Zero Population Growth
http://www.zpg.org

Zero Population Growth (ZPG) is one of the old-line organizations dedicated to the study, and containment, of world population growth. Two key features of its website are "population education" and the "legislative action center." Teachers will find the former quite helpful, as it offers classroom games, role-playing simulations, and other learning materials (some bilingual), as well as a quarterly newsletter for teachers. The legislative action center highlights federal legislation of interest to those concerned about population issues.

Glossary

age-specific rate   The rate of any type of demographic event (births, deaths, etc.) calculated for a particular age group, for example, the "teen fertility rate" is the rate of births to women aged 15–19.

Agricultural Revolution   The shift, first seen in the Middle East about ten thousand years ago, from a nomadic lifestyle to a more stable, settled way of life based on the cultivation of food crops, leading eventually to higher rates of population growth.

antinatalist policy   An effort or program to curb population growth by discouraging births.

Baby Boom   The extra-large generation of people born after World War II; in the United States, the Baby Boom years were 1946–1964.

balancing equation   A simple equation showing that population increases if the number of births plus immigrants outweighs the number of deaths plus emigrants; population *decreases* if the loss of people from deaths and emigration exceeds the gain from births and immigration.

birth control   Actions taken by a couple to permit sexual intercourse without the risk (or with a reduced risk) of conception.

birth rate   The number of births in a given year per 1,000 population (sometimes called the crude birth rate).

Cairo consensus   The acceptance by most parties interested in the population issue of the principle that the best way to lower population growth rates is through efforts to (1) equalize educational and other opportunities for girls and women as compared with men, and (2) make available safe, inexpensive family-planning services that allow for choice about family size. The consensus was reached at the United Nations population conference held in Cairo in 1994.

carrying capacity   The maximum population that could be sustained indefinitely, at a constant standard of living, in a given area.

census   An official count of the population of a specified area (usually a nation), often including details on age, sex, income, and marital status.

childbearing years The age span during which women may conceive and bear children; arbitrarily assumed, in the United States, to be 15 to 44.

cohort A group within the population who share a common characteristic, usually year of birth; for example, the oldest "baby boom" cohort are those who were born in 1946.

contraceptive prevalence The proportion of women of childbearing age (or, sometimes, of couples) who are making use of contraception to space or limit births.

cornucopian A term that refers to those who view population, even rapidly growing population, as a positive thing (opposite of "neo-Malthusian").

death rate The number of deaths in a given year per 1,000 population (sometimes called the crude death rate).

demographic transition An influential notion that countries begin with high birth and death rates, then make a transition, first in their death rates, then in their birth rates, to lower levels of both rates. Until birth rates decline and the transition is completed, population may grow very rapidly.

demography The scientific study of population; often said to have started with Malthus.

dependency ratio The ratio of people considered economically unproductive (under 15 and over 64) to those considered economically productive (ages 15 to 64); a rule-of-thumb concept with obvious arbitrary elements.

depopulation The process of population decline; a future development now expected (and feared) in a growing number of countries.

doubling time The number of years it would take a population, growing at its current rate, to become twice as large. By the rule of 72, it takes a population growing at 4 percent annually about 72 divided by 4, or 18 years, to double; growing at 3 percent annually, it would double in about 72 divided by 3, or 24 years.

emigration An outflow of people from their native country, seeking permanent residence in a new country; one of the sources, along with death, of population decrease.

family-planning Deliberate efforts by couples to change (usually reduce) the number of births or the spacing of births they will have.

famine A situation of food deprivation leading to widespread hunger and starvation, with causes ranging from crop failure to political instability and military conflict.

fecundity The physiological capacity of women (or couples, or men) to produce children.

fertility   Actual childbearing performance, as opposed to theoretical capability of bearing children; one of the basic demographic processes.

general fertility rate   The total number of births in a given year per 1,000 women of childbearing age.

Green Revolution   The development of high-yielding strains of wheat, rice, and other grains, beginning in the 1960s, which led to enormous increases in world food output.

HIV/AIDS   A deadly viral disease, mainly spread by sexual contact, occurring globally but with heaviest impact in sub-Saharan Africa. There life expectancies are falling sharply due to rising AIDS-related death rates.

ICPD   The abbreviation for International Conference on Population and Development, the 1994 Cairo meeting, sponsored by the UN and attended by nearly 200 government delegations. The ICPD reaffirmed and clarified the international community's commitments regarding population and socioeconomic development.

immigration   The entry of foreign persons into a country with the aim of establishing permanent residence; one of the sources, along with births, of population increase.

infant mortality rate   The number of infants under 1 year old dying per 1,000 live births in a given year; a key indicator of socioeconomic well-being.

IPAT   An equation, made famous by Paul Ehrlich, which sees population (P) as one of the variables having a harmful impact (I) on the environment, the others being average level of affluence (A) or consumption, and technology (T); the actual equation is I = PAT.

life expectancy   The average number of years a population can expect to live beyond a given age (that age usually, but not necessarily, being birth).

life span   The maximum age that could be reached by humans under optimal conditions.

life table   A tabular display of the probability of dying at any given age; from such a table, life expectancies can be computed.

Malthusian   Relating to the demographic or economic ideas of Thomas Malthus (1766–1834); generally taken to mean pessimistic about population trends; sometimes modified to "neo-Malthusian."

marriage rate   The number of marriages occurring in a given year per 1,000 people in a country.

maternal mortality rate   The number of deaths among women either from pregnancy or childbirth complications per 100,000 live births in the year.

migration The movement of people across designated boundaries in search of permanent, new places of residence; one of the basic demographic processes.

mobility Demographically speaking, the movement of people within or across borders.

morbidity Illness or disease in a population; a contributor to mortality.

mortality Deaths in a population; a key demographic process, along with births and migration.

neo-Malthusian A policy or attitude favoring slower population growth through the use of various methods of birth control. (Ironically, Malthus himself opposed contraception, on moral grounds.)

net migration rate The difference between migration into and out of a country, expressed per 1,000 population. Currently the United States has a net migration rate of about 2, meaning that it gains 2 persons per thousand, annually, when migration in both directions is taken into account.

nuptiality rate The rate at which people get married; other things equal, a higher nuptiality rate will mean faster population growth.

out-of-wedlock birth rate The rate at which births are occurring to unmarried women, usually expressed as live births per 1,000 women of childbearing age.

population bomb The idea, popularized by Paul Ehrlich, that the world's population is growing at an explosive pace, with possibly catastrophic consequences.

population implosion A term that has been used to describe the effects of declining fertility rates worldwide; a few, mainly European nations are already seeing their populations decline, and many more are on course to experience such an implosion in the coming decades.

population momentum The upward push on population resulting from a large number of currently young people soon to enter their reproductive years; such momentum can exist even if replacement-level fertility has been achieved.

population policy The set of explicit or implicit measures by which a government attempts to achieve certain population objectives (usually in terms of size or growth rate).

population projection An estimation of the future size of a population based on assumptions about fertility, mortality, and migration; demographers work out such projections with great sophistication but no guarantees that they will prove correct.

population pyramid A graph of the age and sex characteristics of a country's population, its shape giving clues to the future growth, stability, or decline of that population. A pyramidal shape, for example, indicates that there are few people in the upper age brackets and many in the lower (younger) brackets, suggesting that future population growth will be rapid.

prevalence rate   The number of people having a disease per 1,000 of population at risk; for example, the prevalence of AIDS in some African countries now exceeds 150 or 15% of the population.

pronatalist policy   An effort or program to increase population by encouraging a high birth rate.

rate of natural increase   The rate at which a population increases solely due to the excess of births over deaths (thus ignoring migration); computed by subtracting the crude death rate from the crude birth rate.

replacement level fertility   The situation that exists when women are bearing just enough children to sustain the current population over the long run; in countries like the United States, this means a total fertility rate (TFR) of about 2.1.

sex ratio   The number of males per 100 females in the population.

total fertility rate (TFR)   An estimate of fertility based on the current age-specific birth rates of all women in a population; complicated to compute, it is basically the average number of children per woman.

United Nations Population Fund (UNFPA)   The main outreach arm of the UN in support of family-planning programs around the world; its initials derive from its original name (United Nations Fund for Population Activities).

vital statistics   Data relating to births, deaths, and sometimes marriage, divorce, and abortion.

zero population growth   A situation in which the births, deaths, and migration movements in and out of a country combine to keep its population constant from one year to the next.

Index

Geoffrey Gilbert has been teaching economics and population issues at Hobart and William Smith Colleges for many years. He is editor of Malthus's *Essay on Population* and of an anthology of nineteenth-century writings in reaction to Malthus entitled *Malthus: Critical Responses* (1998). He is a graduate of Dartmouth College with a Ph.D. from Johns Hopkins University.